Average
to **A+**

Advance Praise for *Average to A+: Realising Strengths in Yourself and Others*

The new focus on strengths is a pivotal moment for humankind. This book is an important milestone in the understanding and practical application of a strengths-based approach to life, as well as to individual and organisational performance. Working with Alex over the last few years has taught me that he has a unique talent for taking academic research into practical application, in a way that will help improve the lives of many people in the workplace and beyond. This book is at the cutting edge of that work.

Alastair Ham, Group Organisational Development Director, Aviva plc

An inspiring book containing a powerful 'call to action' - to realise the strengths in ourselves and others. This book is essential reading for business people who want to harness the power of strengths to distinguish and accelerate individual, team and organisational performance levels.

Andrea Adams, Chief HR Officer, Vertex Data Science Ltd, formerly HR Director, Air Support, BAE Systems

In an era where careful studies have advanced our collective knowledge of strengths, Alex Linley is at the clear forefront of this exciting new science. I am consistently impressed with the degree of sophistication and depth of his thought regarding strengths and their applications. *Average to A+* is a book that is long overdue. It builds on predecessor books but adds vital new information and a dynamic new way for looking at strengths. Linley's work is, bluntly, *the* cutting edge source for using strengths at work, in schools, and in everyday life.

Robert Biswas-Diener, Author, Positive Psychology Coaching

What constitutes capabilities is difficult to measure, mostly misunderstood and a largely undeveloped area, with huge gaps in our understanding. However, Alex Linley in *Average to A+*, has shown through illustrations drawn from both research and his own experience, the crucial importance of being able to recognise, realign and release the talent and capability of people, in order to maximise individual and organisational potential, and to help navigate and respond to changing circumstances. This book is full of wisdom and understanding, and is both timely and foundational. Linley has a real capability in expressing and explaining this important area to us, and has produced a great book that is extremely helpful.

Nigel Sykes, Head of Enterprise Group, Warwick Business School

I will be recommending this book in many spheres, starting with the most important people in my life. It is as relevant to employers and employees as it is to educators and students. It is also a book for parents. In fact, it is a book for anyone who wants to cultivate more positive relationships with the people they know, or have yet to meet. It is a book about history and the past. It is a book about hope and the future. Most of all it is a book about humanity and human nature, and that should interest us all.

Organisations and People

Average to A+

REALISING STRENGTHS
IN YOURSELF AND OTHERS

Alex Linley

CAPP Press
Coventry, England

CAPP PRESS

The Venture Centre
University of Warwick Science Park
Coventry CV4 7EZ
Tel: +44 (0)24 76 323 363
Fax: +44 (0)24 76 323 001
Email: capp@cappeu.org
Website: www.capp-press.org

CAPP Press is a trading name of the Centre for Applied Positive Psychology, a
not-for-profit company limited by guarantee, registered in England and Wales,
company number 05589865

First published in the United Kingdom in 2008

ISBN: 978-1-906366-00-1 (hardback)
ISBN: 978-1-906366-03-2 (paperback)

British Library Cataloguing-in-Publication Data
A catalogue record for this book is available from the British Library.

Printed in the United Kingdom

10 9 8 7 6 5 4 3 2 1

It is the policy of CAPP Press to use paper from sources that are SFI
(Sustainable Forestry Initiative) and PEFC (Programme for the Endorsement
of Forest Certification Schemes) Certified.

To all those
who are striving
to realise strengths
in themselves
and in others

CONTENTS

SERIES EDITOR'S FOREWORD

STRENGTHS ARE AT The heart of CAPP's mission of *Strengthening the World,* and at the heart of the CAPP Press *Strengthening the World* series. As such, it is only fitting that the first book of this series focuses on realising strengths in ourselves and others. We have likely all heard the call to "play to our strengths," yet nowhere has this advice been really unpacked or set out with any clear context, rationale, or recommendation. This volume is designed to do just that, and combines academic rigour and theoretical underpinnings with an accessibility and ease of comprehension that ensures the book can be read by the most general reader.

CAPP's work on strengths blends insights and experiences from a range of diverse areas, and seeks to apply them broadly across a number of different life domains. In this volume, you will find examples of the realisation of strengths throughout everyday life, at work, in children, and as a means for transformative social change – a breadth of applications that speaks directly to the breadth of the strengths approach represented herein. A recurring theme of the book is that using strengths is the smallest thing to make the biggest difference – across so many areas. Ultimately, this is because using our strengths taps into the very core of who we are as human beings, and how we can make our greatest contributions.

The *Strengthening the World* series from CAPP Press publishes books that enable people to understand and realise more of their strengths, and to create the settings and environments that support them in doing so. With this book, I find myself in an unusual position, and one where I am wearing several different hats – as author, as series editor, and ultimately, through my role with CAPP Press, as publisher. As such, I am especially pleased to include this volume as the first book in our *Strengthening the World* series.

Alex Linley
Series Editor
CAPP Press *Strengthening the World* Series

PREFACE

THE IDEA OF focusing on strengths has been around for millennia. And yet, so little has been done to help people to understand their strengths or make the most of them. Strengths are so integral to our identity as individuals and as human beings. They are at the heart of what it takes for us to lead flourishing lives. They are key to us delivering our best performances and being our most fulfilled. Strengths are so centrally important, and yet so little appreciated. Helping people to understand their strengths, and to make the most of their strengths, was my ambition in writing this book.

Those of you who know me will know that I cannot rest until I have got to the core of understanding something – the *Curiosity* that you will meet several times throughout the pages that follow! Equally, you will know my frustration with the academic arrogance that renders so much knowledge accessible only to the initiated few. In writing this book, I have tried – and I hope succeeded in – navigating a path between these two, ensuring a comprehensive level of understanding of the topic, but writing in a way that can be understood by anyone. This is fundamentally important. The messages of the strengths approach have relevance for *everyone*, and everyone should be able to appreciate them.

Average to A+ is my invitation to you to join us in *Strengthening the World*. The world needs all of us, and all of our strengths. We can achieve together what we never could alone. Strengths are the threads that unite humanity, that call for each of us to realise the best we have to offer. It is my firm belief that through realising strengths we will be able to create a world better than we have today, a world of which we can all be proud. We all have strengths, and we all have a part to play in creating this better world. Join us.

Alex Linley
Coventry
February 2008

ONE

Average isn't Good Enough

"Good is the enemy of great"

Jim Collins, *Good to Great*

WHO WANTS TO be average? When people are asked how they would rate themselves on any number of positive characteristics, almost everyone rates themselves as being above average – despite the fact that patently, this can't be true: some of us must be below average, by definition. But it does illustrate the point that we simply don't want to be average – we all want to be better than average. We want to be A+.

What does it take to be A+? That is the subject of this book. The essence of being A+ is that we need to realise strengths in ourselves and others. We need to become and continue becoming the best that we can be, as well as creating environments that support others to grow and develop into becoming the best that they can be. A utopian ideal? There is no promise that it is easy to achieve, and it is even less easy to maintain. But not to do it is to live with the Curse of Mediocrity.

This Curse of Mediocrity is all around us. In our education systems, we see it in the perennial quest to have every student being good at every subject. They are not. At work, we see it in the flatlines of competency models, where everyone is expected to be good at everything. They are not, and this being so, we then focus on what is wrong and what isn't working, trying to fix the weakness. In the world of psychology, we have seen it in the focus on treating disease and overcoming psychological illness: laudable aims in themselves of course, but aims that will never move people beyond the zero-point of being 'not ill,' rather than being 'really well.' Throughout our lives, we are cursed with things being 'okay,' another manifestation of the Curse of Mediocrity. Instead, we should be striving for things to be 'A-Okay!'

As Jim Collins described it: "Good is the enemy of great." When we try to ensure that everyone is good at everything, we are condemned by the Curse of Mediocrity. This book is about breaking that curse. It is about moving beyond average and towards A+. It is about enabling people to realise strengths in themselves and in others. This book is here as a standard bearer for the strengths approach and for everyone who wants to identify and nurture more of what is best about all of us.

The Strengths Approach

What are your strengths? A simple question, but it is one that we often find surprisingly difficult to answer in any worthwhile way. We are unused to talking about our strengths, perhaps wary of people considering us arrogant if we did. The deeper reason, though, is that we simply don't have a language for strengths. Strengths were largely excluded from systematic scientific study – at least until the last decade or so – and as a result we don't have the labels or the language to refer to them.

Even without these labels and language though, the idea of strengths still permeates our everyday conversations. Which of us has not heard the encouragement that we should "play to our strengths"? Thanks to the powerful voices speaking up for strengths throughout recorded human history, the idea of strengths is part of our culture, even if a language of strengths is not yet part of our vocabulary. The strengths approach is a representation of these currents of thought and practice that have carried down to us over years, decades, centuries and even millennia, starting from as far back as the ancient Greek philosopher Aristotle (384-322 BCE). In his treatise *The Nicomachean Ethics*, Aristotle set out to discover what would constitute the good life for people, and how they should go about attaining it. In short, Aristotle argued that to attain a good life, we must "strain every nerve to live in accordance with the best thing in us." From the perspective we now have, "the best thing in us" would be our strengths: Aristotle's call was a call to action - for people to be the best they could be through living in accordance with their strengths.

In more recent times - 1947, to be precise - Bernard Haldane heralded the application of strengths in the modern occupational arena, writing in the *Harvard Business Review*: "…this article proposes to examine what can and may be done to assure better utilization of human talents at the management level," and goes on to provide a compelling account of how his own work had been deployed very successfully to achieve this. Twenty years later, management guru Peter Drucker, wrote - similar to Haldane - with words that now have a near prophetic quality: "The unique purpose of organization is to make strength productive…one cannot build on weakness. To achieve results, one has to use all the available strengths…These strengths are the true opportunities."

You may also have found the strengths approach in social work practice, through the pioneering efforts of people like Charles Rapp,

Ronna Chamberlain, or Dennis Saleebey. Beginning at the University of Kansas School of Social Welfare in 1982, Ronna Chamberlain and Charles Rapp developed the strengths model of case management, based on the recognition and recruitment of individual and community strengths in helping people improve from difficult life circumstances. The success of this approach led to the publication of *The Strengths Perspective in Social Work Practice*, edited by Dennis Saleebey, now in its fourth edition, and ultimately to the work spreading to other states and new populations. For example, if you were a juvenile offender in Riley County, Kansas, after December 1999, you may have experienced Juvenile Intake and Assessment Case Management, a non-traditional correctional program that works to manage at-risk behaviour through strengths-based case management techniques.

You might have heard about strengths through the popular best-seller from Marcus Buckingham and Donald Clifton – *Now, Discover Your Strengths* – or taken an online strengths assessment, being one of the hundreds of thousands of people around the world who have taken the Clifton StrengthsFinder™ (**www.strengthsfinder.com**), the VIA Inventory of Strengths (**www.viastrengths.org**), or the strengths questionnaires on the Personality Strengths website (**www.personalitystrengths.com**).

Or you might have a connection with one of the growing number of organisations who are actively seeking to harness strengths, and exploring what it means to turn towards strengths-based organisation. Household names including Accenture, Aviva, BAE Systems, Microsoft, Norwich Union, Standard Chartered Bank, Sony Europe, Toyota, and Yahoo!, or smaller pioneers such as the Authentic Food Company and Cougar Automation, or the Centre for Applied Positive Psychology, the organisation I founded to put strengths into practice – and which, through its publishing arm, the CAPP Press, is the publisher of this book.

Wherever you found out about the strengths approach, it is almost certain that you won't have been introduced to strengths in any depth. People talk about "strengths" and throw the word around as if everyone knows what strengths are, and we know just about everything we need to know about them. We don't. And until we really start to understand strengths better, we will miss the power of the strengths approach, and the benefits that this approach can bring for our personal growth and development, whether at work, as parents, or in any other domain of life.

Here are the five fundamentals of the strengths approach as I see them:

(1)   The strengths approach focuses on what is right, what is working, and what is strong;

(2)   Strengths are part of our basic human nature, therefore every person in the world has strengths and deserves respect for their strengths;

(3)   Our areas of greatest potential are in the areas of our greatest strengths;

(4)   We succeed by fixing our weaknesses *only when* we are also making the most of our strengths;

(5)   Using our strengths is the smallest thing we can do to make the biggest difference.

We consider each of these fundamentals in more detail throughout the rest of the book, and we will go on to look at what exactly we mean by strengths later in the chapter. But first let's see how these different perspectives started to converge in the movement that really launched the strengths approach into mainstream science and applications: the new science of positive psychology.

The New Science of Positive Psychology

Before the Second World War, psychology had three distinct missions: curing mental illness, helping all people to lead more productive and fulfilling lives, and identifying and nurturing high talent. The advent of the Second World War, and the return of traumatised war veterans to which it led, caused a subtle but significant shift in what psychologists did and where they did it. The establishment of the Veterans Administration (in 1946) and the National Institutes of Mental Health (in 1947), both in the United States, caused psychologists to move towards the study and cure of mental illness. In simple terms, this was where the research funding and careers existed, and psychologists simply followed suit – they had household expenses and mortgage repayments to meet, just like anyone else, and after all, curing mental illness and helping people in distress are worthwhile occupations.

But an unintended effect of this focus on curing mental illness was that the two other missions became almost forgotten. As a result, the aims of helping all people to lead more productive and fulfilling lives, and identifying and nurturing high talent, were left languishing, pursued only by researchers who had sufficient passion to ignite their work in the absence of external resources and rewards. It was in this context, and with this recognition, that the positive psychology movement was born – and from perhaps an unlikely father.

Martin Seligman is recognized as a world authority on depression, pessimism and learned helplessness, as well as an international best-selling author in the popular science and self-help field. In 1998, he was elected President of the American Psychological Association (APA), and on August 21, 1999, gave his Presidential Address to the Annual Convention of the APA in Boston, Massachusetts. The audience likely expected Seligman to talk about new therapies for depression, or his hopes for psychological advances in treating people afflicted by learned helplessness, since these were the areas where he had made his reputation. Instead, what they heard was Seligman making the case that psychology was good, but *not good enough*, because it had neglected the study and application of the things that make life worth living. As such, Seligman argued, the time had come for a positive psychology that would redress this imbalance, and focus research on what was right with people, including happiness, well-being, and human strengths.

This Presidential Address catalysed the positive psychology movement, and was quickly followed by a highly symbolic January 2000 special issue of the *American Psychologist* on happiness, excellence, and optimal human functioning: the first issue of the new millennium. In their introductory article of this special issue, Martin Seligman and Mihaly Csikszentmihalyi offered the following definition of positive psychology:

"The field of positive psychology at the subjective level is about valued subjective experiences: well-being, contentment, and satisfaction (in the past); hope and optimism (for the future); and flow and happiness (in the present). At the individual level, it is about positive individual traits: the capacity for love and vocation, courage, interpersonal skill, aesthetic sensibility, perseverance, forgiveness, originality, future mindedness, spirituality, high talent, and wisdom. At the group level, it is about the civic virtues and the institutions that move individuals toward better citizenship: responsibility, nurturance, altruism, civility, moderation, tolerance, and work ethic…The aim of positive psychology is to begin to catalyze a change in the focus of psychology from preoccupation only with repairing the worst things in life to also building positive qualities"

These calls to research and application created exciting new paths and directions for psychology, and legitimated the study of what was right with people, that had for so long been defined out of the remit of much psychological research and practice. Within less than a decade following its inception, positive psychology has attracted many millions of dollars in research funding, led to the publication of over 16 journal special issues and more than 20 dedicated books, as well as revolutionising how people – both psychologists themselves and non-psychologists – think about psychology and what it does: in short, inviting people to reconsider the questions that they ask and the approach they take. This is a huge achievement by any yardstick, and no doubt an enduring part of Seligman's legacy.

This, then, was the context in which the strengths approach came to life more fully, and it is this context of the new science of positive psychology that informs this book. I have not, however, restricted my attention only to psychology, and certainly not only to positive psychology. Instead, I have reviewed and integrated what is known about strengths and how to develop and apply them from across many diverse fields and practices, including management studies, leadership studies, philosophy, religion, child and adult lifespan development, business, social work, and of course, psychology itself, including my own extensive research and practice in the field of strengths and their applications. Before we can go on and look at these though, it is first important that we establish precisely what we mean by "strengths."

What Do We Mean by "Strengths"?

When people suggest that we "play to our strengths," do we really know what they mean? And, if asked, would we even be able to say what our own strengths were? The answers to both of these questions –

for most of us – are "probably not." For instance, when researchers asked a representative sample of 1,000 people in the UK to say what their strengths were, only around one third of people were able to give a meaningful answer.

We might think of strengths as 'things that we are good at' – and certainly that is an important part of what we mean by strengths. As I will go on to talk about, however, there is much more to understanding strengths than just the 'things that we are good at.' It is important to understand strengths more fully, because this deeper understanding gives us the knowledge and perspective we need to see why strengths are so integral to enabling us to be the best that we can be. So what are strengths, when properly understood? I define strengths in this way:

A strength is a pre-existing capacity for a particular way of behaving, thinking, or feeling that is authentic and energising to the user, and enables optimal functioning, development and performance.

This might seem like a mouthful, or a way of us psychologists over-complicating things to emphasise our own importance. But definitions are important, because they tell us exactly what something is, as well as what it is not. This in turn is important, because we need to be sure that we are all talking about the same thing if we are going to be able to understand each other, and move forward with what we know. There are four parts to this definition, and they all have something important to say about a strength. As such, they all need to be present for the strength to be present, as Figure 1.1 shows.

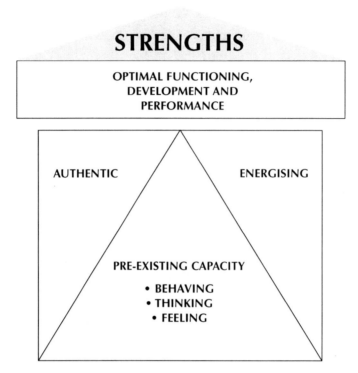

Figure 1.1 The Elements of a Strength

A *pre-existing capacity* means that the strength already exists within us, whether to a greater or lesser extent. Even if a strength is latent – it has not yet been fully developed or used – it still resides within, as being distinct from something that simply isn't there, and yet which is 'added in' to us from the outside. This does not mean that we cannot learn by 'adding in' new things from the outside, but it does mean that we can't just pick and choose the strength we would like to have at any one time.

By pre-existing, I mean that there are already the pathways in our brain that represent the strength. These pathways might have been there when we were born, or we might have developed them as children. The key part about strengths being pre-existing capacities is that there is something about our biological or psychological make-up that predisposes us to have that particular strength. The opposite would be that we were a blank slate on which anything could be written, and that simply is not true. We examine the reasons for this much more in Chapter 2, *Back to the Beginnings*, and look at what it means for developing strengths in children in Chapter 7, *Golden Seeds and Flourishing Children*, suggesting that the strengths approach is a much better way of looking at children's potential than is the 'You can be anything you want to be' mantra, which is common in certain cultures and age groups.

A strength being **authentic** refers to the fact that when people are using their strengths, they feel like they are being 'real me,' not the person that someone else wants them to be, but the person who they really are. Authenticity refers to being true to yourself and following your own directions and preferences in life. It is about being honest with yourself and accepting yourself for who you are. As we will see, using strengths enables people to be authentic because they are acting in accordance with the directions and behaviours that are right for them, something which is an integral part of human nature and a core influence on our well-being and fulfilment.

Part of this authenticity is that strengths are identifiable across many different situations in the same people. Very often, you will be able to recognise themes of your strengths running right throughout your life: people who succeed in what seem to be very different jobs will often identify their success as being the result of simply applying their strengths to different environments. While the environment may change, the core elements of who you are as an individual will not. Protecting this core individuality while simultaneously flexing according to the demands of the situation is at the heart of what it means to be authentic.

A strength being *energising* reflects the fact that when people use their strengths, they feel as if they have more energy available to them. This does not mean that you can use the strength forever and not need to rest (we all have physiological limitations!), but it does mean that your recovery will be faster and you won't burnout when you are using strengths. In a study conducted with my colleague Reena Govindji, we found that people who reported using their strengths more also reported having higher levels of vitality, that is, a sense of energy and zest for life.

Using strengths seems to be able to recharge people as they are using them, perhaps working in the same way as an alternator does in your car engine, recharging the battery as the engine operates. But while this works in the short to medium term, it doesn't mean that we never need to rest when using our strengths, because our energy will deplete eventually - just like the car battery! Even so, our energy will go further when using strengths than it will when we are working from our weaknesses, when the burnout and energy loss will be faster and more severe.

The fact that a strength enables *optimal functioning, development and performance* refers to the idea that using your strengths allows you to be at your best in terms of psychological functioning. People feel more engaged, more alive, more vigorous, and more in flow when they are using their strengths. Strengths also allow optimal development, because - despite many prevailing beliefs - we learn better in the areas where we are already strong. This is because strengths are pre-existing capacities, as I described above: the neural networks – the brain wiring that underpins what we know and what we do – is already there for strengths, and it is easier for the brain to build on the pathways that it already has than it is to develop entirely new ones.

Optimal performance follows naturally from these two. When people are at their psychological peak of functioning, being their most creative, energised, engaged and committed, and when they are learning fastest and applying that learning and development to what they do, it is no surprise that their best performances follow. Realising strengths enables these best performances, enabling people to be A+, rather than just average – because after all, none of us wants to be average.

And in itself, the word *realise* is an integral part of the strengths vocabulary, since it has a powerful and important double meaning. First, *realise* means to see, to identify, to recognise, and to understand. This is the necessary foundation of realising strengths – that we must be able to identify, recognise and understand them. Second, *realise* means to bring into being, to make manifest, to make real, or to bring to fruition. It is about taking something that is potential and making it reality – hence the phrase of 'realising one's potential.' This is the second integral meaning of realising strengths – that once we have identified them, we are able to make them real and realise their potential throughout our lives for the contributions we can make. Realising our strengths is about *knowing* them and then *growing* them (see Figure 1.2).

Now that we have defined a strength, and understood the important dual meaning of realise, you might well be wondering about some pretty fundamental questions. What are the names of different strengths that we might recognise? How many strengths are there? What might be recognised as a strength? How do you identify a strength? Is it possible to overuse a strength? How do you develop strengths? And of course, most fundamentally, how do we realise strengths in ourselves and others? These are all questions that we will consider, but first, it's important to recognise that we don't yet have a fully developed vocabulary of strengths – and as such, one of the first things that we need to do in realising strengths is to build that vocabulary. The words we use to describe things are of fundamental importance. As we go on to explore next, words can define our reality: language becomes life.

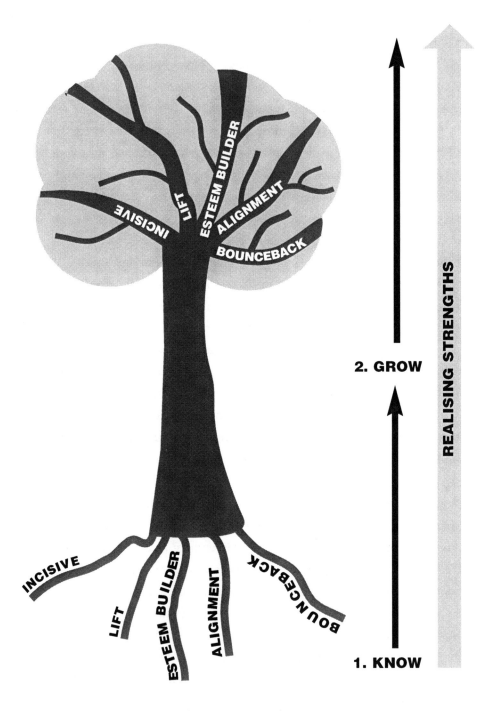

Figure 1.2 Realising Strengths: Knowing and Growing

Language Becomes Life

The words we use to describe everyday things have a powerful effect on us and the people around us. For example, reflect for a moment on the emotions you feel when you read this list of words. Read them out loud, to yourself, slowly:

BAD – SORROW – ASSAULT – LOSS – DEATH – PAIN - WEAKNESS

Contrast this emotional experience with how you feel as you read this second list. Again, read them out loud, to yourself, slowly:

GOOD – JOY – LOVE – GAIN – LIFE – PLEASURE – STRENGTH

They are simply words, but words can have a powerful emotional impact upon us. Have you ever cried when reading a novel? A novel is simply printed words, much the same as this book is – but words carry powerful consequences. The same is true for a language of strengths – except that we don't have a particularly well-developed language of strengths. A major aim for this book is to begin to create a deeper under-standing of strengths, and to enable the development of a much richer, fuller strengths vocabulary. From this basis, we can start to realise strengths much more fully and powerfully.

As we saw above, there are very good reasons why we have such a rich vocabulary of what can be wrong with people – quite simply, psychologists and psychiatrists have spent a huge amount of time and resources studying this over the last 60 years. But we simply have no comparable vocabulary for what is right with people. Words can exert a powerful influence over thought and behaviour. But without words, there is no influence to be exerted. The absence of a sufficiently devel-oped language for strengths sits like a yawning chasm in the middle of strengths research and applications. As we go on to consider in Chapter

2, there are likely to be hundreds of different strengths, and the majority have yet to be explicitly identified, defined, or named, something that my research team and I have been working to address through the Personality Strengths project.

Without a strengths vocabulary, it is very difficult to have any shared understanding of what strengths are generally, or what particular strengths might be. Without the right words, it is very difficult to have a meaningful conversation with someone about what your strengths are, at least in a way that avoids the need for convoluted descriptions and explanations. Without the capacity to describe them, it is easy for our strengths to fall between the cracks of our existence, becoming lost and forgotten rather than identified, nurtured, celebrated, and fully realised.

The entire question of labels and labelling is an interesting one. Simply put, if we give something a name – a label – we pay attention to it. We are able to classify it, to understand it, to put it in its place in relation to the other things we know. But without a label, the 'unknown' things just float around like unconnected wisps of mist in the evening air. They are easily lost, even more easily forgotten.

When we have a name for something, we tend to treat it as real, to reify it. As the medical philosopher Lawrie Reznek said: "Concepts carry consequences – classifying things one way rather than another has important implications for the way we behave toward such things." Having a concept of strengths has many powerful and positive consequences. We are able to know ourselves more authentically. We are able to understand ourselves more deeply. We are able to deploy our talents more fully. We are able to achieve what we want to achieve more efficiently and effectively. Without a concept of strengths, both of our own and those around us, we are left floundering, lost in a forest of life which we cannot escape for not being able to see the wood for the trees.

Given that words shape our reality, that language becomes life, that expressions influence our emotional experience, a major focus of the activity of myself and my colleagues in the strengths approach has been to begin the work of creating a much richer vocabulary of strengths. We have sometimes been able to do this through using existing words, casting them explicitly as a strength. We have sometimes had to do this by creating new words to explain what we mean. Often the words have a resonance with people, and they have an immediate intuitive understanding of what we are talking about. But sometimes they don't, and we have to put the work into explaining and developing the idea. What we do know is that when someone has a strength, and we then reflect it back to them, they have a eureka moment of realisation and recognition. They feel understood, validated, and valued. They feel appreciated for who they really are.

Consider the following examples, and see if any of them resonate with you.

Can you always see the wood for the trees, being the person that everyone comes to when they have a difficult problem to resolve? Do you possess a clarity of insight that renders most problems easily solvable, simply through your penetrating analysis to the heart of the matter. Yes? If so, *Incisive* might be one of your strengths.

Do you just love helping other people to feel better about themselves? Are you able to see quite instinctively the things that they do well, the qualities they have, and use these to help them see themselves in a more positive light? If you are thinking "yes, yes, yes" to this, then you may well be an *Esteem Builder*.

If your colleagues always welcome you being around because you improve the mood of the team with your optimism and encouragement, then *Lift* could be one of your strengths.

Are you the person who always seems able to get things to happen their way, working out who and what you need, and when, and then working behind the scenes to make it happen? And when it does, it looks so effortless to those outside that they think you are one of the luckiest people alive? If this is you, then you are likely to score high on *Alignment*.

Or are you the sort of person who uses negative experiences as a springboard to go on to ever greater things, achieving more than you ever thought? If that sounds like you, you might have the strength of *Bounceback*.

Were you able to see yourself in the above descriptions? Quite possibly - although it is equally likely that you weren't. And the same would have been true whatever selection of strengths I chose to include in the short examples above. Because there are many hundreds of different strengths, the chances of me capturing the ones most relevant to you in such a short space are pretty slim. But don't despair, because in Chapter 4, *Strengthspotting*, I will give you the royal road to identifying strengths in yourself and others – strengthspotting - whether others have developed a label for those strengths or not. The ability to identify strengths is the first stage of realising strengths in yourself and others.

How People Respond to the Strengths Approach

There are four general ways in which people respond to the messages and perspectives of the strengths approach. One group of people will often loudly exclaim words to the effect of:

"This is just great! I feel like I have always been doing this, but without really knowing why, or without really knowing what I was doing. Now I feel like I have a language and a framework for

making sense of it. And what's really great is that it shows me the
ways in which I can build on what I have been doing already, as
well as the areas in which I might have missed something that I can
now start doing."

These people are the **Advocates**, the ones who are already there, and when they find the strengths approach, feel like they have found their home. If you are an Advocate, welcome, let's learn from each other and progress together.

A second group of people are receptive to the strengths perspective, at least to a degree. They are open-minded and think along the following lines:

"There might just be something in this, but I need to be convinced. I
have seen these kinds of things before and they always come to
nothing. But this seems to be a little different. It seems to be based on
something that makes sense, something that I can relate to. There is
something in it, but I need to see the evidence for myself before I am
ready to sign up. But it does fit – in some ways – with what I have
seen work before. Maybe I just need to find out more about it."

These people are the **Undecided**, the people who are receptive to the ideas but who remain to be convinced. They have a crucial role to play in the strengths approach, because they are sceptical but supportive, offering the tough love that any fledgling idea needs: enough to grow, but not enough to become complacent. If ultimately they decide in favour of strengths, they become a **Convert**, and as the saying goes, there is nobody as zealous as a Convert.

The fourth group of people we might call the **Resistors**. They are resistant to the idea of strengths, maybe seeing it as happy-clappy or touchy-feely, descriptions that allow them to dismiss it, especially within tough business cultures where cash is king and the bottom line is the only thing that matters.

There can be a number of reasons for the reactions of the Resistors. People may often simply be resistant to change – as many of us are – and will see the strengths approach as something that necessitates a change in their behaviour, in their modus operandi, and as such, is something to be resisted. This can come from a deep unconscious level, especially if people have been psychologically invested in a process or way of working that would be affected by introducing the strengths approach.

Or it can come – especially in the West – from our sense of a Protestant work ethic: that something worth achieving is hard work, and not meant to be enjoyable, since it's the end result and the moral improvement through the process that counts. There is something about strengths that is just 'too easy' and so shouldn't be taken seriously. But as we will see, there is nothing easy or flippant about developing and building on strengths.

There could also be something deep-seated in the person's history that has caused them to believe that nothing worthwhile can be achieved without going through the pain, suffering and sacrifice that make it worth achieving. On this basis, using strengths simply seems too easy; in fact, it can even feel like it is dishonest – "*I shouldn't be getting paid for something that I enjoy doing so much. Work is not designed to be fun.*"

Yet perhaps the most widespread reason for this resistance is the negativity bias with which we are all endowed – an evolutionary overhang that we go on to consider in Chapter 3. Because we are all faced with this natural predisposition, we need to be even more diligent about how we can overcome it – and when it is appropriate to do so.

And further, it's important to recognise that the Resistors do have a point. Too often, the strengths approach has been presented as an 'all or nothing' focus on strengths that ignores weaknesses and things that simply do need to be dealt with. That is not the approach I take, as you will see through the rest of the book. In contrast, we focus on strengths but recognise that sometimes – if they cannot be made irrelevant - weaknesses do need to be dealt with. Ultimately, what we are interested in is the double-win of highly effective performance that comes from enabling people to be themselves and to do what they do best – and neither are achieved through an imbalanced focus on either strengths or weaknesses.

The strengths approach provides us with a powerful means to counteract our negativity bias, and to focus on building what is best in everyone. It is to create this realisation, through understanding, and to build this realisation, through practice, that I have written this book. We start out with some theoretical background in Chapter 2, *Back to the Beginnings*, where we explore where strengths have come from, tracing them back to our evolutionary origins and linking in with the ways in which we can think about fundamental human nature. In Chapter 3, *Our Negativity Bias and the Golden Mean*, we look at why it is that we seem to be drawn irresistibly to the negative, together with how we can use strengths in the most effective ways, so that they are neither over- or underplayed, but instead used according to the 'golden mean.'

Identifying strengths is the topic for Chapter 4, *Strengthspotting*. We look at the telltale signs of a strength, and examine different ways and means for identifying strengths in yourself and in others. Chapter 5, *Be Yourself - Better*, turns the lens of developing strengths onto us as individuals, seeing how we can find the niches that will allow us to do more of what we do best, doing it ever better.

In Chapter 6, *Harnessing Strengths at Work*, we examine the applications of the strengths approach in organisations, focusing on the experience of the employee and their relationship with their manager and team. Chapter 7, *Golden Seeds and Flourishing Children*, explores how we might develop strengths in children – whether our perspective is as a parent, teacher, or other child professional. We look at the value of planting "golden seeds" that give children an authentic and grounded belief in themselves and their abilities.

Chapter 8, *Making our Greatest Contributions*, stands back to take a wider perspective on that we lead lives that are A+. We consider how we can bring to bear the power of being the best that we can be on the challenges and opportunities faced by our societies. Above all, leading an A+ life is about our contribution to our wider world as well as ourselves, which rests on the three pillars of responsibility of the strengths approach, as we explore here. Chapter 9, *The Smallest Thing to Make the Biggest Difference*, invites you to join us in answering this powerful question.

Average to A+ is your companion to understanding what it takes for you to be at your best, your companion to creating a life where you can spend much more of your time living in the A+ zone in whatever you are doing. For Aristotle – from whom we could all learn much – this was the goal of our existence. It is a goal that we should all consider adopting again: to be the best that we can be. The world, our children, the legacy that we will leave, require us to be just that. Too many of us are content to sit idly by, condemned by the Curse of Mediocrity, and let the world carry on without us. *Average to A+* is a call to action, a clarion call for us to reawaken the best of what each of us has to offer, and to develop that to its highest and most fulfilling extent. Realising strengths in ourselves and in others is a natural, practical and powerful route to making our greatest contributions. After all, who wants to be average?

Key Points

- The Curse of Mediocrity comes from the belief that everyone should be good at everything, and when they are not, we should focus on developing the weak areas.

- There are five fundamentals of the strengths approach: (1) a focus on what is right, what is working, and what is strong; (2) strengths are part of our basic human nature, therefore every person in the world has strengths and deserves respect for their strengths; (3) our areas of greatest potential are in the areas of our greatest strengths; (4) we succeed by fixing our weaknesses only when we are also making the most of our strengths; (5) using our strengths is the smallest thing we can do to make the biggest difference.

- Strengths are defined as pre-existing capacities for particular ways of behaving, thinking, or feeling that are authentic and energising to the user, and enable optimal functioning, development and performance.

- The language we use has a huge influence on the way in which we see the world, but we don't yet have a full language for strengths.

- Realising strengths has a powerful double meaning. It is about knowing our strengths and growing our strengths.

Areas for Reflection and Action

- Think about where the Curse of Mediocrity might have impacted negatively in your life. Recognising this, what can you do to counter it in the future?

- Do you know what your strengths are? How many strengths can you identify in yourself? Are you able to describe your strengths well?

- Where do you stand in relation to the strengths approach? Are you an Advocate, Undecided, a Convert, or a Resistor? Why?

TWO

Back to the Beginnings

"Without the biologically predisposed mechanisms that allowed our ancestors to generate, recognize, and celebrate corrective virtues, their social groups would have died out quickly. The ubiquitous virtues, we believe, are what allow the human animal to struggle against and to triumph over what is darkest within us."

Katherine Dahlsgaard, Christopher Peterson
and Martin Seligman
Review of General Psychology

EVERY PERSON IN the world has strengths. A legitimate question, then, is where do these strengths come from? It seems like a fairly fundamental question, but surprisingly, it is not a question that has received a lot of attention. In this chapter, we explore this question of where strengths come from, looking at explanations and answers taken from a number of different approaches, to see how it is that we arrive at the patterns of strengths that each of us have today.

So that we can understand where strengths come from, we need to bring on board perspectives from a wide variety of areas, including theories of human nature, evolution, nature-nurture, and human development. These perspectives can be brought together to provide a way of understanding the development of strengths that can explain both how strengths developed across people generally, as well as how they developed in individuals more specifically. Figure 2.1 gives a graphical representation of this, and you are invited to refer to it at different points throughout the chapter as the story of where strengths come from unfolds. Having done so, we then look at why strengths matter, showing why using one's strengths is centrally important for authenticity, health, well-being and goal attainment. In order to begin, we need to go a long way back in time.

Strengths, Evolution and Natural Selection

According to Jerome Barkow, editor of *The Adapted Mind: Evolutionary Psychology and the Generation of Culture*, the way in which our brains now function was established when we evolved in the Paleolithic period – around 12,000 years ago at its most recent. At this deep evolutionary level, Barkow would argue, we haven't changed much since!

Going back in time like this, psychologists have shown that evolutionary theory can explain the development of the major features of our personality. In a nutshell, our personality features developed in the way that they did because they enabled us to overcome the challenges that we faced in our day-to-day lives. Essentially, these personality features allowed our ancestors to find ways to survive and reproduce - the two big goals of evolution. In broad terms, survival tended to be about avoiding threats and dealing with problems, whereas reproduction tended to be about making the most of opportunities – whether to impress potential mating partners, or to gather resources to support one's offspring.

For example, one feature of personality, conscientiousness, allowed people to be trusted with tasks which contributed to survival (like finding food and shelter). Agreeableness, as another example, enabled individuals to co-operate with each other for the benefit of the group, again serving both individual and group survival. Particular characteristics came through strongly over time because they provided our ancestors with what evolutionary psychologists call *adaptive solutions* to the situations they faced – that is, ways of dealing with their problems (for example, avoiding the attack of a wild beast) or making the most of their opportunities (like knowing where the best animals were that could be most easily hunted). Because they did this, these characteristics were passed on into the gene pool, from which are taken the genes that make us the people we are today.

Building on this idea, different characteristics evolved to meet different needs. Because these different environments required different adaptive solutions, we evolved particular ways of coping that fitted with particular niches in these different environments. Environmental niches are about the idea that there are particular situations or opportunities that call for particular ways of responding, whether that response is to deal with a threat (like avoiding the attack of a wild beast), or making the most of an opportunity (such as knowing where the best animals could be found). For example, if we lived in an area that had many rivers, we would learn the adaptations we needed about how to catch fish as a source of food. In contrast, if we lived on the plains, we would have learned the adaptations that enabled us to be better hunters of grazing animals. In this way, we evolved particular adaptive solutions to enable us to deal with particular problems, or to make the most of particular opportunities.

On this basis, there are many thousands of adaptive solutions that, at one time or another, conferred an adaptive advantage, allowing our ancestors who held these adaptive solutions to survive and reproduce. And when they did, they passed their genes into the gene pool over generations, meaning ultimately that they are identifiable in us as human beings today. It is through this process that strengths have evolved – because they provided us with ways of either avoiding or dealing with threats to our survival and reproduction, or making the most of the opportunities that were around us, so that we could survive, reproduce and flourish.

Particular strengths are particularly relevant to particular environmental niches. Equally, however, the law of parsimony (which dictates, in terms of evolution, that we don't have more adaptations than are necessary) requires that we should also be able to do the greatest possible number of things with the smallest possible number of strengths – it simply wouldn't be practical to have a strength for curiosity about other people, another strength for curiosity about the shapes of different fish, and another curiosity about the way that weather systems work – instead, we just have *Curiosity* as a strength that applies across these many different domains. From this basis, we end up with any given strength being appropriate and applicable across many of the different situations we face, but by no means being appropriate for all of them.

From the perspective of evolutionary theory, then, modern strengths can be understood as reconfigurations and re-combinations of the many thousands of adaptive solutions that came about through human evolution, and that exist across all human beings. Figure 2.1 shows how adaptive solutions through evolution form the basis from which strengths developed. It also becomes clear that, just as there are many different adaptive solutions, there are also likely to be many different strengths.

Figure 2.1 The Origins of Strengths

The Variety and Combinations of Strengths

Are all these strengths fully distinguishable and distinct? It is unlikely that this would be the case. And, in fact, it is much more likely that strengths - like other psychological phenomena - would tend to be more overlapping with each other than most psychologists would care to admit. Indeed, there is a powerful argument as to why this *should* be the case.

As we found with the law of parsimony above, there is no efficiency in having characteristics that are only suited for one very specific niche (like the curiosity only about shapes of different fish). In contrast, there is a lot of efficiency in having different characteristics that can be blended together, in different ways, to meet a variety of specific needs (like an overall strength of *Curiosity*). This blending of strengths means that the same people could have similar patterns of strengths, but display them quite differently – and this is exactly what we see in practice.

Two people may both be very creative, but express that creativity in very different ways. Beth, for example, is a wonderful artist – creative in the way in which she draws and paints – our typical understanding of creativity. But Charlie's creativity comes through in a very different way. He is very gifted with creativity around visualising strategic futures, and uses that to explore what possibilities might exist for his organisation in the years ahead. Both Beth and Charlie are highly creative, but their creativity expresses itself in quite different ways, according to the different ways in which their different strengths are combined and layered. In Beth's case, this strength of creativity is combined with an appreciation of beauty. In Charlie's case, his creativity combines with a strategic focus and strong commercial acumen.

Another example is the strength of *Relationship Investor*, which blends the more fundamental strengths of *Contact*, *Rapport*, and *Relationship*. Whereas people with *Contact* love to meet lots of new people, and those with *Rapport* love the early stages of getting to know someone and building that connection with them, and *Relationship* is about building deep relationships over time, people with *Relationship Investor* are able to do all of these things very effectively to build networks of relationships that are simultaneously wide and deep – something that very few people are able to achieve. As Figure 2.2 shows, these more complex strengths come about through the layering and combination of more fundamental strengths.

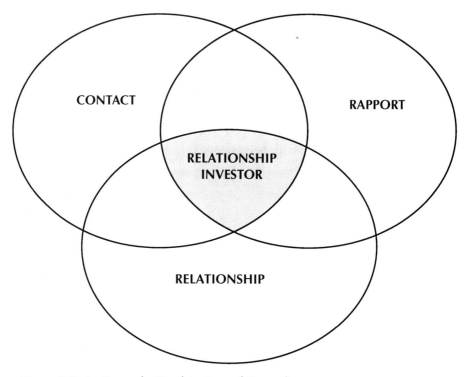

Figure 2.2 An Example Combination of Strengths

When we understand strengths as having the potential to be layered in this way – with the expressions of particular strengths varying according to the combination in which they exist, and with other strengths being built up out of different combinations of strengths – it is possible to understand something of the richness and infinite variety of human beings and their positive attributes: something which we can all witness as we look around us.

Importantly, this is not to say that there is no value in understanding strengths at the most fundamental level: in essence, the more specific we can be about a strength, the greater the chances that we will be able to deploy it most effectively. In contrast, keeping things too general and oversimplified means that we lose sight of what strengths can offer us in the first place. For example, we can act positively on the knowledge that somebody is great at building deep relationships with a few people, since we know how their strength can be best deployed – they have *Relationship*. And we know even more about them and what they can do best if we understand that they are a *Relationship Investor*. But in contrast, the more generic "Good with people" or "Has good people skills" tell us next to nothing. Which people? Doing what? In which way? Over-simplifying things to this level means that they become little use to us in understanding how, where and when people can be at their best.

Ultimately, I hope that we will arrive at the point where we have something like a complete taxonomy of strengths, and are able to understand how all strengths relate to each other - perhaps along the lines of Dmitry Mendeleev's periodic table of the elements in chemistry. But that day is likely a long way off. In the meantime, the most sensible way forward is to continue striving to identify, classify and understand strengths. As rapid evolution attests, we should always be open to the probability that our recognition of hitherto unidentified strengths will develop. Further, we should avoid the temptation of foreclosing too soon on the possible number of strengths in existence. If we were to do so, we would be robbing humanity of its richest diversity, and disenfranchising people throughout the world of what they do best and love to do.

Are There Universal Strengths?

From evolutionary theory, we would expect that there are strengths that exist consistently across individuals, according to the ways in which human beings evolved collectively over time. These general human strengths should be identifiable across all cultures, because they once served an adaptive purpose. Simply put, there are likely to be strengths that everyone has, at least to some degree, because they were (and are) useful to everyone.

In contrast, it also means that there are likely to be many more strengths that are more specialised – because they have evolved as adaptations to a particular niche in our environment. Because of this, there are likely to be many strengths that are more thinly spread throughout the population. In fact, this is exactly what the research points to.

In a key initiative of the positive psychology movement, Christopher Peterson and Martin Seligman developed a classification of "character strengths" that they believed to be universally valued and identifiable across different cultures and different historical periods. The 24 character strengths they proposed were organised under six categories:

1 **Strengths of Wisdom and Knowledge**: Creativity, Curiosity, Open-mindedness, Love of learning; Perspective;
2 **Strengths of Courage**: Bravery, Persistence, Integrity, Vitality;
3 **Strengths of Humanity**: Love, Kindness, Social intelligence;
4 **Strengths of Justice**: Citizenship, Fairness, Leadership;
5 **Strengths of Temperance**: Forgiveness, Humility, Prudence, Self-regulation;
6 **Strengths of Transcendence**: Appreciation of beauty, Gratitude, Hope, Humour, Spirituality.

Given their assumption that these character strengths were universal, they compared the rankings of strengths that were endorsed by 117,676 participants drawn from 54 different nations from around the world. Intriguingly, they found a remarkable degree of consistency across participants from extremely different cultural backgrounds, from Azerbaijan to Zimbabwe, and as varied as Argentina, Britain, China, India, Nigeria, Poland, Uzbekistan, and Vanuatu – cultural backgrounds that are very different by modern standards; and yet which by evolutionary standards should be similar. They found that the consistency of the rankings of the 24 character strengths was 0.78 – a value far higher than many people would have predicted. To explain this further, if all participants had ranked themselves on the character strengths in exactly the same way, this value would have been 1.0. If none of them had ranked themselves in the same way, the value would have been 0. The consistency of the strengths rankings, given the widely different cultures from which people were drawn, was remarkable – but in actual fact, just as the evolutionary perspective would predict.

Equally, in our work with the Personality Strengths project, which is concerned with identifying, defining, measuring and classifying strengths, we have identified – to date – over 100 different strengths, many of which we expect to be more specific and less culturally universal. Again, this fits very well with what evolutionary theory would predict: some strengths may be more universally recognised and valued (they have been developed earlier in our evolution, and apply across different cultures), whereas other strengths are less easily recognised universally, because they have evolved to serve a particular niche in a particular culture or a particular environment. This makes sense, because depending upon the level of specificity with which strengths are defined, we could expect to find either many more strengths or a lot less strengths. For example, if we are looking for strengths that have been around for many generations and are universally valued (such as character strengths), then there are likely to be less of them. In contrast, if our focus is on modern day strengths that may be more specific to the environment in which they are found, there may be a lot more of them – and this is exactly what we are finding through the Personality Strengths project. A reason for this, we believe, is that strengths are examples of rapid evolution, as I go on to discuss next.

Strengths and Rapid Evolution

Peterson and Seligman's character strengths can be considered as a universal grouping, since the strengths listed there can be understood as having a consistent socially adaptive value: they helped people to co-exist and flourish across millennia and generations. In contrast, other strengths now being identified may be arguably less relevant to earlier evolutionary times, and may be reflective of "rapid evolution" – the idea that evolutionary adaptation can happen within a few generations, rather than across the thousands of years first thought. This has now been seen in such diverse species as the blue moon butterfly, the hammerhead shark, and the African elephant. For example, the South Pacific blue moon butterfly produced only male offspring to counter the fact that males of the species were being selectively killed by bacterial attacks that only affected males, a change which occurred in less than 10 generations. In December 2001, a hammerhead shark at the Henry Doorly Zoo in Omaha, Nebraska, gave birth to a live, normally developed female pup - without mating. And over several decades, Iain Douglas-Hamilton has demonstrated that the tusk sizes of African elephants are decreasing, believed to be a result of ivory poaching and the elephants' development of an adaptive solution to protect against it. In each of these cases, the remarkable leaps in evolution were believed to be a means of countering a perceived threat to the survival of the species.

Traditionally, however, the view was that evolutionary change was something that accrued very slowly over many thousands of years. Yet the emerging evidence from the African elephant, the blue moon butterfly and the hammerhead shark – together with very recent radical breakthroughs in our understanding of human evolution – suggest that this may not always be the case. As Steven Pinker, leading psychologist and language expert at Harvard University described it:

"I've had to question the overall assumption that human evolution pretty much stopped by the time of the agricultural revolution…New [laboratory] results have suggested that thousands of genes, perhaps as much as 10% of the human genome, have been under strong recent selection, and the selection may even have accelerated during the past several thousand years…"

In the context of this rapid evolution described by Pinker, it is an intriguing possibility that our psychological strengths are prime candidates to have evolved rapidly over very recent times. This is because our strengths are likely to have continued to evolve (certainly since the Paleolithic period), to enable us to make the most of our rapidly developing environments, whether through avoiding the threats they present or by capitalising on the opportunities they offer.

As technology accelerates, as communications improve beyond our imagination, and as we strive to juggle ever more information and expectations simultaneously, we have developed strengths as the key means of helping us cope with, and succeed in, our complex modern world. Of course, there have always been strengths, but the proliferation of strengths in recent times may be a direct result of the ways in which we have needed to expand our repertoires in order to meet modern challenges and make the most of modern opportunities.

Consider, for example, the strength of creativity, which we used as an example above. In Stone Age times, the sparse evidence we have for creativity is in occasional cave paintings and decorated pottery. Compare this with today, when many more people are involved with creative pursuits – whether as artists, writers, photographers, or musicians, even creative organisational strategists, like Charlie - amongst many others. And equally, almost all of us are now consumers of creative outputs such as music, film, theatre or books. And as our appetite for these creative outputs gets bigger, so too do more people discover and develop their creative strengths to fulfil these appetites. This process reflects the rapid evolution of a strength to meet an opportunity in our environment – an *adaptive solution*, just as evolutionary psychologists have described for our ancestors, but this time with adaptation being much more rapid than evolutionary theory may have traditionally suggested – and just as we have found in the blue moon butterfly, the hammerhead shark and the African elephant..

On one hand, we might consider that the breadth of creativity we see around us today is simply a manifestation of the strength of creativity that existed in our gene pool in the Stone Age, and which is now being deployed according to the needs of our new environment. As is almost always the case with evolution, there is a capability that was selected for previously, on which we are now building. As such, the question is not about whether we have created an entirely new capability (which evolutionary theory would not support), but rather about the speed and extent of change in that earlier capability, in order to meet the challenges and opportunities of our new environment. For example, the need – and hence creativity – to write html code and design internet websites did not exist even thirty years ago. Yet now, millions of people around the world are able to do this, again, building on a strength already present in their gene pool, but adapting that strength exponentially as the situation requires. As Pinker argued, it may well be that selection has accelerated in recent times – and the pace and growth of technological innovation would certainly attest to this.

Nature and Nurture, Chance and Adaptiveness

Many of us will be familiar, at least in outline terms, with the nature-nurture debate. Do we inherit our characteristics from our parents through our genes (nature), or do we develop them through our early life experiences (nurture)? There is now some agreement that for personality characteristics at least, it is some combination of both nature and nurture.

At one level, strengths are very consistent across people and cultures. At another level, strengths are more specific to individuals, and likely reflect the influence of four different factors:

1 **Nature** – our direct genetic endowment;
2 **Nurture** – our early environmental experiences;
3 **Chance** - random variations in our development;
4 **Adaptiveness** - the pursuit of successful performance in a given domain, meaning that we are likely to repeat that approach.

Again, you may find it helpful to refer to Figure 2.1, in order to see how each element in this story of where strengths come from builds on each preceding element: from evolutionary adaptive solutions, to nature, to nurture, to chance, and to adaptiveness.

Given this natural selection for strengths through evolution, it is easy to see how strengths would be conveyed from one generation to the next. It also helps to explain how strengths could be transmitted from parents to their children through genetic heritability – the **nature** side of the nature-nurture debate.

It is also well-established that early childhood experiences (nurture) interact in different ways with the pre-existing capacities and characteristics that people have (nature), which helps to explain how some strengths may be influenced a lot by our genes, whereas others are much more influenced by our early experiences, or **nurture**. Figure 2.1 shows how nurture follows nature, with both nature and nurture building on our evolutionary heritage, and in turn being shaped by chance and adaptiveness.

Chance always has a role to play, since random, unpredictable events can cause our development to shift subtly in one direction or another. As its name suggests, chance is never predictable, and you can never know in advance exactly what effect it will have – but models of development always have to account for chance and random variation, and the model for the development of strengths is no different. Chance events in relation to strengths development could be a passing comment that encouraged us to do more of something (like the 'golden seeds' that we will meet in Chapter 7), or comments that compelled us to stop doing it. These chance events could be finding ourselves suddenly in an environment where we were able to do something that was valuable to us. Or they could be any number of other random things – such is the nature of chance!

A more predictable variation in our development is **adaptiveness**. It is easier to think of tangible examples of adaptiveness, since we all have them throughout our lives. Adaptiveness refers to doing more of the things that we find we are good at, and avoiding doing the things we are not good at (as long as there aren't external pressures compelling us to do them). For example, at school I was hopeless at Design and Technology, so as soon as I had the opportunity, I stopped taking the course. In contrast, I was quite good at French, and so I studied it all the way through to leaving school. I am sure you will have your own examples – but just occasionally they might point in the opposite direction, like my friend John who took an Open University degree and specialised in chemistry – because it was his weakest subject and he wanted a challenge – quite possibly the strength of *Bounceback* in someone who loved a challenge!

Taken together, nature and nurture, and chance and adaptiveness, interact to create patterns of neural wiring within our brains. We can think of the neural structure of our brains as being like a densely packed fishing net in our heads. There are hundreds of thousands of different connections, with each connection leading to several other connections, and groups of connections together, or particular pathways through the connections, representing different elements of our personality, strengths, characteristics and abilities.

These patterns of connections represent the pre-existing capacities that we identified within the definition of a strength in Chapter 1. As such, they help to explain why strengths get stronger when we use them: just like the natural footpath that gets established over time by people taking a shortcut through the field, so our neural connections get stronger and faster the more we use them. In contrast, the ones that we don't use tend to fall into decay and disrepair, just like disused footpaths.

Recognising this, we can start to understand why it is that strengths get stronger when they are used, but weaknesses are always more difficult to develop – and, even when focused on, are never able to be developed to a top level of performance. Understanding the neural wiring of our brains, and how it has developed, also helps us to understand why it is that using strengths is authentic and energising – simply, because we are doing the things that are most natural for us, and following the directions that are right for us. But to put this in the proper context, we need to understand our fundamental assumptions about human nature, which is where we turn next.

Strengths and Human Nature

Strengths are rapid evolutionary adaptations that allow us both to cope with the demands of a fast-changing complex world and to make the most of the opportunities that such a world provides. An evolutionary perspective helps to explain where strengths come from, and how the development of strengths over time is in turn influenced by both nature and nurture, while being shaped by chance and adaptiveness. Strengths can be understood further within the context of theories of human nature. Understanding strengths within this context allows us to make sense of the authenticity and energy that people experience when using their strengths, and the benefits they reap through using them in terms of achieving their goals and enhancing their happiness, well-being and fulfilment.

What is our fundamental human nature? People can have some quite negative views of human nature. As George Mandler describes in his book *Human Nature Explored*:

> *"What happens if we ask people to list the characteristics of human nature?*
> *Usually the result looks something like this:*

Greed	*Violence*
Competition	*Intelligence*
Ambition	*Joy*
Jealousy	*Aggression*

> *... Though the list may contain some positive aspects, it is usually loaded on the negative side. On further exploration, many people will explain the negative aspects by noting that these characteristics are typical of most other people, but less so of themselves, while the positive aspects are more likely to be their own characteristics."*

And yet, even though there may be this immediate reaction that humans are inherently bad and destructive, that is very unlikely to be the case. As Mandler continues:

"It is only after some probing that the positive side of human nature emerges in everyday discourse. It is often referred to as one's "essential humanity," which refers to the caring, empathic nature of the beast....In fact, the majority of human interactions are positive or neutral. It may be the very relative rarity of true acts of malice, aggression and destructiveness that makes them stand out and be memorable, thus distorting our view of the relative probability of positive and negative human acts."

Mandler is right, but there is also a deeper truth at play here – and one which we explore more fully in Chapter 3 – our inherent negativity bias. From this basis, it is understandable that the unthinking assumption about human nature is a negative one. Broadly speaking, there are three grand theories of human nature. We consider each in turn.

Human Nature is Inherently Destructive. The first view of human nature argues that human beings are by their very nature self-serving and destructive, and so they need to be controlled and managed to ensure that they do not do harm to others. This view is often associated with Sigmund Freud. It is, however, difficult to accept this view as a fundamental of human nature, since people have done, currently do, and will continue to do good deeds, and it is very difficult to argue that these good deeds are solely for the benefits to themselves.

Human Nature is in Conflict. The second view argues that human beings are pulled between two different inclinations, the first positive and life-enhancing, the second negative and life-destroying. As such, this view continues, the role of society is to uphold the positive side of people while keeping down the negative side – this actually seems to be the position taken by Katherine Dahlsgaard and colleagues in the opening quote for this chapter, but the view is most typically attributed to Rollo May, a hugely influential existential psychologist. It is easy to see why it may be considered to have merit: if we look around us, it is a simple task to identify people who do good and people who do ill, and this theory of human nature would seem to account for that. It does little, however, to account for why people follow a path that we might deem good, and other people follow a path that we might deem bad.

Human Nature is Inherently Constructive. In contrast, the third view argues that human beings are naturally motivated toward their own growth, development and actualisation, and also the growth, development and actualisation of the people around them. Human beings have an intrinsic tendency to strive towards developing themselves to become all that they can be, and given the right social environmental conditions, this is what they will do, as well as being more inclined to do the same for others. The social environmental conditions, however, are not always right, and so sometimes people will be pulled off course. It is when they are pulled off course that they will act in ways that are negative and destructive. This view is most associated with the humanistic psychologists Carl Rogers and Abraham Maslow, although others who share it include the psychotherapist and writer Karen Horney, and our friend Aristotle, with his invitation to "strain every nerve to live in accordance with the best thing in us."

Given the right social environment, people's tendencies will always be towards these pathways to growth and development, in both themselves and others. As Horney, described it, when people's natural tendency toward self-actualisation (that is, our tendency to want to realise our potential) is given expression:

> "…we become free to grow ourselves, we also free ourselves to love and to feel concern for other people. We will then want to give them the opportunity for unhampered growth when they are young, and to help them in whatever way possible to find and realize themselves when they are blocked in their development. At

any rate, whether for ourselves or for others, the ideal is the libera-
tion and cultivation of the forces which lead to self-realization."

Authenticity and Goal Attainment

The essence of the self-actualising view is that we all have directions in life that are right for us. Importantly, we also have an inner
compass that lets us know – at least if we listen to it – whether or not
we are keeping on track, whether or not we are being true to ourselves.
This state of being true to ourselves – of following the directions in life
that are right for us – is called *authenticity*. We talk about authenticity a
lot in modern times, especially in relation to its counterpart – inauthenticity. Often, we have a sense of when someone or something is being
inauthentic, not being honest, not being true to themselves, or even
being a downright fake - just think about inauthentic works of art -
attempted copies of some of the great masters, that lose their value
massively when their inauthenticity is exposed. Similarly, we don't like
people to be inauthentic.

When we are following the directions that are right for us, we are
being authentic. We feel authentic. We feel like we are fully alive, being
the person who we really are. Following and using our strengths are
great examples of this authenticity, since by using our strengths we are
doing what we feel naturally drawn to do, and acting in accordance
with what is best about each of us. When we do this, we feel like we are
being ultimately true to ourselves. As Alastair Ham, Group
Organisational Development Director at Aviva, puts it:

*"When I am using my strengths fully, I feel like I am in flow, in
the zone, fully engaged and energised. I feel like I am being fully
me, the person who I really am and who I want to be."*

Authenticity is a very powerful feeling because it comes from an alignment between who we are, what we believe, and what we are doing. Strengths contribute to these feelings of authenticity because strengths are an aspect of who we are (our pre-existing capacities) and it feels very natural, authentic and congruent for us to be using them. As we explored above, this is because we are using the pathways in our brain that already exist, and that feel natural and appropriate for us. When we are doing this, it feels good and it feels right – just as authenticity would predict, and just as the research evidence shows.

Authenticity is associated with enhanced well-being, better health, reduced psychological distress, and improved relationships. For example, Ken Sheldon from the University of Missouri, a leading figure in the positive psychology movement, found that higher levels of authenticity were associated with higher levels of self-esteem and lower levels of anxiety, depression and stress, as well as lower levels of physical symptoms of illness. In our own work, we have shown that authenticity is associated with higher levels of happiness, fulfilment, gratitude, emotional intelligence and self-esteem, and lower levels of anxiety, stress and negative emotion. Further, we have demonstrated how using your strengths more is associated with higher levels of authenticity, happiness, fulfilment, and positive energy.

When people are acting authentically, they are acting in alignment with themselves and their core nature. Because of this alignment, they are able to function more effectively and have more energy available to themselves. We can think of this alignment as being like when a bicycle wheel is turning and is set perfectly straight, working most efficiently. But when the wheel is slightly off-centre, and is catching on the brakes, that alignment is missing, and so it takes more effort to achieve less – because we are trying to turn the wheel against resistance. When we are behaving in ways that are authentic, we are like the wheel turning when it is perfectly aligned – at our most effective and efficient.

Using strengths is such a powerful proposition because it builds on our natural capabilities and preferences, and does so in a way that is authentic and in keeping with the directions that we naturally want to follow – we have clear alignment and hence greatest efficiency by acting in the ways that are most natural and authentic to us. This alignment and efficiency is a powerful source of our psychological energy. Because using our strengths represents this alignment in practice, we find using our strengths energising, enabling us to feel fully alive and as if we are being 'who we really are.'

Another area where this really matters is in relation to our goals, and how effective we are at achieving them. In one study by Ken Sheldon and Andrew Elliot, participants were followed over a period of time to see how effective they were at achieving their goals, and if there was anything about the nature of the goals that made the goals more or less likely to be achieved. Sheldon and Elliot found that people were more likely to achieve their goals if those goals were more intrinsic, that is, consistent with the person's developing interests and core values, which they labelled as self-concordant goals (we might also describe them as authentic goals). Further, when people did achieve these types of goals, they were better able to satisfy their psychological needs, and so to increase their well-being as a result. In a second series of studies, Ken Sheldon and his colleagues showed that people who were more successful at attaining their goals, and who satisfied their needs and enhanced their well-being as a result, were subsequently more likely to achieve further goals in the future. As a result, they suggested that the attainment of self-concordant goals (which were consistent with people's authentic selves) caused an upward spiral that increased need satisfaction and well-being, and enhanced later goal attainment as a result.

When I was an academic at the University of Leicester, I conducted some research in which I was interested in the question of whether people were more likely to attain their goals, according to how closely the person's strengths fitted with their goals. For example, if a person set themselves a goal of doing better in their exams, and they had a strength in love of learning, they might be better placed to achieve that goal. If they set themselves a goal of making new friends, and they had a strength of social intelligence, they might be better placed to achieve that goal.

The study started in early October, at the start of the Christmas term, with 230 second year undergraduates serving as participants. First of all, they completed the VIA Inventory of Strengths, and provided information about their top three goals for the term. Many of these goals were about doing well in their studies, but also included things like making the university netball team, taking part in a production by the amateur dramatics society, or making new friends. The most amusing goal must be the one given by the person who said "To find someone who is my equal" – I don't think that modesty was one of their top five strengths! At the same time as completing the strengths inventory and writing down their top three goals, the study participants also completed measures of need satisfaction and well-being.

Then, six weeks later, I asked them how they were doing in relation to attaining their goals, their need satisfaction, and their well-being. Also, I asked them how much they were using their top five strengths in helping them to achieve their goals. To assess this, I designed a *strengths X goals* matrix, whereby people rated how much they had used a particular strength to achieve a particular goal. This procedure was repeated after ten weeks, so that we had two sets of data following on from the initial phase of the study, which allowed us to look at how strengths and goal attainment, as well as need satisfaction and well-being, might be related over time.

What did we find when we looked at the data? Across the three different goals, people were more likely to attain their goals if they used their strengths more as they were trying to achieve their goals. Simply put, when strengths fitted better with the goals that people were pursuing, they were more likely to achieve those goals, because they were using their strengths to enable them to do so. Further, when people attained these goals, they were more effective at satisfying their psychological needs and achieved greater well-being as a result. Overall, these findings indicate that we are better at achieving our goals when we are using our strengths, and when we do, we will be happier and more fulfilled as a result.

This is the essential promise of the strengths approach, and why we believe that realising our strengths is the smallest thing that we can do to make the biggest difference. When we realise our strengths we are becoming the best we are capable of being. We are following the developmental directions that nature intended for us, and for which our actualising tendency guides us. As we do this, we feel authentic and energised, being connected to our true selves and doing the things that are right for us. When we are acting in this way, our performance improves, whether specifically at work or in life more broadly. We achieve our goals more effectively and are better enabled to make our greatest contributions in work and life – in just the way that nature intended for us. And as we do so, we are happier, more engaged, and more fulfilled as a result. For all of these reasons, realising our strengths is the royal road to optimal development and performance. As Figure 2.3 shows, *realising our strengths is the smallest thing we can do to make the biggest difference.*

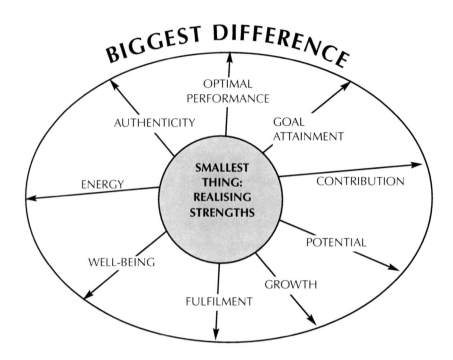

Figure 2.3 The Smallest Thing to Make the Biggest Difference

Having gone right back to our evolutionary heritage, and then seen how we are shaped by nature, nurture, chance and adaptiveness, we can observe how our strengths have evolved over time and developed in us as individuals. Having established where strengths come from, and how they are central to our well-being and optimal functioning, it is now time to turn our attention to how we go about using our strengths to best effect. To do so, we need to counter another evolutionary over-hang - our negativity bias - and recognise the role of the golden mean and optimal strengths use – to which we turn in the next chapter.

Key Points

- Strengths are adaptive solutions that have evolved throughout human history. It is likely that this evolution has become more rapid in recent times.

- The development of our strengths is shaped by evolution, nature, nurture, chance, adaptiveness and our actualising tendency.

- Some strengths are universally recognised and valued; others are likely to be more specific to particular cultures.

- When we are using our strengths, we are more authentic and energised, have higher levels of well-being and fulfilment, and are more likely to achieve our goals and deliver better performance.

- Using strengths is the smallest thing that we can do to make the biggest difference.

Areas for Reflection and Action

- Are you able to identify events in your earlier life experiences that shaped the development and direction of your strengths?

- What is your view of human nature? What are the implications of this for what you think about the strengths approach?

- From your own experience, do you feel a sense of energy, authenticity and well-being when you are doing the things that you do best? Are you better able to achieve your goals when you are doing these things?

THREE

Our Negativity Bias and the Golden Mean

"Moral virtue is a mean...it is a mean between two vices, the one involving excess, the other deficiency...For in everything it is no easy task to find the middle...but to do this to the right person, to the right extent, at the right time, with the right motive, and in the right way, that is not...easy."

Aristotle, The Nicomachean Ethics

ALL OF US, to some degree – and some much more than others – tend to focus on the negative, on what's wrong, on what isn't working. Why could this be, and what could we have to gain from it? Perhaps most importantly for our current concerns, what does it mean for our ability to realise strengths in ourselves and others? These are the questions with which we are concerned in the first part of the chapter, where we investigate where this negative focus comes from and why. In the second part of the chapter, we explore another aspect of why this focus on the negative is appropriate - to ensure that we don't take our strengths too far – the topic of the golden mean and optimal strengths use.

The reason that we tend to notice what's wrong and what isn't working is our inherent negativity bias, something that we carry with us from our evolutionary past. Across a whole range of things - including our reactions to events, the effects of positive and negative emotions, the impact of good or bad parenting, – whatever the topic, the pattern is depressingly consistent: bad is stronger than good. In fact, even when researchers have tried to find instances of where, all other things being equal, good may be stronger than bad, they have failed.

If you are one of the people who finds it difficult to attend to strengths and what is working, finding yourself being constantly pulled back to focus on weakness, problems, and deficit – you are not alone. You are just a typical, regular member of the human race. Welcome. And you are in good company – as Parminder Basran, the wonderfully positive Business Controller of the Authentic Food Company describes:

"Working from the strengths approach can be counterintuitive, and I am finding it harder than I thought it would be. It's difficult to implement – and that's not to say that we are not doing it – but I am finding it harder than I thought it would be. Is it in everybody's make up to look at the negative side in people? It happens in our business all the time. You can box off somebody's strengths, taking from that the very wrong idea that they are rubbish in every other area. But that is not the case, so you need to be careful to pay attention to other areas too. You really have to train yourself as a leader and a manager to work in this way, and if I'm finding that tough, then there must be other people who are as well, and so we need to work together to overcome it. The strengths philosophy is a very important part of what we are doing at the Authentic Food

Company, but doing it every single day, every single week, every single month, is tough."

Why could it be that Parminder finds this so tough to do? What could we have to gain from this tendency to focus on the negative? The reasons, as will become apparent, are very good, healthy, and adaptive ones. But they only tell part of the story.

If you think about the human body, we all need a heart, lungs, liver, stomach, and brain, amongst many other things, for the body to function effectively and successfully. Remove any one of these component parts, and the body simply does not work anymore. Yet equally, having only one of the component parts is in no way sufficient and complete. For a human body to be successful, it requires that each component part fulfils its function. When even one of them breaks down, the body begins to dysfunction, and ultimately, to die. So, no matter how many well-functioning parts there are, the attention needs to be on the single failing part.

Paul Rozin and Edward Royzman identify five other reasons for the negativity bias that seems inherent to all of us:

- Negative events are more potent than positive events;
- Negative events become more negative more quickly than positive events become more positive;
- Combining negatives and positives, the negatives always come out stronger;
- Negative things are more varied and numerous, and engender a wider repertoire of reactions, than do positive things;
- Taken together, these four elements of negativity bias create a fifth reason - negative events are more **contagious** than their positive counterparts.

It is the contagious nature of negative events, like the contagious nature of germs, that renders them so potent. For example, somebody being sad around us is much more likely to make us feel sad, than somebody being happy around us is likely to make us feel happy. Similarly, a wasp flying into our jar of raspberry jam renders the jam inedible, but putting a spoonful of jam into a wasp's nest does nothing for the edibility of the wasps! For all of these reasons, we seem quite naturally to pay attention to the negative.

Understood in this way, we can begin to see why it might be that we are attuned to the negative, to what is bad or dangerous, to threat. Evolution has shaped us in this way, because, simply put, if it had not, we would *not* have evolved to survive and reproduce through passing our genes into the gene pool of the next generations. Attending to the negative is adaptive; it enables us to survive. But this now creates a paradox, for two reasons.

The first reason is that we don't, typically, live under the conditions of imminent threat that our ancestors did (at least those of us in the developed world). We have greater physical security and freedom from physical threat. Nutritious and sustaining foods are easily available. We have homes that at their most basic provide us with shelter and protection, but often provide us with great comfort or even luxury. We have access to healthcare and medication that renders us significantly less vulnerable to injury and disease, thereby improving our quality of life and extending our longevity. And all of these ensure living conditions that are more benevolent for us today than our ancestors ever experienced throughout human history. As a result, much of our attentional focus on the negative is wasted, an evolutionary over-hang from times past.

The second reason is that giving so much focus to the negative leaves us with a significant opportunity cost – the cost of failing to pay attention to, identify and build on what works. If all our attention and energy is spent on looking for threats that aren't there, or worrying about problems that are never going to happen, then we have missed the opportunity to deploy that energy, effort and time to better effect in looking at how we can build on success and strengthen what works. The biggest casualty of this negativity bias can be the attention and focus we give to our strengths – of course, a major theme of this book. As such, we need to be aware of this negativity bias, and we need to do what we can to counter it, recognising that it does have a role to play, but that it should not dominate everything we do.

Countering the Negativity Bias

Just as none of us want to be average, we have seen that we do seem to be hardwired to focus on negativity. In the context of strengths and weaknesses, we attend to what *isn't* working, rather than what *is* working. Many people I have spoken with – like Parminder Basran - think that this attention to the negative is something that is peculiar to them: it isn't. In fact, it could be one of the most universal manifestations of human psychology that exists. People everywhere, in all sorts of different contexts and through all manner of different tasks and activities, focus on the negative.

If it is the case that the negative focus wins out each time, and as Roy Baumeister and his colleagues argue, that "bad is stronger than good," what can be done about it? First and foremost, simply being aware of this evolutionary over-hang can be a powerful antidote to it. When we catch ourselves falling into the negativity trap again, we have taken a big step to overcoming the hold that it has upon us. As Parminder again describes:

"A lot more often now, I catch myself slipping into focusing on the negative, on what someone hasn't done well. But at least I have caught myself and done something about it – it bothers me to think what things would be like if I didn't catch myself, and I guess that is a challenge that all of us will have to overcome."

We can also start to counter our negativity bias by taking off the critical, evaluative spectacles that we tend to wear. Arvinder Dhesi, Group Talent Management Director at Aviva, provides this wonderful analogy of how we would behave if we were to apply this negativity bias to machines, in the same way we tend to apply it to people:

"Think back to how you reacted when you were given your first bicycle. Did you question the fact that it only had two wheels? Were you concerned that your parents had invited you to ride on something so inherently unstable? Did you ask for a full list of risks and concerns, and what had been done to mitigate them? Did you ask to see a business case to prove it would be better than your tricycle? Did you insist that someone calculate the 'Return on Investment' for the time it would take you to learn how to ride? I suspect you didn't.

When we take off our critical, evaluative spectacles, we can feel that sense of wonder again. When we keep them on all the time, we are always looking for what's missing and what's broken.

You would never complain about your refrigerator in the same way. You wouldn't say, "Well, it's pretty good at keeping food cool, but it's useless at washing dishes!" Does your fridge have a 'development plan' stuck to it, listing your disappointments? "Over the next twelve months I expect you to become more like the microwave oven!"

Yet this is our entrenched mentality when it comes to people. Unleashing the talent in employees begins with an appreciation of their capacities rather than their deficiencies."

Another way in which we can get round the power of the negative is through strength in numbers: having more good can overwhelm, or crowd out, the bad. Simply put, we need to have more good experiences than bad experiences in order to function positively, and we need to experience more positive emotions than negative emotions to be at our best. Indeed, this is what we see from the research on well-being and optimal human functioning, where scientific studies have now shown that we do indeed need a larger number of positives to outweigh the more potent negatives.

For example, Barbara Fredrickson and Marcial Losada examined the extent of positive emotions experienced by people relative to the extent of negative emotions, and assessed what ratio might be found among people who are flourishing. They found a ratio of 3:1 – people needed three positive emotions, events, or experiences, for every negative one. And equally important, it wasn't the case that having infinitely more positive emotions was better: when the ratio moved beyond eleven positives to every one negative, people got stuck going round in circles. On this basis, it does seem that it is entirely possible to have too much of a good thing, but somewhere between a ratio of 3:1 and 11:1 positive to negative emotions should be optimal. Except for relationships, that is, where marriage researcher John Gottman found that long-lasting, happy and successful marriages reported positive to negative emotion ratios of 5:1 or more – so there is no room for complacency when we get home from work!

Intriguingly, using strengths is one powerful way in which we can experience these positive emotions. As my research with Reena Govindji has shown, people who use their strengths more are more likely to be happier, more fulfilled, and have a greater feeling of positive energy. Thus, at the same time as we can counter the negativity bias by focusing more on our strengths, so does using our strengths create the positive emotions that enable us to flourish and hence become less inclined to focus always on the negative – thus creating a virtuous circle whereby attending to and overcoming our negativity bias enables us to focus on our strengths more. In turn, using our strengths more fully and creating positive emotions in the first place then renders us better able to overcome our negativity bias, as Figure 3.1 shows.

Strengths and the Golden Mean

Just as we need to overcome our negativity bias, we should not wish to switch it off completely, for it does have an important role to play. As always, the right path exists between two extremes, and this again is a central message of the strengths approach, properly applied:

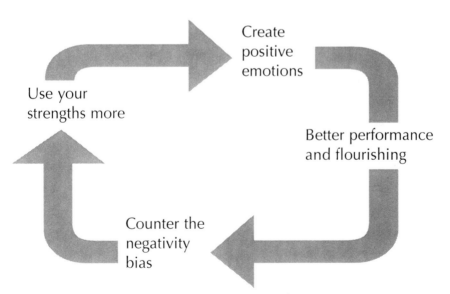

Figure 3.1 The Virtuous Circle of Using Strengths

the golden mean. Using strengths most effectively and optimally means that we should not overplay them or underplay them, but rather use **the right strength, to the right amount, in the right way, and at the right time**. The golden mean is not intended to suggest 'everything in moderation,' or a bland average, but is rather about doing things so that the best overall result is achieved. As such, the golden mean points us to be aware of both strengths overused and strengths underused, while always focusing on how to use our strengths in a way that is *just right*.

The key question, here, though, is how we know what the right thing is, how much is the right amount, which is the right way, and when the right time? It is for contexts like these – which surround us every day - where the answer about what to do is not obvious, that we need practical wisdom, or *phronesis*, as it was labelled by Aristotle. Barry Schwartz and Kenneth Sharpe identified that there are three primary reasons why practical wisdom is needed in the judgment of our everyday actions:

- First, we need to decide what is relevant. Strengths don't come with a user's instruction pack that dictates where and when they should be used – we are left to work that one out for ourselves;
- Second, using any two strengths may appear equally appropriate, if for different reasons, yet the choice leaves us with a conflict. Which strength, which course of action should we choose, if both appear valid and yet they are incompatible?
- Third, there is the issue of specificity. Having decided which strength is most appropriate to use, what exactly should we do to deploy it? Practical wisdom enables the exercise of appropriate judgment in changing circumstances and evolving contexts, where a constant re-evaluation and re-weighing of possible choices and their consequences is required. Ultimately,

we should aim to arrive at a decision that is the right thing, to the right amount, in the right way, and at the right time – or, more simply, the golden mean.

Extending this issue of which is the right strength to use, and when, the ancient Greek concept of *antakolouthia* (the mutual entailment of virtues), is concerned with the question of how strengths are used in relation to other strengths. The essence of *antakolouthia* is that no virtue is a virtue by itself, since true virtue requires us to balance the deployment of opposites. Thus, just as with Aristotle's concept of the golden mean, the route to best performance lies between doing something too much and doing it too little, but also doing it in relation to the other things that one should do. The example that is often cited to illustrate the principle of *antakolouthia* is that '*honesty without compassion leads to cruelty.*'

Imagine, for example, the situation where a bride-to-be is putting on her bridal gown two hours before the ceremony on her wedding day. "What do you think to my wedding dress?" she asks. From the perspective of *antakolouthia*, this would not be the moment to say that you don't like the colour and that she would have better with something that was less closely cut (honesty): her reaction could legitimately be one of distress, even devastation (the result of our perceived cruelty). Rather, compassion suggests that the brutal honesty of the answer is mitigated, and we save the feelings of the bride-to-be by a measured response about how beautiful she looks, and how fortunate her groom is to have her as his bride. The mutual entailment of virtues directs us to consider the extent to which any given strength (e.g., honesty) is used, while being mindful of a higher and more important end (e.g., compassion rather than cruelty), rather than just blindly using the strength to its fullest degree.

Understanding the golden mean and strengths in relation to one another are very powerful ways to start using strengths optimally. When we fail to do so, it is likely because we are either not making the best use of our strengths (strengths underplayed) or we are doing them too much (strengths overplayed). We now consider each of these in turn.

Strengths Underplayed

To many of us, it may seem counterintuitive that a strength can be underplayed, because a lot of what we might have heard about the downsides of strengths concerns strengths being taken too far (more on that below). Even so, strengths underplayed can be as much a problem for optimal effectiveness as strengths overplayed, not least because strengths underplayed represent a potential that is not being realised, and to paraphrase an old saying, we should not be content to hide our talents under the bushel of inactivity or underdevelopment. As we discussed in Chapter 2, this is not how human beings are made; it is not what we were designed to do. Our actualising tendency is focused on us becoming all that we can be, and developing, polishing and refining all of our strengths is central to this. Realising our strengths is a lifelong activity, a process of becoming rather than a destination at which we finally arrive.

Why might it be that a strength is underplayed? The most frequent reason is that we simply don't recognise our ability in an area as a strength. We may simply take it for granted, assuming that everyone else can do it at least as well, and get frustrated and impatient with them when they can't. In fact, this can be a first indication of a strength not being recognised in ourselves, if we consistently get frustrated with other people's inability to do things as well, or as quickly, as we are able to do them ourselves. If this happens to you, it is worth pausing and asking yourself the question of whether, in fact, you have a real strength in this area that you have not yet fully recognised or realised.

Given that strengths are pre-existing capacities that feel authentic and energising for us, we can be forgiven for thinking that they have always been there. As a result, we can fall into the trap of not recognising them as anything special, instead taking them for granted and assuming that it's the same for everyone else. Further, because of the dominant focus on weakness – through both our evolutionary tendencies and the Curse of Mediocrity – we may well be unlikely to have paid any systematic attention to our strengths. As a result, our developmental focus is almost exclusively fixed on weaknesses: how can we get better by improving on the things that we are not good at?

This is compounded by people's difficulty in accepting and internalising positive feedback, of which feedback on strengths would be a significant part. There are difficulties and misconceptions around both giving and receiving positive feedback, which we consider in more detail in Chapter 5, *Be Yourself – Better*. As a result of these difficulties, we may be resistant to taking on board the idea that we have a particular strength. Not recognising a strength in ourselves can be the single biggest blocker we face to our taking ownership of that strength, internalising it, and making the most of what we have to offer.

Once we are prepared to accept that we might just have a particular strength, how can we go about developing our strengths that are being underplayed? The practice of building strengths which were underused is simply around using them more, trying them out and monitoring the results – always looking for the feedback and calibration of whether one can do it more, or whether there is a need to turn it down because we have gone too far.

If we don't, we run the risk of the two major and limiting implications of leaving an strength underdeveloped. Having a strength and not using it is the equivalent of having a million pounds but keeping it under your mattress: you not only lose the potential for investment income, but your capital is also depleted by inflation. The corollary for underplaying strengths is that we lose the opportunity to be our most effective (lost investment income), at the same time as the strength becomes rusty and in need of development (capital depreciation). In contrast, when a strength is polished and honed, the pay-offs can be enormous, both psychologically, in terms of well-being and fulfilment, and through enhanced performance and delivery, whether that is at work, in relationships, or elsewhere in life.

Strengths Overplayed

Just as we may lose the possibilities of what we are capable of by underplaying our strengths, so too can we undermine our best performances by taking a strength too far. Strengths can be overplayed – taken too far – for two major reasons:

- First, because using the strength worked and was highly effective before, and yet the context has changed, but we haven't.
- Second, strengths can be overplayed because we believe – implicitly – that using that particular strength is the only thing we know, and we don't feel that we have anything else in our toolkit to be able to respond more accordingly.

Consider, for example, Ginger Gregory's story about how she learned to use her great strength of creativity to its optimal degree, rather than too much. As the Global HR Head for Novartis Institutes of Biomedical Research in the United States, having too many creative ideas can be unsettling for the people around her - not least because the HR team looks to Ginger for direction. If she is always in idea creation mode, coming up with new ways of doing things and novel things to do, then her team are left unsure about what they should be focusing on themselves. In order not to lose the value of this strength, but also acknowledging that it could not always be used in her current leadership role, Ginger described how she managed her situation:

> *"One of my greatest strengths is around having ideas, and so I have built this into my working week in order to enable me to support my team. We have a weekly brainstorming session where people bring along ideas and projects, and we choose one or two to focus on for that week. We come up with ideas, create new perspectives, and come up with wacky ways of looking at things. If we didn't do that, sometimes I would be in that sort of setting, and sometimes I wouldn't – and so I would be missing the opportunity to make the most of this strength around idea generation. Now, as a leader, I can't always be in idea generation mode, because it can be confusing for people. But through setting up these brainstorming sessions, we have created a way of working that means that I get to use my creativity, but that also allows other people to recognise that we are in this brainstorming mode, and to respond accordingly. Without this, it would be much more difficult, and much less effective."*

When strengths are taken too far, it almost always leads to imbalance, since focusing too much on one side almost always means that the other side is being neglected. For example, Alex Bailey, Head of Organisational Effectiveness at Aviva, tells the story of how her strengths combine in ways that make her more vulnerable to overplaying them than most. Alex's strengths are all focused on the future: having a strategic view of things, always looking forward, and always wanting to achieve more, each and every day. Taking these strengths in combination, it's easy to recognise that she isn't your average happy-go-lucky kind of character. Instead, she is someone who has a view of what she wants and how she is going to get there – and someone who will work as hard as it takes to make that happen. But the flipside to these strengths being overplayed – and they easily can be – is that she isn't too good at taking time to stop and celebrate her successes, or taking stock of what she has achieved, something to which Alex has now found a solution, with the help of her husband:

> "My husband is great at encouraging me to do that. Every so often, he'll buy a bottle of champagne, and while we're enjoying a nice meal, he'll encourage me to take some time and stop to recognise – and celebrate – what it is that I have achieved. In this way, I have learned to be more grounded and appreciative – and to make sure that the strengths that I have are not taken too far."

As Bob Kaplan and Rob Kaiser describe it in their book *The Versatile Leader: How to Make the Most of Your Strengths – Without Overdoing It*, we might consider that leadership has two fundamental dimensions: a forceful-enabling continuum and a strategic-operational continuum. To the extent that, as a leader, you are extremely forceful, the corollary is that you may not be being sufficiently enabling. Similarly, to the extent that you are overly strategic, the day to day details of operations may be overlooked. The argument is not that we should be all things to all men (the Curse of Mediocrity again) – because, inevitably, we have natural strengths, preferences and inclinations – but the argument is that we should all strive to demonstrate versatility: the ability to do more or to do less, to turn the volume up or down on a particular strength as the situation requires.

Tracy Wood, a Partner at the Big Four professional services firm Ernst and Young, describes exactly this from her own experience:

"I'm a very focused individual and I am very task-oriented. When I know what I want to do, I will just go out there and get it done. That can be very positive, because it means that I will be brave and enthusiastic about what I want to get done, and I'll make it happen. But about five years ago, I hit a point in my career where I suddenly had to realise that it was actually turning people off, and I needed to do something about it. I had some really tough feedback from the team that I was working with, and I wasn't expecting it at all. The people I reported to thought I was a star, but the people who worked with me and for me couldn't stand me at all. When I heard this, I was mortified! I realised that I had taken my strength of focus and task-orientation too far, because I would do anything and everything to please my clients and keep to the work agenda, but I had failed to bring my people along with me. When I realised this, I knew that I had to learn to flex my style more and to be able to do both – and since I've learned this, things have been so much better all round."

This concept of a volume control for strengths, rather than an on-off switch, has transformed the understanding of many of our clients. Recognising their ability to do something less, or to do it only in certain circumstances, rather than feeling the need to stop doing it entirely (especially when, quite rightly, they consider it has been a key enabler of their success to date) is an understanding that is central to the successful application of the strengths approach. Being able to do more or do less, according to the demands of the situation and what is most appropriate, is a hallmark of wise strengths application, which is always determined by context and situation. The concept of the volume control shows how reference to the golden mean enables the most effective and optimal use of strengths, according to the requirements of the situation, as Figure 3.2 shows.

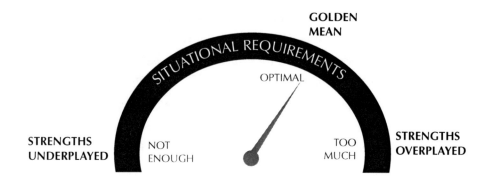

Figure 3.2 Strengths Use and the Golden Mean

Some of us will be able to turn our strengths up or down intu-itively – without even realising it. For example, when I asked Alastair Ham about whether he had ever being aware of overplaying his strengths, he replied "No, never," but then on reflection, continued:

> "Well, yes, as I think about it, I suppose that I do automatically tone down my strengths when I need to. I don't always think about it consciously, but I am increasingly aware that I need to give other people the space to do what they do, allowing them to reach their own decisions, rather than trying to impose my own solutions on them before they have been able to think things through for themselves."

In acknowledging this, Alastair was recognising the golden mean of optimal strengths use. Using strengths just to the right amount, not too much and not too little, through understanding how to use them appropriately as the situation requires, while avoiding getting to the point where a strength was being used too much.

One of the ways in which we can calibrate whether we are using a strength too much or too little is, quite simply, by asking others. While we may be resistant to positive feedback, we should actively develop our receptivity to feedback from people about how effective we are being. Asking others whether we are doing something too much, or even too little, can be a powerful way of building this feedback culture. As Bob Kaplan, a partner in the US leadership consulting firm Kaplan DeVries describes it:

> *"Over time, I have learned how to dial up or dial down on my strengths according to what the situation needs. I have learned how to calibrate off other people by asking them if I am doing too much – and I always remember the answer I got once about overplaying my persistence, when one of my colleagues replied to me, 'Bob, you're just like the sea, you just keep coming back!' Since that remark, I have learned to ask the question about whether I need to dial down a little!"*

For others, though, this insight may be less obvious and they may need a little more prompting before the eureka moment when they realise that some of the things that they are doing – while they started out as strengths – are no longer helping. And, in fact, they might have become potentially fatal flaws that are undermining their performance. In each case, the point being made is that there is a strength being used to excess that causes people to come off the rails, to 'derail' as the management literature describes it. It is not using the strength per se that is the problem, but rather using the strength too much – as the executive derailment literature shows.

Strengths Overplayed: The Case of Executive Derailment

Executive derailment is about the idea that strengths become so-called weaknesses which then cause senior executives to fall off the track, or derail, doing damage both to themselves and their organisations. Typically, this is because strengths have been overplayed – and this has been used by some authors to argue that we shouldn't focus on strengths at all.

Two of the leading writers on executive derailment are Michael Lombardo and Robert Eichinger. In 1989, they published what was to become a highly influential guide, *Preventing Derailment: What to do Before it's Too Late*. The opening sentence of this guide read as follows: "Many of the strengths that lead high-potential managers to early promotions become weaknesses," so setting in place the implicit assumption that was to permeate executive development going forward: *Don't focus on strengths, because strengths become weaknesses, and weaknesses will derail you and your organisation*. Lombardo and Eichinger's assertions continued, with the claim that "Regardless of the particular combination, many future leaders have big strengths and corollary big weaknesses." Again, the message they want to convey is clear: *Don't focus on making a strength stronger, because it will become a weakness that derails you*. Unfortunately for them, there is much more to it than this.

It is likely that executive derailment is itself a misleading reflection of our pervasive negativity bias playing out yet again. That is, we simply notice executive derailment because the downfall is so spectacular, while not paying attention to the many, many, many more executives who deliver their work successfully, even spectacularly well. In the same way, we remember aircraft crashes because they are rare and spectacular, but we pay far less attention to car accidents because they are more commonplace - and yet, irrationally, many more people suffer from fear of flying than suffer from fear of driving.

Why is this? It is well-established that people attend to negative events that are extremely salient, and consider them as occurring much more frequently than they actually do. One explanation for our fear of flying relative to our fear of driving is the greater salience of air crashes, and our flashbulb memories for these events. Air crashes are rare, and so are given major television coverage. As emotive events, we remember them vividly because the memory is encoded in a particular part of the brain, the amygdala, which stores emotional memories. It is very likely that executive derailment follows a similar pattern.

The spectacular downfall of once major players such as Nick Leeson at Barings, Bernie Ebbers and Scott Sullivan at WorldCom, and Kenneth Lay and Jeffrey Skilling at Enron, and the damage that their derailment leaves behind, makes for headline news. Headline news creates emotional salience, and emotional salience creates an emotional flashbulb memory. The result is that we remember derailment much more vividly, and the vividness of our memories tricks us into thinking that it is much more commonplace than it actually is. This also helps to explain why the "strengths become weaknesses" mantra is so powerful, and hence can become so deeply embedded.

The executive derailment and strengths-become-weaknesses arguments are powerfully presented, and can easily hook into our evolutionary predisposition to pay attention to the negative. But they ignore the weight of evidence that focusing on strengths actually enables higher performance, and that people get stronger at the things they were already good at. For example, research with 19,187 employees by the Corporate Leadership Council (CLC) showed that focusing on performance strengths *increased* performance by a massive 36.4%. In contrast, focusing on performance weakness caused performance to *decline* by 26.8%. In CLC terms, strengths are an A-driver: one of the top factors that enable high performance. Similarly, the opportunity to use one's strengths at work every day is a core predictor of engagement and performance. So much for anecdote and assertion, the empirical data tell a different story: using our strengths is key to us being A+.

But is this to say that Lombardo and Eichinger are entirely wrong? No. As ever, there is a middle position that is closest to the truth, and which contains the best of the arguments from each side – people with the strength of *Balance* will likely have already spotted what this is! In essence, an extreme form of the strengths approach could be '*Focus on strengths and ignore weaknesses*' – and it seems to be this to which Lombardo and Eichinger are responding. But their equally extreme position of '*Don't focus on strengths at all, because strengths become weaknesses*' also misses the reality of the situation – as the Corporate Leadership Council data, amongst others, clearly indicate. The more accurate position is that one should focus on using strengths *as much or as little as the situation requires*, while still *managing weaknesses* to the extent that they cannot be made *irrelevant* – themes which we consider below in Chapter 6, *Harnessing Strengths at Work*. In essence, whenever we are using strengths, we should be striving to do so optimally, according to the golden mean: the right thing, to the right amount, in the right way, and at the right time. Good advice that has lasted over 2,000 years!

Key Points

- We all have an inherent negativity bias that means we focus on the negative, on what's wrong, on what isn't working. This is an evolutionary over-hang, and is adaptive – as long as we don't do it too much.

- To use strengths optimally, we need to do so according to the golden mean: the right strength, to the right amount, in the right way and at the right time.

- If we underplay our strengths, we miss the opportunity for making our greatest contributions. We may underplay strengths because we take them for granted or don't recognise them as strengths.

- If we overplay our strengths, we will damage our performance. We may overplay strengths because the context has changed and we haven't, or because we think that it is the only thing we know.

- To be most effective, we should learn how to turn strengths up or down, according to the situation and need – with reference to the golden mean.

Areas for Reflection and Action

- Are you aware of your own negativity bias? Does this get in the way of things? What can you do to counter this negative focus?

- Can you identify strengths that you might be underplaying? If so, you are missing opportunities to contribute. What can you do to turn them up more?

- Can you identify strengths that you might be overplaying? If so, you are damaging your performance. What can you do to turn them down?

FOUR

Strengthspotting

"Each of us has much more hidden inside us than we have had a chance to explore."

Muhammad Yunus,
Banker to the Poor: The Story of Grameen Bank

DO YOU KNOW what your strengths are? Do you know the strengths of your husband or wife? Your mother or father? Your children? Your colleagues at work? Of course, having read this far into the book, you are at an advantage compared to many people, because, sadly, studies to date have shown that only around one-third of people have any meaningful understanding of what their strengths are. You should now, however, be able to take a giant stride forward, just by starting to pay attention to strengths, by acknowledging that strengths exist, and by being aware of the inherent negativity bias that can get in the way of us recognising our strengths. You should also have some sense of what strengths are and what they look like, both of which are integral elements to how we can go about identifying them. The topic of identifying strengths in yourself and others – or what we call strengthspotting - is the focus of this chapter.

If you think about it carefully, you can probably spot the things that you really look forward to doing. The things in which you just lose yourself. The things that make you feel like 'the real you' – fully alive, fully engaged, and fully immersed in the activity. For some of us, we don't even need to think about them – we just know. We are so used to doing them and have spotted them often enough to know that they are something important that merits our attention. For others of us, we might need to think a little more carefully – either because we haven't learned to look at things in this way, or because the answers just don't seem so immediately clear cut. But for every one of us – you can be sure – when we do find the strengths that make us feel this way, life and work will take an important step towards being more productive and fulfilling. As Jonathan Hill, a business psychologist who has worked with strengths for many years, describes it:

> "The best evidence for strengths is an attraction to a particular type of activity, or rapid learning in particular areas, or evidence of partic-ular aptitudes at a young age. The distinctive feature of the strengths approach is that it leads us to a philosophy of human development that focuses on what is right with people and the best that they have to offer. It focuses on rapid learning and optimal development, but in a way that acknowledges continual growth and development over the lifespan, thereby recognising that people are developing all the time. But to be best enabled to do that, people first need to know what to look for in themselves that might be their dominant strengths."

By now, I hope you will be starting to gain a better understanding of your *own* strengths, and in this chapter we explore the different ways in which we can identify strengths. By the end of the book, I hope you will be a skilled observer of strengths, able to both identify and build on strengths in yourself and to recognise and enable them in others, thereby realising strengths in both senses of the word.

Broadly speaking, there are two major ways through which we can start to identify strengths. The first are individually focused observational techniques, whether through informal self-reflection and observation of others, or through a more formal *Individual Strengths Assessment*, as we go on to discuss below. The second approach to identifying strengths relies on predetermined classifications of strengths, which are then assessed through a strengths-based interview, or through one of several psychometric tools. These too are discussed below, but let's begin by seeing how we can go about spotting strengths every day, in every walk of life.

Day-to-day Strengthspotting

Day-to-day strengthspotting is exactly what it sounds like: spotting strengths in people – whether oneself or others – as we go about our daily activities. As we do so, what are the telltale signs of a strength that we should be looking for? These signs would not necessarily be found together, at least at any given moment in time. But observed over time, it is very likely that patterns will emerge and that the same things will keep coming up time and again. The telltale signs of a strength include the following:

- A real sense of energy and engagement when using the strength;
- Losing a sense of time because you are so engrossed and engaged in the activity;

- Very rapidly learning new information, activities, or approaches that are associated with the strength;
- A repeated pattern of successful performance when using the strength;
- Exemplary levels of performance when using the strength, especially performance that evokes the respect and admiration of others;
- Always seeming to get the tasks done that require using the strength;
- Prioritising tasks that require using the strength over tasks that do not;
- Feeling a yearning to use the strength, while also feeling drained if you have not had the opportunity to use it for a time;
- Being irrevocably drawn to do things that play to the strength – even when you feel tired, stressed, or disengaged.

Strengthspotting is a highly engaging activity – I find! – and most importantly, can be deployed in what might seem like the most unusual and unexpected situations where one might expect to see strengths. For example, on a hot June morning I was one of many hundreds of people stuck in a wall-to-wall queue, packed solidly like sardines in a tin, waiting for access to the London Underground at London Euston train station. It was rush hour, and all the trains were delayed: there had been the ubiquitous 'signal failure.'

I was due to be the first speaker at a conference, and I was in a rush – no doubt like many of the other people stuck in this queue. As the temperature started to rise, with all the bodies being squeezed against each other, people got impatient and tempers looked like they were starting to fray. At that moment, a London Underground representative emerged from the 'Up' escalator, equipped with a loudhailer:

"Ladies and gentleman," he began, "I do apologise for the delay to your journey this morning. There has been a signal failure further up the line, which has caused significant delays to all services. I do appreciate that this is difficult for you, and I would like to reassure you that we are doing everything possible to keep the delay to your journey to a minimum. Thank you for the patience that you have shown."

In a few seconds, the angst and anger was averted. There was an almost palpable collective sigh of relief from the gathered crowd. What had changed? The London Underground spokesman had read the mood of the crowd, and acted swiftly to avert the rising impatience and anger. How had he done it? In my view, he did so through the very effective use of two core strengths - empathy and emotional intelligence. He used *Emotional intelligence* to read the mood and sense the frustrations of the crowd (a cynic might argue that was hardly difficult to do in the circumstances, but nonetheless, he got it exactly right), but then used his *Empathy* to convey that, not only did he recognise our predicament, but he understood and shared our frustrations. Having conveyed this, he drew the sting of the situation by reassuring us that everything was being done to resolve the situation, and thanking us for our patience, thereby reinforcing the positive behaviour that he hoped to see continue.

I relate this as an example of day-to-day strengthspotting, and strengthspotting in an unusual place. The point illustrates that strengths can come to the fore at any time, from anyone – even from possibly unlikely people in unlikely places. Indeed, there are some strengths that are much more context-dependent, or phasic, than others. *Bravery*, for example, is difficult to display in the absence of situations that call for brave acts, whereas in contrast one can have *Curiosity* about anything at any time. As such, it is likely that there are some strengths

– the phasic strengths – that we may have to look much harder to find, or at least be particularly alert to them when the situations permit.

What does it take to be a strengthspotter? In essence, to spot strengths in whatever we are doing, wherever we are, with whomever, requires only the prepared mind that knows what to look for, and knows what a strength is when it has been "spotted." Importantly, as we discussed in Chapter 2, there are very likely several hundred different strengths, and by no means have all of them yet been identified, labeled or categorised. Given this, it is very likely that we will spot strengths in people, but that we won't immediately have a name that we can use to describe what it is that we have seen in them.

Much of our work in strengths research is concerned with exactly these questions of identifying, labelling and categorising strengths. But, for any given person at any given time, this absence of agreed names need not be an obstacle to having a strengths conversation with someone. Even if it seems impossible to name the strength succinctly in one or two of words, the impact of validation and recommendation that comes through having somebody identify a strength in you is equally as powerful when both people just agree the description of what has been identified, even if it cannot be given a specific name. Some examples of our day-to-day strengthspotting are set out below to give you more of a flavour of how this can happen – and we would love to hear your examples too. If you'd like to share them, please visit our website at **www.averagetoaplus.org**

Consider how we identified the strength of *Esteem Builder*. Jenny works for Children's Services, and spends a lot of time with people who are in difficult circumstances and who, on first impressions, don't seem to have too much going for them. Yet, what she is able to do, quite remarkably, is to see the glint of possibility and potential in somebody, and to cherish it, nurture it, and develop it in them. She describes how she will spot something that they have done well, a previous success, or a natural but possibly latent talent, and bring it to their attention, polishing it, encouraging it, and making sure that they don't dismiss it as irrelevant.

This is hard enough to do with people generally (we are all resistant to positive feedback!), but especially so when people find themselves in persistently difficult life circumstances. Yet once Jenny has spotted that glimmer of positivity in somebody, she won't let it go. Instead, it will be held up to the light, brought to the person's attention, and explored and developed with them until they cannot help but agree that there is something that they are good at, something that they have done well, or some talent that they had somehow lost in the fog of their life circumstances. And with this realisation, they start to shift. It might only be a small shift at first, but a shift nonetheless. They feel better about themselves. They start to see that they do have something to offer the world. They start to see that they are not a worthless person. Suddenly, life is not as bad. Buds of hope and optimism for the future start to sprout. Their self-esteem improves. The *Esteem Builder* has been at work. And when they have achieved something they didn't at first believe themselves capable of, the Esteem Builder's catchphrase comes back loud and clear in response, *"I knew you had it in you,"* thereby implanting the person's belief in themselves yet further and yet deeper.

Figure 4.1 Jenny, the *Esteem Builder* at Work

Lift is another example. Nicky works with CAPP, where she is an important and valued member of our team. Her strength of *Lift* helps to explain why. Nicky has an infectious enthusiasm and optimism that can't help but catch your mood and lift it too. But this isn't any Pollyanna-like utopian ideal. Nicky's strength of *Lift* also combines a tenacity and determination that ensures that she – and those around her – can face difficult times with the fortitude and pragmatism that the situation requires. In whatever she does, her positivity, drive, and commitment is there for all to see. It pulls people up by their bootstraps, sending the message, very powerfully, that this is the way that things get done round here. And they do get done, because the positive emotional climate ensures that people want to be part of things, they want to be around, they want to be on the team. *Lift* isn't a feminine emotionality to be dismissed (although this has happened to Nicky in the past). Instead, it is the bellwether of the emotional mood of the team and, of critical importance, the bellwether of the same emotional mood that in turn influences productivity and team performance, as studies are beginning to show.

Have you ever worked with somebody who seemed to be connected to everyone? Who was always just happening to bump into the right people? Who had a telephone directory of a memory that was always putting different people in touch with each other? Who was always seeing the links between ideas that other people missed, and then connecting those ideas with the people who could make them happen? Both Linda and Sally are just such people, for they have the strength of *Connector*. "*Let me introduce you to X*" is a favourite line, as is "*You really must meet so-and-so, let me arrange it for you.*" *Connectors* are the people who keep the relational networks of the world turning, since they get such a buzz from connecting people with people, or people with ideas, such that they appear to have an uncanny ability to get the right people together in the right place at the right time – their own *Connector* version of the golden mean!

These are just three examples of more than one hundred strengths that we have found through our work in this area. The richness of the language, and the richness of our understanding, increases each time we are able to identify, name and understand a new strength. We are completely focused on building this database of strengths over time, identifying them, understanding them, measuring them, and enabling people to apply them in their work and their life. The work is not easy, and it takes a long time to get it right – but it is fundamentally the right thing to be doing.

Listening for Strengths

Given the passion and energy that strengths ignite in people, I became very interested in the question of what strengths 'sound like.' I was particularly interested in whether there were identifiable differences that occurred when people were talking about strengths, relative to other topics, or other types of conversation in which we might engage. Starting with a class that I used to teach by telephone (class members were drawn from half a dozen countries around the world), I developed an exercise where I asked someone first to spend about five minutes talking about a weakness, or about something with which they were struggling. Then, second, I asked them to spend about five minutes talking about a strength, or about when they are at their best – it's important always to do the weakness exercise first, and the strengths exercise second, as will become apparent from the results below.

So, what happened when I asked people to do this exercise? Remember, the first times I used the exercise were by telephone, where there is no medium of communication other than the speaking and listening that the telephone allows. Equally, it does mean that people will be carefully attuned to what is being said, even if they don't have access to additional physical cues, like body language or facial expressions. Here are the sorts of observations that characterized the answers of people when they were asked to describe what they experienced when the person was talking about an area of weakness:

- They are more hesitant and struggle to express themselves;
- Their voice sounds dejected and deflated;
- There is a harder emphasis on things;
- They are more critical and unforgiving of themselves;
- Their attention narrows to focus only on the problems they are talking about, rather than their solutions;
- Their tone is heavy and self-critical;
- They express annoyance at their failings;
- They sound disengaged from the conversation, like they are holding something back;
- They express impatience at themselves and their situation;
- They seek avenues of withdrawal from the situation, offering rationalisations and justifications;
- They are more likely to be retrospective and backward looking;
- They tend to feel weaknesses as being constrictive, narrowing their attentional focus;
- The conversation may have more stops and starts, and be harder to progress.

Even just reading through that list again, I can feel my own energy start to drain away. In contrast, when after five minutes or so I asked people to switch over and to talk about their strengths, these were the sort of observations that characterised them:

- The sound and tone of their voice changes in pitch, becoming clearer and more focused;
- They speak rhythmically, having found their own natural pace and flow;
- There is a sense of energy and uplift in their voice;
- They seem happy and relaxed when talking, but also very energised;
- They have a great sense of confidence;
- They sound very authentic, honest, integrated, and complete;
- They use more elaborate language and can explain things graphically;
- They use phrases like "I love" and "it just fits;"
- They are specific in their choice of words and descriptions;
- They demonstrate an insightful and rich knowledge of the topic;
- They find it easy to visualise and explain what they are talking about;
- The passion in their tone and voice is evident;
- They are fully engaged with the conversation and fully present within it;
- They are more likely to be forward looking and optimistic;
- The conversation is very free flowing;
- The description / conversation is much richer, with many more themes interwoven with each other and connections being made;
- Using a musical analogy, people shift from a "minor key" to a "major key;"
- There is a sense of absorption in the subject and a loss of self-consciousness;
- Their responses are more immediate;
- Examples to illustrate strengths themes are often brought from many different areas of people's lives;
- People can talk about recognising the strength in their childhood

and the early years of their life, making sense of the patterns over time.

The differences here are stark – and remember – the first time I did this, it was on the telephone with about 30 people listening to the one person who was speaking. As such, there were no clues as to body language, posture or physical gestures through this medium – and still the differences were absolutely stark.

Further, as I extended these observations into working with much more diverse groups in physical locations, rather than telephone settings, I was able to build the database of observations and reflections – both from the participants themselves, and from independent external observers who were present, but were not taking part in the activity. Here is some of what these independent observers noticed when people shifted to talking about strengths:

- The energy levels significantly increase;
- The noise levels significantly increase;
- The exercise takes longer to stop;
- There is a shift in bodily posture around the room – people display body language that is much more open, engaged and confident.

But my biggest – and most amusing! - lesson came when my first telephone group asked me about my strengths. I started to talk about the things that I did best, the things that I felt made me uniquely me, and that I loved to do......and they all started to laugh. I stopped to ask what the joke was, and the class replied that I was doing exactly what they had just listened to in the other participants: my energy and engagement had increased, I was in flow, I was speaking confidently and graphically about my experiences......and I hadn't even realised it.

I have subsequently run this exercise with many diverse groups of

Figure 4.2 Listening for Weaknesses and Listening for Strengths

people, including executive coaches, therapists, HR professionals, educational psychologists, occupational psychologists, corporate boards, insurance claims advisors, recruitment managers and regular people just like you and me – even a group of 120 military leaders drawn from across the army, navy and air force. In each case, the findings have been the same, with participants both experiencing and witnessing the shifts in energy and engagement that I found initially in the teleclass experiment. Of course, the findings are not always identical. I have found that educational psychologists – across several different experiments – demonstrate a remarkable degree of humour and resilience when talking about weaknesses, so much so that the differences with this group have tended to be the least pronounced of all the groups with whom I have run this exercise.

This leads to an important caveat, which is that while there are certainly remarkable consistencies across these different groups and diverse populations in listening and observing for strengths, there can also be important individual differences: not everyone responds in the same way, and it is very important to keep this in mind. If we do not, we run the risk of misinterpreting the responses of people who are simply different. This caveat applies to all psychological research, which is almost always nomothetic (seeking to create generalisable laws that apply across people), despite being applied in ways that are idiographic (specific to a given individual).

So, why is it so important to do the weaknesses exercise first, and the strengths exercise second, as I mentioned at the outset? You may well have already worked this one out for yourself, but it is all to do with the state in which we leave people when the exercise is finished – in any intervention with people, we have both a professional and a moral responsibility. For almost all people, talking about weaknesses was a negative experience. For almost all people, talking about strengths was a positive experience. Hence, our professional and moral responsibility is to leave people in a positive place, rather than to leave them in a negative place when the exercise is finished.

Underpinning this, as well as our responsibilities to the people taking part, is the scientific case. As Barbara Fredrickson's work on positive emotions has shown, positive emotions can undo the negative effects of negative emotions, and the experience of positive emotions builds psychological, social and physical resources which help people long into the future – some of the evidence indicates very strongly that positive emotions can account for people living up to nine years longer. Further, positive emotions increase our creativity and capacity for learning, as well as our inclinations toward prosocial behaviour, so doing a lot of good all round. More broadly, these implications of the beneficial effects of strengths use and positive emotions apply across many different areas – in school, at work, and throughout life – thereby again supporting our fundamental view that *using strengths is the smallest thing we can do to make the biggest difference.*

Individual Strengths Assessments

Strengthspotting and listening for strengths are both naturalistic activities – that is, they can and do happen in everyday life, as people are going about their everyday business. They are limited, however, by their reliance on the strength being identified when it happens to come into play. As powerful and validating as this is – I have seen people transformed by having a strength identified in them – it does depend on that strength coming up at that particular moment in time. Given this, at CAPP we have been working on developing a more structured, but still free-flowing means of identifying strengths in people - the Individual Strengths Assessment, or ISA.

The ISA combines the strengthspotting skills of a strengths coach with the telltale hallmarks of a strength that we explored through the listening for strengths exercise. It involves the strengths coach in asking a series of questions, in a semi-structured and free-flowing way, that then allow the person to talk about their strengths in an easy, natural manner, as part of a conversation. As this conversation is happening, the strengths coach is noting and identifying the strengths that shine through. The strengths are not typically fed back to the person as they are identified – this would often break the flow of the conversation. Instead, they are noted by the strengths coach, who then seeks additional validation and support for what they have heard, by asking additional follow-up or supporting questions. Towards the end of the conversation, or at another appropriate point, the strengths coach then feeds back what they have heard to the client.

It is amazing just how powerful – and transformative – this process can be. In our experience of delivering ISAs, we have seen numerous examples of people who became more confident and integrated with themselves as a result of being able to understand their strengths more fully – and to understand them more fully in context, a critical consideration. One example was a client working in a civil engineering firm – we'll call him Nigel - who was disengaged from his work and wondering what he was going to do in terms of his future career. Following the ISA, he felt in touch with who he really was for the first time in a long time, recognising his great strengths in creativity and appreciation of beauty that were simply not being used in his current role. Equipped with this knowledge, he started to re-design how he spent some of his time outside work, so that he could do more that played to these strengths. And at work, feeling more confident and integrated, he went to see his line manager, explored the work options where he could make his best contributions through his strengths, and negotiated increased responsibility and a pay rise as a result!

Or consider another client, who we will call Victoria. Lacking self-confidence, despite having lots of things going for her, Victoria was someone who had many different strengths, but had never had the opportunity to acknowledge, celebrate or really use them to any great extent. Following the ISA, she was like a person re-discovered – in touch with herself and with all the many things that were good about her, in such a way that she was more confident, more integrated with who she was as a person, and more able to work out her own right directions and right decisions in life. Again, as a direct result of the ISA, Victoria has been able to start thinking in a much more meaningful way about her future career options and directions.

What does the ISA look like, and how does it work? As I began to describe above, the ISA is a conversation with a strengths coach about your strengths – but the beauty of it is that it is not explicitly about your strengths, but rather it gets to explore your strengths through the 'back door' into your consciousness – remember that only about one-third of people could give a meaningful answer to the question "What are your strengths?" In contrast, the ISA uses questions like the ones I include below, all designed to encourage people to talk about their great experiences, their enjoyment, their best successes, about who they are, at their core, when they are at their best.

The ISA questions cover each of the emotional, thinking and behavioural aspects of people, and range over the past, present and future, always looking for consistent themes that would indicate the presence of a strength – and it is hugely important that each of these aspects is covered. Here is one example of why. We once ran an ISA with a client – we'll call her Jane - who was proving to be very difficult to connect with and to get the sort of responses and indicators that we would typically look for in identifying strengths. This continued – right until we started to ask questions about the future. And then everything changed. It was like a light bulb went on for Jane – and for us, it was a real eureka moment too! Talking about the future, Jane came alive. All the passion, the energy, the verve and desire that come through when talking about strengths were there in bucket loads when she was talking about the future. The reason? Quite simple, really. Jane's strengths were all future-focused. She was always inimitably geared towards what she was going to do next, what her plans were for tomorrow, next week, next month, next year, even next decade – and not remotely interested in what she had done before, or what she was doing today – unless and until it connected with her path into the future.

As this example illustrates, it is important to recognise that the ISA doesn't work according to a script. It is, unfortunately, not a foolproof process, whereby anyone can read the questions from the list, and establish what someone's core strengths are. In contrast, it is a subtle but powerful combination of the questions of the ISA and the expertise of the strengths coach. The ISA questions move people into the right territory to be thinking about their strengths. The coach's own strengths, together with their skill and experience, allow them to draw those strengths out through the conversation, before feeding them back to the client in such a way that the client understands, values, and engages with the strengths.

To that end, we have an ongoing debate about whether the language used to describe the strengths when they are fed back should be the language of our emerging classification, or in contrast whether it should be anchored firmly in the language used by the client as they provided their descriptions. Neither approach is entirely right, but what is always right is to follow the client's agenda and direction, and to do what is right for them. Sometimes clients find it helpful to connect to a larger classification of strengths, and value feeling the security of a context for the strength that has been mapped and explored by others before them. For other people, using this pre-existing language and classification can get in the way of what they perceive – often quite rightly - as being their unique and idiosyncratic descriptions of what it means to have *Delivery*, to be a *Talentspotter*, or to be *Proactive*. Given this, the right way is always the way that is right for the client – whatever that may be.

Here are some sample ISA questions for you to consider. You may wish to think about your own answers to these, and to see what strengths your responses may lead you to identify in yourself. Or you might want to try them out with some of the people around you, seeing what sort of responses you receive, and what you can glean about that person from how they respond:

- What sort of everyday things do you enjoy doing?
- What makes for a really good day for you? Tell me about the best day that you can remember having?
- What would you describe as your most significant accomplishment?
- When you are at your best, what are you doing?
- What gives you the greatest sense of being authentic and who you really are?
- What do you think are the most energising things that you do?
- Where do you gain the most energy from? What sorts of activities?
- What are you doing when you feel at your most invigorated?
- Tell me about a time when you think that "the real me" is most coming through.
- Do you have a vision for the future? What is it about?
- What are you most looking forward to in the future?
- Thinking about the next week, what will you be doing when you are at your best?

All of these questions start to open up the dialogue around strengths, around what energises and invigorates people, what gives them a sense of authenticity, and enables them to be at their best.

Even so, it is also a very useful approach to ask some questions as part of the ISA that are focused on weaknesses and the activities that drain the client. Very often, people's responses to these questions will serve to reinforce and re-affirm the messages that have been coming through about their strengths, but equally they will sometimes open up new and fertile ground that helps the strengths coach to understand the person better in context – to understand them more holistically, in relation both to what they do well and to what they don't do so well, or even what they wish they could stop doing or avoid altogether!

People's responses to these types of questions can also serve to validate the indicators that were coming through for strengths, by showing the differences in response, whether it is through vocabulary, tone, energy, passion or even engagement in the conversation. We would expect to see lots of these when people are talking about strengths, and have equally seen them disappear almost immediately when the conversation turns to talking about weaknesses. When this happens, it provides good supporting evidence for the effect of both strengths and weaknesses – and on those few occasions where it doesn't happen, it serves as an important reminder that there are always exceptions to the general rule. Knowing this requires the strengths coach to be carefully attuned to the conversation and to ensure that they pick up on the other cues that are present, as well as paying attention to the differences that may exist in the nature of the conversation itself.

The weakness questions look like this:

- What are the activities that you really dislike doing? Why is that?
- Are there things that you never seem to get done, or things that you always try to avoid? What are they?
- What are the activities that drain you when you have to do them? Has it always been this way?

It's important to note that, in the case of all these questions, the ISA conversation is just that – a conversation. It is not an interview, or somebody reading from a scripted list of questions. As such, the strengths coach is always at liberty to tailor the questions as is appropriate for them to feel comfortable, and for them to feel that they fit within the context and flow of the conversation, as well as the needs and expectations of the client.

Very often, when the questions are written down formally as they are here, they can feel presented in a formal and constraining way – but conversational language is almost never like that, so the strengths coach should feel at liberty to speak as they would naturally speak through the ISA. They should use the questions as a helpful framework and prompt, rather than as a gilded cage that constrains and gets in the way of what would otherwise be a nicely flowing conversation!

As the conversation draws to a natural conclusion – when the responses are all pointing in the same direction, and little new material or indicators are coming through – it is very often helpful to ask people what, on the basis of the conversation, they think their strengths are. This can also be a good opportunity to introduce the question around other feedback that people may have had through formal or informal processes, and whether that feedback is consistent with what they have started to identify through the ISA conversation.

Even though only around one third of people can meaningfully identify their strengths when asked, through the process of an ISA conversation people will typically be able to start to identify key themes and emerging consistencies that point them in some helpful directions to recognising and realising their strengths. Inviting the client into this discussion is also a great way to engage them in the feedback process.

ISA Experiences. There are a number of recurring topics that tend to come up through our experience of developing and delivering ISAs, and it is worth considering them here. First is always the question about *"What are my top strengths?"* Paradoxically, answering this question without appreciating the wider context and implications for it can be unhelpful. This is because we need to know, top strengths for what? When? How many? Misinterpreting the subtext of these questions can lead to faulty assumptions and hence faulty responses and recommendations.

It's an open question as to how many strengths a given individual has, and also an open question as to how many of those strengths are 'top strengths.' As we see below, psychometric strengths assessments typically report back on a predetermined number of strengths, often the top five strengths from the assessment. But that does not helpfully indicate the strengths that may be equally as powerful and important, but for a number of reasons came out somewhere just below the 'top five' in the assessment. It also does not take any account of how those strengths may shift, some moving out into the foreground and others receding into the background, as the context and hence need changes. As such, talking about 'top strengths' needs to be qualified with the understanding:

(1)   that there is not any fixed number of 'top strengths' that people may have;

(2)   that strengths may recede into the background, or advance into the foreground, depending on context and need, so that;

(3)   strengths need to be understood in context, and so;

(4)   the number of strengths that we should focus on at any one time depends on the requirements of the situation - some situations may require a wider combination of strengths, other situations may require just one or two.

A second question that almost inevitably comes up at the end of an ISA is "What next?" Of course, this is impossible to answer in the abstract, since next steps are always a result of the particular combination of strengths and situations that a person is presented with at any given time. These next steps are typically to do with questions of how the client can use their strengths more effectively in their work and in their life more broadly. Often, this can be about helping the client to find or create situations where they can deploy their strengths more, or exploring ways in which they can have conversations with others (spouse and supervisor being classic examples) about what they would like to do to maximise their strengths more in the future.

Almost always – and almost inevitably – the conclusion of an ISA is characterised by the client's realisation of a deeper insight and understanding of themselves, particularly when they are at their best, and what they can do to achieve that more often. There is also a marked shift in realisation towards the practical steps that can be taken to re-shape and refine their life and work on this basis.

If you wondered about the value of an ISA for people who have already received a lot of feedback – and indeed who might already know their own strengths well – consider my own experience. I have spent the last seven or more years working in this field, explicitly focused on identifying, understanding and assessing strengths. So when I arranged to have an ISA with Janet Willars, one of our expert strengths coaches, I was very interested to see what would come out.

And what did come out? A *lot* of validation for what I already knew, as well as two new insights that built on this. First, I was able to recognise a strength that had been latent for quite some time, but which was now being more fully developed through – yes, you've guessed it – a change in circumstance and need that was inviting this strength to move into the foreground. And second, I realised another strength to a far greater depth than I had ever done before: recognising that the extent of this strength went far beyond the traditional definition, and as a result, that there was actually something that was subtly, but importantly and powerfully, different about it – something that was much more uniquely me - and all that within a 45-minute conversation!

As you can see, ISAs are a tremendously powerful way of opening up a conversation about strengths, and enabling people to talk in ways that allow the expert strengths coach to identify and draw out the core strengths that the person is describing through their responses. As well as the ISA, there are also several other approaches to the open-ended identification of strengths, as we go on to consider next.

Other Open-ended Approaches to Strengths Identification

Bernard Haldane and The Dependable Strengths Articulation Process. Bernard Haldane (1911-2002) is arguably the person who first introduced a systematic focus on strengths, and especially the appropriate identification of strengths. Despite this, he is sadly not well-recognised within the modern strengths field, but was known as a leading innovator in career development. Writing in the *Harvard Business Review* in 1947, Haldane provided an explanation for people's lack of efficiency at work:

"One of the reasons for this neglect and waste of manpower is that very few top-management men know and recognise the varieties and number of human aptitudes. Another is general lack of information on how these aptitudes combine to form personality and work patterns. A third reason is a failure to realise the results of misapplication or neglect of talents."

The same might be argued today, in spite of advances in our understanding of 'human aptitudes.' Haldane's work was pioneering and is perhaps best characterised by his view that, because you are unique, there is something you are better at than anyone else. It was from this basis that Haldane's methods for identifying strengths were all focused on using a person's own language, rather than prescribing the strengths to be assessed according to a predetermined classification. Haldane developed a number of open-ended approaches for the identification of strengths, but these ultimately converged around the Dependable Strengths Articulation Process for which he is best known.

When completing the Dependable Strengths Articulation Process, participants are first asked to identify a number of experiences of which they feel proud, which they did well, and which they enjoyed. Participants then tell the stories of these experiences to other people in their group, who are asked to try and identify the strengths that they see being illustrated in the experiences (what we might now refer to as "strengthspotting"). The participant then sorts through the strengths identified, and identifies six to eight strengths that they believe are their Dependable Strengths®. Further information about articulating Dependable Strengths can be found through the Center for Dependable Strengths at **www.dependablestrengths.org**

Mike Pegg and the Strengths Way. Mike Pegg is a British consultant and writer who has been working with people to build on their strengths for the last 40 years. His model is based on three steps to success, which he describes as (1) Strengths, (2) Specific goals, and (3) Success. *Step 1: Strengths* is about knowing your strengths, which Pegg describes as the activities in which you consistently deliver As, that you find fulfilling, that give you positive energy, and where you find yourself at ease but where you also excel. *Step 2: Specific goals* is about achieving clarity around the specific goals that you want to achieve, and focusing on them. *Step 3: Success* contains the three themes of *Strategies* (clarifying the strategies that give the greatest chance of success), *Solutions* (finding creative solutions to challenges and also to managing weaknesses), and *Success* (focusing on an inspiring environment, effective implementation tools, and enabling people to integrate their learning in their own way).

Marcus Buckingham and the SIGNs of a Strength. Having left The Gallup Organization where he made his name through co-authoring *Now, Discover Your Strengths* with Donald Clifton, Marcus Buckingham turned his attention to the identification of strengths through more open-ended approaches, developing the S-I-G-Ns of a strength in his later book, *Go Put Your Strengths to Work*. According to Buckingham, the S-I-G-Ns of a strength are that you feel *Successful* when you are using it; that it feels like an *Instinct*, something that you feel drawn to do; that you experience *Growth* through using it; and you feel that you have satisfied a *Need* when you have been using it. Buckingham suggests a 3-step process for strengths identification from this basis: (1) Capture (making a note of what you are doing when you feel powerful, confident, natural, etc., and also when you feel drained, frustrated, forced, etc.); (2) Clarify (in each case asking yourself where this applies, where it does not, and how far it can be generalised); and (3) Confirm (testing possible strengths against a set of 12 questions which relate to what you do, the way you do it, how you feel about it and how successful you are in it).

Each of these more open-ended approaches to the identification of strengths converge around similar themes that are the telltale signs of a strength – telltale signs that we consider in detail in this chapter particularly and throughout the book more generally. But as much as open-ended approaches are valuable, there are also situations where the focus is instead on a more formal assessment of the *presence* or *absence* of particular strengths. This is where strengths-based interviewing and psychometric strengths assessments come into focus.

Strengths-based Interviewing

Listening for strengths in day-to-day situations and Individual Strengths Assessments are both open-ended and free-flowing ways of assessing the strengths that exist in a given individual. In contrast, strengths-based interviewing is concerned with assessing the presence or absence of particular pre-determined strengths, and then establishing the degree to which those strengths may exist in any given individual. Just as more traditional competency-based interviews seek to assess the extent to which candidates have the particular competencies that are required for the role, so strengths-based interviews are designed to assess that candidates have the particular strengths that are required for the role.

There are, however, some important distinctions and differentiators between the two approaches. Whereas competency-based interviews are very much grounded in past experience, strengths-based interviews are not constrained by the search for evidence that someone has before done the particular thing in question. In contrast, strengths-based interviews draw from people's natural talents and preferences for particular ways of thinking, feeling or behaving, and these natural aptitudes, recurring over time, are indicative of what it is that the person is most likely to continue doing – with energy and engagement - into the future. As such, the evidence used to support decision-making in strengths-based interviews comes from a much wider body than just previous relevant work experience: it could extend to any parts of a person's life where that strength has been at play, thus rendering the process much more inclusive and a more level playing field. Further, competency-based interviews tend to steer away from expressions of emotion and passion, and yet, as you will now know, these are some of the hallmarks of what shines through when people are talking about strengths.

Strengths-based interviews typically begin with some generic warm up questions, such as *"What has been your best day at work? Why?,"* *"When are you at your best?"* and *"What are the things that most energise you?"* These questions are not included as part of the scoring, but are used to settle the candidate into the interview, and to help them move into a frame of mind that is conducive to the questions that follow. That said, very often people's responses to these opening questions can be very revealing and tell the interviewer a lot about the person.

The interview questions themselves will all be designed to assess a specific strength in the person. Typically, an interview would include between three and six questions for each strength that was being assessed. The candidate's responses are scored using a deliberately spaced distribution of 0, 3, or 5. Candidates who clearly are failing to demonstrate the strength score 0. Candidates who are able to demonstrate some of the strength, but are not completely consistent with it, score 3. And candidates who exemplify the strength are scored 5. The spacing between the scores helps to ensure that interviewers think carefully about how to score any given response, rather than just shading into the next score bracket without due consideration.

In every case, the interviewer is listening for a particular set of 'listen-fors' – typical responses provided by people who have the strength to a very high degree, and hence who may be considered the prototypical exemplars of that strength. Some sample strengths-based interview questions, and their scoring keys and listen-fors, are provided below:

Time Optimizer -

How would you say that you manage your time?

0   I don't / unsure

3   Quite / fairly / reasonably well / effectively. May describe occasions when this does not happen

5   Make the most of every minute / Very effectively / Superb / Effective use of time comes naturally to me

Explainer –

How does it make you feel when you have explained something to another person?

0   Nothing / alright (noncommittal answer)
3   Pleased that I have been able to explain it
5   Get a real buzz from explaining things to people / need to hear enthusiasm / energy

Planful –

Would you describe yourself as someone who is eager for action or do you like to plan carefully before doing something important?

0   Eager for action only
3   Plan carefully but with some pullback
5   Always plan carefully

Of course, the secret - as with any interview - is to be looking for consistency across responses, and congruent lines of evidence all pointing in the same direction. That is why we always ask several questions about any given strength, to ensure that people's responses are not skewed or misrepresented by their misunderstanding or misinterpretation of one of the questions. Second, asking several questions about any given strength allows us to ensure that there is consistency across the interview responses as a whole. Seeing this consistency is a good indication that the strength is possessed to a high degree, as well as being both stable and reliable within the person.

Experiences of Strengths-based Interviewing. Our experiences of designing and delivering strengths-based interviews have been very rewarding. Not only have we delivered substantial organisational benefits, including enhanced retention and improved performance, to clients like Norwich Union, but we have also heard and seen many examples of candidates who simply found the process to be much more open and effective for them. In fact, it is not unusual for people to take part in a strengths-based interview, but then to decide for themselves that they do not want the job – and not necessarily because they are not able to do it, but because they realise themselves that the *fit* between what the job requires and what they are bringing to it is not a close one. It is far easier to withdraw oneself, or ultimately to face rejection, on the basis of closeness of fit and circumstance, than it is to do so through lack of ability or competence.

Another key element of this approach is that it enhances the candidate recruitment experience, something that is increasingly important to consumer-facing firms, for whom the candidate may already be an existing client, be related to other existing clients, or be a potential future client. At the very least, having a positive recruitment experience does the organisation's reputation no harm; at best, it can build both the organisation's consumer and employer brands in tandem. Strengths-based interviewing approaches have consistently delivered this improved candidate experience - as well as, fundamentally, delivering people better able, interested and motivated to do the job. Unlike traditional competency-based recruitment, which focuses on getting people who can do the job, strengths-based recruitment is about recruiting people who not only *can* do the job, but also *love* to do the job. I am always reminded of the claims advisor whose colleagues described her as "leaving skid marks on the carpet because she cannot get to her desk fast enough to start work." How much does that say about what she thinks of her job?

Figure 4.3 The Effect of Strengths-based Recruitment

The process described so far works well for generic roles where there is a degree of consistency across the role and the work that is required. But how does this translate to roles that are less easily defined, more variable and fluid? In such cases, it is important to recognise the potential for role shaping – the idea that it is much easier for roles and jobs to be shaped to fit the person, than it is for the person to be shaped to fit the role or the job!

Role shaping is most applicable and effective in roles where there may be a number of different ways in which the outcomes can be delivered, and so where different people may deliver the same outcomes but in quite different ways. Where this is the case, the recruitment focus shifts to examine the strengths that people naturally bring to the role, rather than being focused specifically on the presence or absence of pre-determined strengths.

Through this approach – which we often conduct using the ISA described above – one is able to gain a sense of where the candidate's attention is most likely to be focused. The question becomes one of where they naturally pay attention, thereby indicating their natural focus and preferences, rather than assessing the presence or absence of particular strengths. This focus of attention underlies where the candidate is likely to direct their energy, time and focus, and provides an answer to the fundamental question of *"What would this person do if they were appointed to this role?"*

This question is often at the heart of leadership appointments, since, by definition, people in leadership roles manage their own time and priorities (as well as those of others), thereby having a large degree of freedom and autonomy to determine on what they focus. And it is here that an understanding of strengths adds a richer depth and context to those recruitment discussions, through the consideration of the fit between the strengths and attentional focus that the individual brings, and the needs of the organisation at that point in time.

As I have aimed to demonstrate in this section, strengths-based interviewing is a very effective way of assessing people for the presence or absence of particular strengths in a comprehensive way. It can, however, be time-consuming and resource-intensive. This being so, other approaches to identifying strengths may be more appropriate and scalable across larger numbers of people, among them the use of psychometric strengths assessments.

Psychometric Strengths Assessments

Psychometric may seem like a frightening word, but it simply refers to the measurement of psychological phenomena, or things – in this case, strengths. Psychometric strengths assessments traditionally have followed the same sorts of approaches as many standard person-ality assessments. That is, they invite people to agree or disagree with a series of statements that are then combined in particular ways to estab-lish the strengths that an individual has. Those strengths are then attrib-uted to the individual to a greater or lesser degree – typically as a func-tion of the extent to which she agreed or disagreed with the different statements in the assessment. Approaches such as this, however, are fundamentally limited, since they are able only to assess a predeter-mined number and selection of strengths. It seems obvious to say, but they can only assess what they assess. In contrast, approaches like listening for strengths or the ISA are more fully able to capture and identify strengths as they naturally exist and arise in the person, without the limiting framework of a particular predetermined set of strengths.

That said, many people have been introduced to strengths through taking an online strengths assessment, such as the Clifton StrengthsFinder^{TM} or the VIA Inventory of Strengths, and strengths assessments such as these have been instrumental in raising people's awareness of strengths and beginning to create a language around strengths that people can use. Here are brief details of the major strengths assessments that are available. You can find out more about each of them by visiting the websites provided for each below.

Clifton StrengthsFinder^{TM}: The Clifton StrengthsFinder^{TM} was developed by Donald O. Clifton and colleagues at The Gallup Organization, in the United States. Don Clifton is recognised as the father of strengths psychology, and received a presidential commenda-tion from the American Psychological Association to that effect in 2002. Clifton was interested in the fundamental question of what you discover when you study what is right with people, and dedicated his life to doing this. In order to establish the factors that facilitated top-level performance across a number of different professional occupations, Clifton and his team of researchers at The Gallup Organization interviewed thousands of professionals with the aim of identifying the themes of talent that differentiated the top performers from the rest.

Strengths were developed from one's innate talents, they argued, through the application of knowledge and skill. Working from these definitions, Clifton and colleagues identified hundreds of themes of talent from their interviews with professionals, but condensed these to what they described as the 34 most prevalent themes. Details of the 34 talent themes are given in the bestselling, *Now, Discover Your Strengths*, by Marcus Buckingham and Donald Clifton. These themes are assessed through the online Clifton StrengthsFinder^{TM}, available at **www.strengthsfinder.com** or through the access code included with many of the books published by The Gallup Organization. The assessment takes around 30 minutes to complete and you receive a feedback report that details your top five of the 34 themes.

VIA Inventory of Strengths: Developed by the leading positive psychologists Christopher Peterson and Martin E. P. Seligman, the VIA Inventory of Strengths (VIA-IS) measures 24 character strengths that are believed to be universally valued across culture and history – and as we discussed in Chapter 2, the cross-cultural data certainly support this. The VIA-IS was developed through extensive literature searches of historical inventories of strengths and virtues; the examination of writings that addressed good character from psychiatry, youth development, philosophy, and psychology; together with brainstorming with colleagues and conference participants.

The 24 character strengths identified are conceptually clustered under six broad headings: *Wisdom and knowledge*; *Courage*; *Humanity*; *Justice*; *Temperance*; and *Transcendence*. Character strengths are defined as "the psychological ingredients – processes or mechanisms – that define the virtues. Said another way, they are distinguishable routes to displaying one or another of the virtues." As such, an explicit focus of this approach was that character strengths were held to be morally valued and to be enablers of the "good life." The VIA-IS consists of 240 items (10 items for each of 24 strengths) that respondents rate using a five-point scale. Typically, it takes 30-45 minutes to complete. The VIA-IS provides a free report detailing the respondent's top five character strengths, known as "signature strengths." It has been completed to date by more than half a million people around the world, and the UK data for the VIA-IS has been reported by myself and my colleagues. The VIA-IS is freely available through either **www.viastrengths.org** or **www.authentichappiness.org**

Inspirational Leadership Tool: Drawing on studies of more than 2,600 workers from across a range of companies in the UK, who had been interviewed about what inspired them to follow a leader, this tool was developed by Caret Consulting on behalf of the British Department of Trade and Industry (DTI). As well as this research, the authors also looked at other studies and literature reviews of leadership, including the work of Beverley Alimo-Metcalfe, Warren Bennis, Richard Boyatzis, Jim Collins, and Daniel Goleman.

The ILT measures 18 attributes of leadership that were identified as inspiring followers to follow leaders. These 18 leadership attributes are clustered in four dimensions of inspirational leadership: *Creating the future; Enthusing, growing, and appreciating others; Clarifying values;* and *Ideas to action.* Respondents to the ILT choose between 54 paired statements using a five-point scale, and the tool typically takes around 15-20 minutes to complete. It provides a free report detailing the ranking of the participant's 18 leadership strengths, together with more detailed coverage of their top six and bottom four leadership strengths, with developmental suggestions for each. Given that the ILT was developed specifically for use with leaders, many of the items are only relevant to people working in leadership positions. As such, unlike other psychometric strengths assessments, it is not appropriate for general use. The tool is available at **www.inspiredleadership.org.uk**

You may well have taken one of these several strengths assessments that are available. These are certainly a valuable starting point, and can begin to provide a language and perspective on strengths that otherwise can be missing. But it is important to recognise that they are not the complete and final answer to your question of *"What are my strengths?"* Indeed, it was my sense of gnawing discontent and dissatisfaction when I had taken some of these assessments that led me into the work I now do on strengths. And that same sense of unease has been shared by many of the thousands of people that I have worked with on strengths since.

The problem is this. It sounds obvious (and it is when you see it), but any strengths assessment tool is, by definition, limited to the strengths that it assesses. Whatever the number of strengths, the assessment has limitations, because, as we discussed in Chapter 2, the number of strengths likely runs into hundreds or more. No single strengths assessment gets anywhere near assessing that number, so they are unlikely effectively to capture *your* individual strengths in a way that is comprehensive. Similarly, it is typically the case that when an assessment is reported back, only a given number of "top" strengths are reported. So not only are we assessed on the basis of a limited number of pre-selected strengths to begin with, but we then receive a feedback report focusing on a subset of these pre-selected strengths.

What happens, then, if your top strengths were not even covered by the initial selection of strengths assessed? You may well feel, like myself and many others, that while the feedback report does indeed capture some accurate, helpful, and insightful elements of who you are at your best, and does provide a language and framework for you to start thinking about how and where you can make your best contributions, there is still something missing. A nagging sense that something isn't quite right. That somehow, it isn't the 'whole me.'

As it happens, my top strength on the VIA Inventory is curiosity, and equipped with this knowledge, it probably won't come as a surprise that I couldn't rest with this nagging sense that something wasn't quite right. Why? What was it? What was missing? Why did I feel this way? These questions flitted in and out of my mind with such persistent regularity that I couldn't ignore them. I wanted to get to the root of why I felt this way – and also to see if other people had had the same experience.

So, at conferences, on courses, and in conversations with people around the world, I asked them. Not everyone shared my disquiet – some found their assessments to be insightfully complete – but many people did. And as we discussed it, the disquiet became more lucidly clear: while the strengths assessments had captured *some* elements of who we were at our best, they had not captured our unique individuality in any complete or total way. Of course, it is unfair to expect that they would do – but in seeking to realise our strengths more fully, we do need to acknowledge the limitations of these assessment approaches. It is for these reasons that using more open-ended approaches to strengthspotting, in conjunction with more structured assessments, is so important.

Second Generation Strengths Assessments: Realise2

As a result of these concerns, together with my team at CAPP, we have been working to establish a means of assessing strengths that combines the best of both of these approaches, and minimizes the limitations of each, while still delivering a gold standard experience of strengths identification and development. Realise2 is the product of this work.

Realise2 assesses a large number of strengths according to *energy*, *performance* and *use* (see **www.realise2.org**). Our strengths work shows consistently that being *energising* is the core hallmark of using a strength, and that when this is the case, people are always acting authentically. As such, assessing for whether an activity is *energising* provides an efficient but reliable means to establishing the presence of a strength. The performance dimension is concerned with how good we are at something. The use dimension is concerned with how often we do it. By assessing each of these dimensions, across a large number of strengths, Realise2 is able to identify strengths - whether they are realised or unrealised, and weaknesses - whether they are exposed or unexposed, together with the possible strengths and possible weaknesses, and learned behaviours, that may exist somewhere in between.

Realise2 enables people to see their strengths and weaknesses much more comprehensively, and provides them with action planning tools to maximize the contribution of their strengths, while minimizing the impact of their weaknesses. Having a deep knowledge of your strengths and weaknesses, and then being able to do something effective about them, is at the heart of realising strengths in yourself and others. This is why CAPP has developed Realise2 – in a single word, to *realise* strengths both through knowing them and through making the most of them – the dual meaning of realise, and the dual meaning of Realise2.

Realising strengths is what this book was written to achieve. In the chapters that follow, we go on to look at how we can each do more to realise strengths, whether that realisation is in ourselves (Chapter 5, *Be Yourself - Better*), through our work (Chapter 6, *Harnessing Strengths at Work*), or in children (Chapter 7, *Golden Seeds and Flourishing Children*). You can realise, too.

Key Points

- When people are talking about strengths, they are more positive, energetic, and engaged. Their body language is open and receptive, and they are enthusiastic about the conversation.

- When people are talking about weaknesses, they are more negative, hesitant, and disengaged. Their energy levels drop and they appear more withdrawn. Their body language is closed and defensive, and their attentional focus is narrowed.

- Approaches to strengths identification can be qualitative and open-ended, such as day-to-day strengthspotting and Individual Strengths Assessments, or quantitative and psychometric, such as strengths-based interviews or psychometric strengths assessments.

- Traditional psychometric strengths assessments are constrained by assessing only a limited number of strengths and then typically reporting back only on a certain number of 'top strengths.'

- In contrast, we all have a symphony of strengths that advance into the foreground or recede into the background as the situation requires. As such, strengths identification approaches should combine both qualitative and quantitative approaches wherever possible.

Areas for Reflection and Action

- See which and how many strengths you can spot in the people around you through your normal daily interactions. Discuss your observations with them, and see if and how they resonate with the person whose strengths you have spotted.

- Pay attention to the tone, flow and energy of the conversations you are having with people, to see what indicators they may provide for the presence of particular strengths. Discuss your observations with others to invite their perspectives as well.

- Take a strengths assessment. See how the results compare with the ways in which you view yourself, as well as the results of other personality profiles you may have completed. Discuss the results with people close to you who will also be able to provide their own perspectives on what they see as your strengths.

FIVE

Be Yourself - Better

"Everything that every individual has ever done in all of human history and prehistory establishes the minimum boundary of the possible. The maximum, if any, is completely unknown."

John Tooby & Leda Cosmides, in *The Adapted Mind*

IT IS SAID that when travellers visited the Ancient Greek Oracle of Delphi, they were greeted with two inscriptions: "Know thyself" and "To thine own self be true." These edicts are as true for building your strengths as they were for the ancient Greeks in their philosophy for human growth and development. If we are to be ourselves - better, as this chapter argues, then we need both to understand ourselves, and to act in ways that are consistent with our true selves, striving to be authentic through following our inner compass and the directions that are right for us, just as we discussed in Chapter 2.

Being yourself – better – is about getting rid of the blockers that interfere with us accepting our selves for the best that we can be. It is about knowing our strengths more intimately and harnessing them more fully, through being open to the potential of our own growth and development. It is about stopping the perennial focus on what doesn't work, and instead paying attention to weaknesses only when we need to – that is, when they get in the way, and cannot be made irrelevant. It is about finding our niches and making the most of them, through building and refining our best abilities. It is about making the most of habit (doing this consistently) while managing against habituation (losing the effect of doing this, because we become used to doing it and always do it in the same way). And ultimately, it is about understanding and practising the art of the possible, setting out to envision what can be and then taking the responsibility, and putting in the effort, to make it happen. Each of these aspects we explore more fully in the sections that follow.

Get Rid of the Blockers

It can be easier to see strengths in others than it is to see them in ourselves – and for very good reasons. Given that strengths are pre-existing capacities, we can easily take them for granted and not see anything special about them – they come easily to us, and so we expect that it is the same for everyone else. As a result, we can fall into the trap of thinking that everyone else has the same aptitudes as we do, and thus, that what we can do is nothing special – because everyone else can do it too.

There are, however, two challenges that we should make to this argument. First, it's easy to think that, because we can do something without even thinking about it, that everyone else can too – easy to *think* it, but actually in reality it is very rarely the case. If we feel that way about something, it is very often because it is one of our own natural strengths that we have taken for granted. This is especially so if we then get frustrated with other people because they can't do it as well as we can – one of the telltale signs of an unrecognised strength! Second, even if other people can do it well too, it doesn't mean that it should be any less of a strength for us. It's important to remember that when we are focusing on being ourselves – better, we are measuring our strengths relative to how effective we have been with them before, or how effective a particular strength is relative to our other strengths. We are not measuring our strengths relative to other people's strengths - nor should we be, when our focus is on being ourselves - better. Taking a strengths focus is about being the best that we can be, not necessarily about being better than anybody else.

The positive feedback trap is another important blocker that can get in the way of us really knowing our strengths. The positive feedback trap is that little voice inside our heads that warns us about the complacency and arrogance that can come from us claiming a strength for ourselves, or even acknowledging that we might just be good at something. *"You arrogant so-and-so"* it says, or *"Watch out, or your head will get so big you won't get through the door!"*

Whatever the message, the underlying meaning is the same: that we should not accept positive feedback or praise – and certainly not administer it to ourselves – because otherwise our downfall will swiftly follow. This mindset leads to five entrenched reasons why we may not take positive feedback on board, because:

- We are concerned about becoming arrogant or big-headed;
- We fear becoming complacent and 'taking our foot off the gas;'
- We risk the pressure of ever-higher expectations - if we accept the praise this time round, then the expectations next time will be even higher;

- As we raise the bar of expectation, we increase the risk of failure – and so we try to avoid raising the bar by avoiding the positive feedback;

- And most fundamental of all, because we simply don't see the positives ourselves. As such, we find it difficult to relate to them, and not least to integrate them into our view of who we are.

As if these blockers to knowing our strengths were not enough, they are exacerbated by the fact that the people around us – especially at work – seem to be disinclined to tell us what it is that we do well. As Mike Westcott, Group HR Director for National Grid put it:

"How often do people hear the message from their boss at work that they are doing something well? Hardly ever. Those messages tend to come from our partners, our parents, our teachers, our friends, or our colleagues. But hardly ever do we get them at work - and this simply isn't good enough."

Not only are we resistant to hearing these messages of positive feedback, but other people seem to be resistant to giving them to us. Our managers and leaders may feel this way for any one of at least four reasons:

- They have an implicit belief that people want feedback that gives them something to work on, and they assume (wrongly) that positive feedback doesn't do that (this is part of the irony of 'strengths' and 'areas for development' in performance appraisals – implying that there is nothing we need do to work on or develop our strengths);

- They may think that praise and positive feedback are simply part of the 'feedback sandwich' that is used to fortify people ready for the negative feedback that is to follow. As such, positive feedback is simply a buffer, rather than having any intrinsic merit – and if there isn't negative feedback to deliver, they don't need to bother with the positive;

- They may believe that praise and positive feedback is only used as a tool to make people feel good, and so they don't need to be overly concerned with it;

- And the most damaging reason of all, they may believe that giving people positive feedback allows them to slack off on future performance – when, in fact, the opposite is so often true: praise provides the encouragement that people need to deliver even better performances in the future.

Through my work with corporate executive boards, I am very familiar with the staunch resistance that people may have to giving and receiving positive feedback. For example, I was once running an event where I covered some of the difficulty of these issues around giving and receiving positive feedback. Having done so, I invited the board members to actually *practise* giving and receiving positive feedback with each other. Two senior board members got up and left the room – as it later transpired, to find a quiet corner, away from everyone else, where they could conduct the exercise with each other but out of earshot from their colleagues. When – to my great relief – they returned, one of them described the experience of giving and receiving positive feedback thus:

> "*Positive feedback - it sounds simple, but that was one of the hardest – and most powerful – things that I have ever done.*"

To be sure, getting rid of the blockers is not about creating a huge ego-driven positivity-fest, where we sit around and pat ourselves on the back for being so fantastic at being who we are. But it is about shifting the balance away from always beating ourselves up about the things we are not good at, and spending all of our time and energy focused only on those things that we are not good at. As is so often the case, there is a balance to be struck, and that balance is once again the golden mean that we encountered in Chapter 3: *the right thing, to the right amount, in the right way and at the right time.*

In terms of getting rid of the blockers, it is about ensuring that we are not defeated by our ability to take positive feedback on board. At the same time, though, we need to be careful that the positive feedback we accept is both appropriate and accurate. To enable us to judge this to best effect, positive feedback should be **specific**, **targeted** and **with evidence**:

- *Specific*, because it is tied to a particular event or moment in time;
- *Targeted*, because it is about a particular behaviour or action;
- *With evidence*, because the outcome to which it led is encompassed as a core part of the positive feedback message.

In this way, we can be more confident of the positive messages that we are allowing ourselves to take on board – and they are also more likely to stick. As Carol Kauffman, Founding Director of the Coaching Psychology Institute at Harvard Medical School describes, we can think of *negative feedback* as being too often like *Velcro* (super sticking power) and *positive feedback* as being too often like *Teflon* (non-stick). We need to reverse that, so that positive feedback sticks and negative feedback delivers its lesson but doesn't undermine us forever more. Seeking out positive feedback that is *specific, targeted* and *with evidence* is one powerful way of doing so. Through accepting this positive feedback, we are better equipped to know our strengths.

Know Your Strengths

We discussed a number of ways in which to identify strengths in Chapter 4, and it is worth now recapping on some of those and referring back where that would be helpful to you. Specific techniques for strengthspotting that we discussed included:

- Day-to-day strengthspotting;
- Listening for strengths;
- Individual Strengths Assessments;
- Dependable Strengths Articulation Process;
- S-I-G-Ns of a strength;
- Strengths-based interviewing;
- Psychometric strengths assessments
- Realise2

When we are focused on knowing our own strengths, we can often find the answers through looking at the consistent themes that emerge over long periods of time and throughout many different facets of our lives and experience. Certainly, when I have asked people about how they first came to realise what they were good at, many of them talked about early memories from childhood of actions and activities that grew into what they now consider as their strengths. This development might have been intentional, although it was more often accidental rather than conscious and deliberate (probably because it is natural and instinctive) - but in all cases, the early threads of the strength can be traced through right to the present day. For example, leading psychologist and author Howard Gardner, who is the Hobbs Professor of Cognition and Education at the Harvard Graduate School of Education, describes how:

"Even as a young child, I loved putting words on paper, and I have continued to do so throughout my life. As a result, I have honed skills of planning, executing, critiquing and teaching writing. I also work steadily to improve my writing, thus embodying the second meaning of the word discipline: training to perfect a skill."

My colleague Dr. Janet Willars tells an amusing anecdote that reinforces this concept. When interviewing for a Financial Controller for a major financial institution, Janet asked the candidates what they remembered doing in their childhood. Such a broad question could elicit any number of possible responses, across an immense range of possible topics: playing hide and seek, cooking with grandma, watching *Muffin the Mule* or *Jamie and the Magic Torch*, building a den or falling off your bike. But no, the successful candidate did not reply with any of these – or indeed anything like them. His response, totally unscripted, was: *"I used to play post offices, and I was always the postmaster. I used to take the money in and pay it out, and make sure that the records balanced at the end of each day."* Of course, we might consider, cynically, that it was a pre-prepared answer to the question that fitted what the prospective job would entail, but I am assured it was not: the answer was, simply, what the candidate remembered doing in childhood - and yes, they were offered the job. And yes, they were highly successful in doing it.

Thus, a royal road to working out where our strengths may lie can come from looking back over the course of our lives to see what themes and patterns we can identify that consistently emerge. The context and circumstances may change, but the vital essence of the strength will remain. If you are an *Esteem Builder*, you likely have a long track record of helping people to feel better about themselves: right from recognising the creativity of the girl with different coloured socks when you were in primary school, to seeing the compassion buried deep in the drug addicted mother of four that you are now working with as a professional. If *Lift* is one of your strengths, for example, you will likely be able to see it working its magic in school, with your family, regularly throughout your social network of friends, as well as at work. Strengths endure, and these enduring themes can be key markers for spotting strengths in others and knowing our own.

Other staging posts on the royal road to knowing our strengths include paying attention to the things in your life that just *always seem to get done*. The things that might not even make it on to your 'to do' list, because they are always there, top of mind, and you actually feel drawn to do them. The things where it feels just right to be doing it: authentic and energising, like you are being the 'real you' – as some people have often described it - "*Doing what I was put on this earth to do*." The things where you get so absorbed and engaged with them that you might lose a sense of time – in the term coined by Mihaly Csikszentmihalyi where you are 'in flow.' Rob Kaiser, a partner in the US leadership consulting firm Kaplan DeVries, provides just such an example:

> "*When I'm working from my strengths, I feel on top of the world, and get a real clear sense of losing myself in the task. For example, one time I had a really big database to analyse in preparation for a conference presentation, and I sat over the computer analysing that data for days on end. One Friday, I came in at 5 in the morning, analysed the data all day, went home for dinner, went and coached the kids T-ball practice, came home and put the kids to bed, talked to my wife a little, she went to bed at 9.00pm, I was back in the office around 9.30pm, and I didn't pull away until 9.00am, in time to go home, get a shower, and go to the kids T-ball game! I had something like a 3-hour break in a 36-hour session of analysing that dataset, because I was so absorbed in it*"

It can also be possible to see strengths reflected in ourselves by recognising what it is that we value in other people. When you look up to someone, what is it that you admire about them? Why do you admire it? Often, it can be that we tend to recognise and admire our own strengths when they are reflected in other people. There is something about seeing a strength in someone else that can make it easier to identify. This is because when we see a strength in someone else, we have a degree of detachment and objectivity that enables us to recognise it as a strength, without having to be concerned by the implications (such as arrogance and complacency) of accepting it as a strength in ourselves. Equally, it may well be that we value the strength in a person whom we admire, because it gives us someone to look up to, something after which we can aspire.

Traditionally, comparing ourselves to other people who were doing better than us (upward social comparisons, to use the academic terminology) was considered a bad thing to do: we would feel bad about ourselves when comparing to someone who was better. In contrast, psychologists often recommended, we should compare ourselves to people who were worse off than we were (so called downward social comparisons), so that we could feel better about ourselves. But this framework does not allow for what we might gain from studying our heroes and role models, and groundbreaking work by social psychologist Michael Cohn at the University of Michigan showed why.

Cohn discovered that when we compare ourselves with people, we are likely to do so along two different dimensions. The first dimension is the direction of our comparison. We might compare ourselves *upwards*, with people who are perceived to be better than we are, or we might compare ourselves *downwards*, with people who are perceived to be worse off than we are. The second dimension is the nature of the comparison that we make with the person. We may either *contrast* ourselves with them (meaning that we are unlikely to become like them), or we may *assimilate* ourselves with them (meaning that we could become the same as them).

The direction and nature of our social comparisons have important implications. For example, when we make *downward comparisons* and *contrast* ourselves, we may feel more positive about ourselves (for example, superiority, confidence, relief). But when we make *downward comparisons* and *assimilate* ourselves, we can fear becoming like the person who we perceive to be worse off than we are, leading to anxiety and self-doubt.

The same pattern applies to upward comparisons, but in reverse. That is, when we make *upward comparisons* and *contrast* ourselves, we may be concerned that we will never be able to achieve our target aspiration, thereby leading to feelings of inferiority, jealousy and regret. But when we make *upward comparisons* and *assimilate* ourselves, we see the pathways through which we can learn and develop, and the sort of person we aspire to become, leading to inspiration, motivation and learning – as Figure 5.1 illustrates.

Understood in this way, positive upward social comparisons enable us both to admire and to learn from someone who deploys a strength exceptionally well. When we have that strength ourselves – albeit possibly to a less developed degree – we feel a sense of connection, an emotional engagement, a buzz from seeing someone else use it at a level of mastery as a maestro or virtuoso. Of course, we may well also admire the strengths of others for the very reason that we don't have that strength ourselves – but when that is the case, we are easily able to identify that our admiration comes from the absence of the strength in us, rather than being an admiration inspired by our desire to hone and perfect the strength in ourselves.

And, of course, another useful way in which we can start to identify our strengths is to ask others. What do they see in you when you

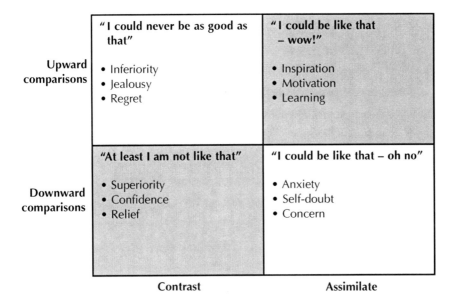

	Contrast	Assimilate
Upward comparisons	"I could never be as good as that" • Inferiority • Jealousy • Regret	"I could be like that – wow!" • Inspiration • Motivation • Learning
Downward comparisons	"At least I am not like that" • Superiority • Confidence • Relief	"I could be like that – oh no" • Anxiety • Self-doubt • Concern

Figure 5.1 Positive Social Comparisons

are at your best? When do they see you as being your most energised? What are you doing when they see you as delivering your best performances, and making your greatest contributions? When answering these questions, be sure to guide people to give feedback that is specific, targeted and with evidence, for in doing so, you maximise the chances of that feedback being helpful, and also maximise the chances that, like Velcro, it will stick. To help you with asking these questions, we have designed an online system that enables you to email people quickly and easily with your request to tell you about what they see as your strengths. Simply visit our supporting website at **www.average-toaplus.org**.

Harness the Power of the Growth Mindset

For over twenty years, Carol Dweck, a Professor of Psychology at Stanford University, has argued that the way in which we think about ourselves has enormous implications for what we believe is possible – and as a direct result, for what we then go on to achieve. Dweck distinguishes between having a *fixed mindset* and having a *growth mindset*. People with a fixed mindset believe that their qualities are pretty much carved in stone – they have a certain amount of intelligence, a certain personality, a certain outlook on life, and of course, certain strengths – all that are fixed and unchanging. What we have is what we've got, according to the people with this fixed mindset.

In contrast, people with a growth mindset are quite the opposite. They hold the view that our basic qualities are things that we can cultivate through our own efforts. Although of course people do differ, and do have natural talents, aptitudes, interests and temperaments, these only provide a baseline against which people can grow and develop. Nothing is fixed, nothing is unchanging or unable to be altered by effort and persistence, according to those who have this growth mindset.

For example, Dweck re-tells the story of Christopher Reeve. Thrown from a horse, his neck was broken and his spinal cord was severed from his brain. He was completely paralysed below the neck. The doctors' view was *"So sorry. Come to terms with it."* But for Reeve – a veritable Superman in life as well as in role – that was unacceptable. Having a massive growth mindset, he started an exercise program to teach his body to move again. Five years later, he started to regain movement – and in doing so, changed the entire way in which the medical profession thinks about the nervous system and its potential for recovery. Reeve's growth mindset had redefined what was possible – just as John Tooby and Leda Cosmides suggested in the opening quote for this chapter.

This theme is one that I have employed in my own teaching – and to great effect. Teaching third year undergraduate social psychology, I sought to equip my students not just with what they needed to pass their exams, but with some of the fundamental skills they needed for life. The growth mindset was one of these things, since (as Dweck's research over the last twenty years has shown), believing that we can grow and develop is most likely the single most important belief that we can hold about ourselves. Dweck cites Howard Gardner's conclusion to his book *Extraordinary Minds*: "[exceptional individuals] have a special talent for identifying their own strengths and weaknesses," going on to conclude herself "It's interesting that those with the growth mindset seem to have that talent." I agree – very interesting – and also very important.

This is where the nature of our mindset comes centrally into focus in the development of our strengths. Simply, if we are operating from a fixed mindset, we are unlikely to think even that we *can* develop our strengths – we will be of the view that what we have is what we are born with, and there is not much else that can be done about it. As a result, however well we can do something, is however well we can do it, end of story. Further, if we have *Rightfinder* as a strength, but we don't have *Time Optimizer*, then there is nothing that we can do about it, again, end of story. What we have is what we have, full stop.

When, however, we have a growth mindset, our view of the world looks completely different. First, we believe absolutely that we can build, develop, and grow our strengths – just as we can anything else. As a result, we are not just open to the possibility of how we can realise our best selves, we are actively focused on it. Second, we recognise that just because certain strengths came out as the top rankings in our recent strengths assessment, that absolutely does not mean that they are fixed and unchanging. Instead, we see them for just what they are – the strengths top-of-mind at that moment in time, likely influenced by our context and whatever our situation called for. And, as Dweck suggests, having a growth mindset in the first place likely enables us to have a more accurate view of our strengths and weaknesses, which can only be a good thing.

For example, when I was working full time in academia, my top strengths came through on a particular strengths assessment as being academic strengths about learning and reflection. When I retook the same strengths assessment, but this time as the Director of CAPP, the strengths that came through were all about strategy and achievement. Am I fundamentally a different person? Not at all. But my *context* is certainly different, and so the strengths to which I relate most closely at that moment in time reflect that context. There is nothing at all wrong with this – just so long as we recognise that we have a symphony of strengths that move out to the foreground and then recede into the background, as our situation and context requires. Having a *growth mindset* helps us to understand, accept and capitalise on this. Having a *fixed mindset* means that we are forever confusing ourselves by trying to make static sense of a dynamic subject.

There is also, however, a further distinction that should be drawn – and again, it will be no surprise to you that we can understand this distinction by reference to one of the guiding principles of realising strengths, the golden mean. This distinction is about recognising that even with a growth mindset, we are not signing up to the view that 'Anyone can do anything, you just have to try hard enough.' Given that strengths are pre-existing capacities, this mantra is, quite simply, wrong. So at one extreme, I am not suggesting that 'anyone can do anything,' while at the other extreme, neither am I suggesting that 'what you have is what you have got.' What I am stating, fundamentally, is that there are some strengths to which we are more pre-disposed and naturally inclined than others, and that within these strengths, there is a lot of room for growth and development. Equally, we might still be able to do something to improve a weakness (more on that below), but we will never be able to take something that is a basic liability for us and turn it into our greatest asset – whatever the extent of our growth mindset, and however hard we work at it. As ever, the question is one of balance and one of degree.

Debunk the Weakness Focus

As paradoxical as it might seem at first glance, realising strengths is not about ignoring weaknesses – far from it. But it is about, wherever possible, making them irrelevant. As management guru Peter Drucker so presciently described it forty years ago:

> "[Making] strength productive...cannot, of course, overcome the weaknesses with which each of us is abundantly endowed. But it can make them irrelevant."

To make weaknesses irrelevant, though, we first need an accurate sense of what they are. This accurate sense is not achieved, however, through the 'weakness gloss' that is the legend of job interviews: "Yes, I do have weaknesses, people tell me that I am a perfectionist, that I work too hard, and that I am overly focused on getting the job done." In contrast, the accurate sense that we require comes through understanding both weaknesses and strengths in context and in relation to each other. We are far more likely to be able to talk authentically about our weaknesses if we have also been able to talk authentically about our strengths. This is not only a matter of self-awareness, but also self-esteem: recognising our strengths tends to make us feel sufficiently good about ourselves, so that we are also able to recognise and admit to our weaknesses.

Recognising and dealing with one's weaknesses is increasingly being identified as a key part of what it takes to be an authentic leader, and should also be seen as a key part of what it takes to be an effective individual – that is, being ourselves - better. Just as the Delphic oracle prescribed, "Know yourself" and "To thine own self be true" – neither of which are possible without an accurate sense of both our strengths and our weaknesses. We have already dedicated a lot of attention to knowing our strengths, and you might recall that in Chapter 4, we also contrasted strengthspotting with what weaknesses looked and sounded like. Yet paradoxically, and likely because of our negativity bias, we are all pretty adept at knowing what it is that we are *not* good at – the evidence is there all around us, and we are only too conscious of it.

To spot our weaknesses, we simply need to look at the things that we never seem to get done. The things that are always on our 'to do' lists, and are crossed off only under threat of sanction; or because we have left them so long that they have become irrelevant anyway; or through the acceptance that comes with the realisation that, actually, we are never going to get round to doing it anyway – there's just too much else that is far preferable before we even get there! Chapter 4 also provided some key weakness 'listen-fors,' so if you did want to investigate your weaknesses more systematically, you may wish to refer back to them.

When weaknesses are identified to exist – as inevitably they will be – what we can do about them? The first and fundamental question that we need to ask ourselves about our weakness is simply: *"Does it matter?"* Does the weakness really matter in terms of what we are trying to achieve? Or, is it simply irrelevant? For the vast majority of us, the vast majority of the time, the weakness will simply be irrelevant – because our role, work, and lives will have evolved, both intentionally and unconsciously, to make it so. If we are extremely bad at doing something, and hate it, we will not tend to pursue a career that requires us to make a virtue of it. For example, my playing of the recorder was never great, and I gave it up at the first opportunity I had – I was about 8 year old at the time – and I haven't looked back since! As such, we would be remarkably unfortunate if we had somehow managed to construct a life for ourselves that was fundamentally constituted around the things that we were no good at, which we had to force ourselves to do, and which left us feeling hollow, devoid of energy and fulfilment.

This being so, it is far more likely to be the case that the weakness with which we are dealing is just one element of a much wider array of activities, some of which we excel at, others of which we perform acceptably or competently, and just a few of which we might struggle with and need to do something about. Just as Drucker advised over forty years ago, that 'do something about' should be first and foremost to make the weakness irrelevant. If irrelevant, our objective has been achieved.

If the weakness isn't irrelevant yet, can we make it irrelevant? This means looking at ways in which we can stop doing whatever it is that is proving a weakness for us, either by doing something different, by doing it in a different way, or by teaming up with someone else who can do it better than we can – most husbands and wives operate in this way, with a fairly clear division of labour across the household chores - even though that division of labour may often reflect traditional stereotypes!

In organisational terms, role fluidity, role shaping and role re-design are all about redefining the boundaries and parameters of any given role so that the weakness-inducing task is defined out of our responsibilities, and so made irrelevant. Together with complementary partnering and strengths-based teamworking, we explore these topics further in Chapter 6, *Harnessing Strengths at Work*, since they can be best described within a working context.

The most important aspect of debunking the weakness focus,

however, is that by spending less time being focused on our weaknesses, we are able to spend more time on building and developing our strengths. There is nothing wrong with fixing a weakness per se, it's just that star performance and optimal functioning never comes just through fixing weaknesses, but more through building on strengths. How many sports stars have you ever heard say that they succeeded through eliminating the things that they weren't good at? Of course, they will almost certainly have dealt with the things that got in the way of their best game, but *that is it*, they stopped there.

Arvinder Dhesi, Group Talent Management Director of Aviva, relates a story of exactly this from his own experience:

> *"Early in my career, I was put in charge of an international project that spanned 22 countries across Europe. This was a huge step up for me. It was the first time I'd been asked to make something happen in more than one country and the project was not only big in terms of scale, but it also had high visibility in a complex terrain of internal politics. The daunting nature of the task and my total lack of formal project planning experience was keeping me up at night.*
>
> *At first, I did what so many people do when faced with an area of weakness – I just worried about it, tried to avoid it and prayed that I'd somehow survive it. I avoided it, that is, until my new boss asked to see my project plan. Behind my smile, I was utterly terrified. I had no project plan, I barely knew what a project plan was, and yet here I was being expected to deliver one that covered a complex set of activities across 22 national boundaries.*
>
> *There was, however, a window of opportunity. My boss was going away for a two week holiday, and I happened to have two weeks off work immediately after him. So I had four full weeks to get my head*

around the issue and conquer my fears. I grabbed this opportunity with both hands. I put myself on the most basic, introductory level project management course I could find. I immersed myself in two or three books on the topic - and crucially - reached out for help from current and former colleagues. Through doing this, I was able to get over my fear, learn the basics, build a support network and develop a level of competence that enabled me to put my newly acquired knowledge into immediate use, to do the job I needed to do.

I am still no expert on project planning – but at least now I know the fundamentals and that I can do it if I have to. Thankfully, most of the time, I am able to work with great team members who can do it far better than I can – and that is such a better way to work."

Arvi's story illustrates the fundamentals of what we need to do in dealing with weakness, and that is simply to make it irrelevant so that it is not getting in the way of the performance we can otherwise deliver. In contrast, one of the tenets of the Curse of Mediocrity is the idea that we can all become super-rounded performers by fixing the things we aren't good at. Good in theory, but in practice people simply aren't built that way – just think about the negative feedback that you might have had over a period of time, whether from a parent, spouse, friend, colleague or boss, and see how often it is the same things that keep coming up – even going right back to your school reports! The fact is, weaknesses don't shift much, but they can be managed. The real potential for us to move from average to A+ is through building and developing our strengths more – and finding the niches in which we can do so to the best effect.

Find Your Niches – and Expand Them

So far in this chapter, we have dealt with the blockers, got to know our strengths better, harnessed the power of the growth mindset, and debunked the weakness focus. We turn now to finding the areas in which we can apply our strengths more, and also to understanding how we can build on and develop what we do best.

It is important to recognise that strengths are only strengths when they can be effectively deployed. A strength without application in the right situation is nothing more than untapped potential. As such, an integral part of our work in realising strengths has to be dedicated to understanding the particular niches where our strengths may be more effectively deployed – and then making the most of them.

There are two distinct opportunities here:

- Finding new niches where our strengths can be applied equally as well or even better;
- Finding ways to apply those strengths even more effectively in the areas where they are already at work.

Sometimes this will involve just doing more of what we already do (while being mindful of the danger of *over*playing strengths), other times it will involve creating entirely new niches where we can carve out an environment for ourselves that allows us to deliver the best of what we have to offer. Usually, however, the identification and development of a new niche for our strengths lies somewhere in between these two extremes. This may involve tweaking an existing role or job a little, to enable us to do more of what we do best and less of what we don't do well. Or it could be about moving to a different role that we think provides a better fit for what we have to offer.

For example, Dominic has a great strength in being constructively critical – we call it *Counterpoint*. He had always known that he was able to do this, but it hadn't always been appreciated. When he started working with CAPP, where this strength was not only recognised, but also valued and invited, he found that he was able to give his *Counterpoint* strength a new lease of life. As a result, Dominic has given some feedback to one of his colleagues that he would never have dreamed of giving before, and has been able to extend the previously very small niche where he had been able to use this strength.

Another example of somebody expanding their niche to realise their strengths more is Philip. He is always recognised as someone who seems to know everyone. And he doesn't just seem to know everyone, but he always seems to know everything. Of course, not everyone and everything throughout all time, but always the things or the people that it worked out he needed to know. Or at least, that was the way it seemed to the people around him.

Philip had *Alignment* as a major strength, and so was the sort of person who always seemed to be able to connect ideas, passions, resources and people with the right opportunities to realise them. When he looked back over his life, it had always been this way, but he was increasingly aware of the power of his *Alignment* strength as he became more mature. As a result, he took increasingly bold decisions to play to it, expanding the niches in which it could be used until it was at the heart of his professional life. Now, his full time role as leader of an organisation is all about *Alignment*: making sure that he joins up people, passions, projects, programmes and resources. And if they don't exist, he will go out and find them. That is *Alignment* at work, and an illustration of how a niche can be expanded – massively – to make the most of what the strength has to offer.

Of course, not all of us will be able to deploy our strengths on the same scale – but we don't have to. Expanding our niche can be as simple as re-shaping elements of our role, whether at work or elsewhere in life, that enable us to do even just a little more of the things that we do best. One may think that a bag packer at the end of a supermarket checkout line, for example, has little scope over what he or she can do to shape their role around their strengths. But Martin Seligman tells a different story. He worked with one such bag packer who had a strength in social intelligence. She crafted her role not so that it was focused on her ability to pack people's shopping most effectively, but on ensuring that, as far as possible, the shoppers had their best interpersonal experience of the day when they came to buy their weekly groceries. She used her social intelligence to deliver a meaningful social connection in an otherwise largely mundane experience, for her own benefit and the benefit of her employer and her customers.

Hence, the size and scope of the niches in which we are able to deploy our strengths are by no means fixed or unchanging. At one level, we might make simple but effective changes in the way in which we characterise our current role, like the bag packer. At another level we might make substantial leaps in the reach of our strengths application. Indeed, we may even go so far as to create a job that is built around us and what we bring. Alastair Ham, Group Organisational Development Director of Aviva, describes just such a process:

> "I have never had a pre-defined job. In every role that I have held, I have crafted that role, and the responsibilities within it, according to the strengths that I bring. Because I have done this at the contracting stage, people have generally been supportive, but problems can arise when things change in midstream – and what is needed then is the conversation that deals with it. Ultimately though, I – just like everyone else – deliver my best performance when I am being my unique self and am valued for that."

Much earlier in her occupational lifespan, my daughter Lucy returned from a visit to a fortune teller, as a seven-year-old, to announce "My job doesn't exist yet." My hope is that the reason for this, at least in part, is because she will be able, in time, to shape a job around her own unique talents and strengths – just like Alastair has been able to do.

As we think about job shaping that will enable us to build more of our daily activities around what we do best, it is important to keep in mind two central tenets. The first is that we should not – despite the inclination of many career guidance inventories – assume that there is a linear relationship between a particular aptitude or strength, and effective performance in a particular job. Research by Chris Peterson and his colleagues, examining the strengths profiles of people across different occupations, indicates that, in general terms, people who report themselves as being in more senior professional roles (e.g., chief executives, professors, doctors, lawyers) also reported themselves as being stronger across almost all of the 24 character strengths assessed by the VIA Inventory of Strengths. In contrast, there were not particular strengths that predicted high performance in particular roles.

There are, of course, trends between strengths and roles that are meaningful, but we should always be mindful of the fact that a strength does not play itself out in only one context, or only one niche. Strengths are transferable across many different areas, so being strong in *Curiosity* could be great for a research scientist. Or a private detective. Or a journalist. Or a teacher. You get the idea: quite different jobs, but jobs that have common themes running through them. As such, it is possible to trace the same strength being deployed in very different ways across very different contexts and in very different job roles. This is bad news for career guidance inventories (they need to move beyond the advice I was given at school: "You're good at maths, become an actuary" and "You're good with foreign languages, become an interpreter"), but good news for us as individuals. With some more careful consideration, and a better understanding of what jobs *actually* involve, we are likely to be able to find a job that is even better suited to us.

Herminia Ibarra's research on career changes demonstrates the point. People are very unlikely to make great leaps into new careers when they have 'finally' worked out what it is that they want to do. In contrast, we tend to make small shifts, one step at a time, trying on new identities and trying out new roles through getting a bit closer with each move we make. This may be through shaping our current role so it fits better, moving into a new role that is a step closer to where we think we want to be, or taking up a hobby that allows us to build something that gets us ever closer to becoming a viable, income-generating alternative to our current job. In the best of all worlds, people are able to combine all three strategies at the same time, and thereby to explore their 'possible selves,' to know who they are and, perhaps more importantly, who they want to be. And it's worth remembering that, like snakes, sometimes we need to slough off our old skin in order to let the new one shine through. Finding the niches where we can realise our strengths more fully is likely to mean stopping doing some things in order to give ourselves the time to do the new things that come through our strengths – the old has to give way for the new.

As we transition and try on different 'possible selves,' we create the opportunities for our different strengths to come into play. A key part of these transitional attempts is to enable us to explore the strengths that we have peeking out from the background, but that are not being deployed yet. They are held in reserve awaiting their opportunity. Whenever this is the case, there is a potential that lays dormant in us, and we are not being all we are capable of being. As you get to know yourself better, and get to listen to the inner voice of your strengths, this becomes an increasingly unacceptable way of being. As we discussed in Chapter 2, our strengths are aspects of our core inner nature. Our actualising tendency prompts us to use them and to follow them. When we know our strengths and use them, this journey toward self-actualisation is accelerated. Our strengths need to be, they require expression: when they are, we are happier, more fulfilled, more confident, more capable, and more likely to achieve what is most important to us in life.

We may find that we like using some strengths more than others, that some are particularly suited to application in our worlds, or that some just leave us feeling more fully authentic and in touch with who we are. Exploring our strengths can be like letting the genie out of the bottle – once open, we cannot simply put the lid back on, for things will never be the same again. Nor should we expect them to be, because growth inevitably involves change, and change requires loss, if only the loss of the way things were before. As Karen Stefanyszyn, Head of Organisation Development at Norwich Union, described it:

> *"Once you have started to recognise your strengths and to play to them, you can't go back. It's like letting the genie out of the bottle – it won't go back in. Once you have realised the things that you are good at and that you love to do, and you have found ways to spend your time doing them, it's impossible to go back to a life where you are not doing that. And who would ever want to?"*

Changing circumstances and contexts provide us with changing opportunities - opportunities to bring latent strengths to the fore, to try out new ways of being, and to see what fits, what we like, and what we want to keep. The process of strengths exploration itself may be unsettling and discomforting, but these are natural reactions to change and a journey into a world that is less well-known to us. The key is to keep our confidence and live through the exploration, rather than trying to short-circuit the process. Once we have developed a better grasp of who we are and what we want to become, we are well on the path to building the strengths that will become the basis of our contribution and existence, forming the bedrock of our movement from average to A+, through being ourselves - better.

Practise and Refine Your Strengths

Having found your niche and started to deploy your strengths more, the next stages in building your strengths are to practise and refine them. Practise is as practise does – it is simply about using your strengths more – and if it really is a strength for you, you won't need to be invited twice! Intrinsic motivation and discretionary effort – doing something for the sheer enjoyment of it and doing more of it than you are required to – are both hallmarks of a strength in practice. Deploy your strengths accordingly for best effect and greatest contribution. When you know a strength better and start to explore where you might use it more, you are likely to find myriad opportunities, including those outside your previous circle of action and influence.

Take Richard, for example. He is a senior manager in a major FMCG company (FMCGs are Fast Moving Consumer Goods – for example, foods and household products). Several years back, he took a strengths assessment that showed empathy to be one of his highest strengths. He took the assessment results and used them as a book-mark, finding them serendipitously several years later. There is nothing unusual in that, you might think – except what had happened in the intervening years.

Richard had become increasingly disillusioned in his job. Although a veritable expert in his field, he was a classic case of someone high on competence (he was very good at doing it) but low on strength for the role (doing it didn't come naturally, and in fact over time it drained him). As a result, Richard experienced a quite tortuous period of soul-searching and questioning about what he was going to do with the rest of his life, while continuing to support his young family. Finally, he arrived at the recognition that his job didn't give him enough opportunity to be himself – and, in fact, he came to realise increasingly that there were large parts of who he was that were cut off and excluded from his day to day reality. He was feeling increasingly inauthentic and disengaged because he was not using his strengths anywhere near enough.

Equipped with this knowledge, he started to explore what those neglected parts of himself were, and identified strengths in empathy and the ability to listen and connect with others. In a quite surprising turn of events for someone of his age and in his field of work, he applied to join the Samaritans, an organisation that provides 24-hour listening and support services for anyone who finds themselves in crisis. Richard relished the training, finding it to be the most powerful validation he had ever had of who he was and what he was about. At last, here he was able to be valued for what he did best. Now, over a year on, Richard is a regular volunteer for the Samaritans, spending up to eight hours per week listening to and supporting people in crisis.

He didn't change his job, but became much more engaged and productive, paradoxically by virtue of connecting with himself and what he had to offer outside of work. And as so often happens, his greater engagement outside of work is having a knock-on effect within work. People have started to recognise and appreciate that Richard possesses a possibly rare combination of strengths, deep empathy and listening skills, combined with acute business understanding. In time, it is likely that this recognition of Richard's strengths more fully by the people around him will present its own opportunities for Richard adapting his role ('role shaping'), to allow him to bring into work more of what he does so well outside it.

In this context, in a turn of events in equal parts sad and ironic, it was at this time that Richard found his strengths assessment results from so many years before, and started to wonder how his life could have been different if he had acted on them sooner. Who knows what the future will hold for him? What is clear is that now Richard has found a niche to practise and refine his strengths of empathy and connection, his life is much more authentic, in balance and integrated, both outside work and increasingly also at work.

As Richard's example shows, the practice and refinement of our strengths need not be restricted to our work environment – or even to the particular environment where that strength is predominantly used. Just as with expanding our niches, we may find a surprising variety of opportunities for practising and refining our strengths, just so long as we keep ourselves open to the possibilities.

This practice and refinement is not so different from how sports people and athletes might develop their physical strengths. To a degree at least, we can liken psychological strengths to physical strengths, or the strength of a muscle – something that Mark Muraven and Roy Baumeister looked at specifically in relation to self-control (which we would recognise as a psychological strength; it is called self-regulation in the VIA Inventory of Strengths). They were interested in the question of whether self-control resembled a muscle. That is, does exerting self-control use up the energy of self-control, reducing the amount of self-control available for subsequent self-control actions? They found that it did: people were more likely to fail in attempts at self-control when recent demands on their capacity for self-control had depleted their limited inner resources for self-control. They extended their findings to suggest that this strength model of self-control could also be taken to imply that by systematically exerting the muscle of self-control, and then allowing time for recovery and renewal, people would be able to increase their muscle capacity for self-control. Just as muscles build when we exercise them beyond our comfort zone, but then take time for recovery and renewal, so too, Muraven and Baumeister demonstrated, did self-control.

This approach is echoed in the work of Jim Loehr and Tony Schwartz with high-performing athletes and sports stars. In their book, *The Power of Full Engagement*, Loehr and Schwartz similarly demonstrate how the world's best performers have in place rituals for practice and performance that systematically take them beyond their comfort zone in order to build capacity and capability, but then recover through allowing time and resources for recovery and renewal. Given that strengths themselves are energising, the practice of building strengths could itself become a virtuous cycle, because as Loehr and Schwartz suggest: "Any activity that is enjoyable, fulfilling and affirming serves as a source of emotional renewal and recovery." As such, using and building our strengths can simultaneously renew and recharge us, thereby creating the virtuous cycle shown in Figure 5.2.

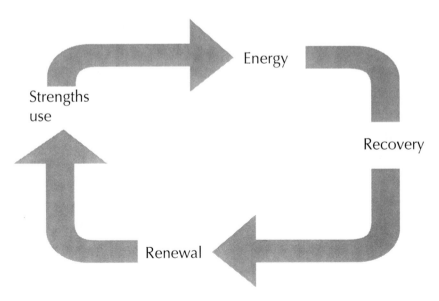

Figure 5.2 Using Strengths Provides Energy for Recovery and Renewal

This model of having a limited inner resource of strength, but a resource that, just like a muscle, can be grown and developed through systematically using and extending it, then allowing time for recovery and renewal, provides a useful analogy for building psychological strengths. In essence, to build our strengths, we need to use them more and more, going systematically beyond our comfort zones to apply them in new and different areas. But at the same time, we need to allow time for recovery and renewal, while also ensuring that the strengths are not overplayed, in the way that I described in Chapter 3. One of the most effective ways to do this is through developing habits of strength, while guarding against habituation.

Habit and Habituation

The power of habit was thrust back into popular discourse with the publication of Stephen Covey's international bestseller *The Seven Habits of Highly Effective People*. Turning on its head the popular conception that habits were 'bad' (for example, biting your finger nails, picking your nose), Covey reintroduced the idea that habits actually constitute the things that we do quite naturally everyday, and that if we can adopt and develop good habits – such as these seven habits that characterise highly effective people – then we too can become highly effective. Likely one of the reasons that Covey's book sold - and continues to sell - so well, is because we can all relate to the idea of habit, and recognise those things that we do naturally and repetitively each day. The idea of replacing our own inefficient habits with the habits of highly effective people is a very tantalising one, not least because implicitly we understand habits as the ways in which we act automatically, without needing to think about them. Habits require less effort and resources, both psychological and physical.

Understood in this way, we can begin to see how using strengths can represent a positive, constructive, 'good habit.' We are already predisposed to use our strengths, because they are pre-existing capacities within us that we are motivated to use, and we feel rewarded when doing so through the feelings of authenticity and energy that come from using our strengths. It is little surprise then, to find that in an experiment where people were asked to use their strengths in a new and different way for one week, they continued doing so months later – without prompting - and as a result, reported increased happiness and lower depression that was sustained over time.

This is one of a variety of initiatives recommended for the increase of happiness. Other happiness increase initiatives point to the need to develop the habit of taking new actions to refresh our happiness, while avoiding habituation (that is, getting used to doing something so that it loses its novelty and effect). We can think of habituation in relation to eating chocolate pudding after every meal. After the first meal, maybe even the second meal, possibly even the third meal, the chocolate pudding is a welcome pleasure. But, the more chocolate pudding we eat, the more we get used to it, and the less pleasure it gives us. In economic terms, the pleasure of eating the chocolate pudding is a diminishing marginal return. Simply put, over time, eating chocolate pudding after every meal loses it's effect, that is, we *habituate* to it.

Thus, the recommendation should be that we get into the habit of doing different activities to enable our happiness, but that we avoid falling into the trap of doing the same things, because we habituate to the activity, and so it loses its effectiveness. This habituation effect refers to the 'hedonic treadmill' of which you may have heard – the idea that people get used to changes in their circumstances, and as a result, happiness levels tend to be relatively stable over time – famously even in the case of people who have won the lottery, or who have been seriously disabled in accidents.

Building strengths through habit requires us to develop the good habit of using our strengths more in different contexts on a daily basis, while being careful to avoid habituation and overplaying the strength. As Jerry Porras and his colleagues identified in *Success Built to Last*, the secret of sustainably successful people was all about making use of constructive habits: "Builders achieve enduring success when they pour themselves into constructive habits – limiting their 'addictions' to the passions that serve them."

What constructive habits could you adopt or develop around the understanding and use of your strengths? Answering this question will not only increase your effectiveness and satisfaction, but also help you to develop the 'art of the possible.'

The Art of the Possible

When, like Richard, you start to use your latent strengths more, one of the first challenges will be to get the measure of what you can do. The challenge here is often not the fear of what we can't do, but rather the fear of what we can. As Marianne Williamson famously wrote in *A Return to Love*:

> *"Our deepest fear is not that we are inadequate. Our deepest fear is that we are powerful beyond measure. It is our light, not our darkness that frightens us. We ask ourselves, Who am I to be brilliant, gorgeous, talented, fabulous? Actually, who are you not to be?"*

Suddenly, possibility and potential seem to exist beyond what we might ever have dreamed. There is a lesson in itself in mastering this anticipation and stepping boldly into the realms of what can be. Consider the experience of Roger, a design engineer at Cougar

Automation, winner of the 2007 Customer Experience Awards. Cougar Automation is a strengths-based organisation that builds computerised control systems for clients including food manufacturers, airports, and utilities. Cougar Automation's work can basically be divided into two parts, the design brief and then writing the software. Clive Hutchinson, the Managing Director, described it like this: "Design brief – greens; writing software – dessert."

But it transpired that Roger didn't see it that way. When Cougar Automation were implementing the move towards using strengths more in their organisation, Roger put himself forward to do more of the design briefs, on the basis that, simply put, for him they were like eating the delicious dessert rather than chewing his way through the healthy but hateful greens. And the results? Whereas the previous average time taken to produce a design brief was 2-3 days, Roger is now consistently producing them on a *daily* basis. But the moral of the story is that he would never have got there, had he – and Clive, and the organisation - not believed in the art of the possible, but instead had continued to labour under the Curse of Mediocrity – the belief that everyone should be good at everything.

Examples like this can make it look easy, but that would be to miss the fear of the stretch. Indeed, if you don't feel the fear of the stretch when you are honing a strength more towards its greatest contribution, then it is unlikely that you are using it to anything like its fullest extent. I remember the experience of editing my first book, *Positive Psychology in Practice*. I was a PhD student at the University of Warwick, UK, and decided that I was going to edit a book on the applications of positive psychology, because in my view it was needed in the field, and nobody else at that time was working systematically in the area.

With a certain dose of confidence (and in retrospect, probably more than a dose of arrogance!), I started to edit the 42 chapter book, working with my PhD supervisor, Stephen Joseph. I invited contributions from some of the biggest names in the field – people who were, simply, my heroes, and whose work I was now going to judge and adjudicate, with all the experience that you can muster with a three year Honours degree and a year's graduate study under your belt. It was certainly a stretch, and halfway through the process, I started to feel the fear of that stretch in ways that I couldn't have anticipated. "Can I really deliver this? What will happen if I have taken a step too far and it all falls down around my ankles?" But it worked - the volume was a great success, and through the process I honed my strengths of writing and editing even further. As the saying goes, failure was not an option, but the stretch really showed me what can be possible when you start to build your strengths. It is a lesson I have taken to heart ever since, and I fully encourage you to do the same. Why should you not strive for your greatest achievements through using your greatest strengths?

When we start to get rid of the blockers that get in the way of us making the most of our strengths, harness the power of the growth mindset, and find the niches in which we can most effectively develop, refine and deploy our greatest strengths, we are able to redefine what we consider to be the art of the possible. The art of the possible is what we believe our own possibilities and potentials to be – and they are effectively without limit. As Christopher Reeve's story showed, and as John Tooby and Leda Cosmides set out in the opening quote for this chapter:

> "Everything that every individual has ever done in all of human history and prehistory establishes the minimum boundary of the possible. The maximum, if any, is completely unknown."

Realising our strengths provides the single most effective route for making the art of the possible our own reality. It is the most potent means through which we can be ourselves – better.

Key Points

- Realising strengths in ourselves requires us: (1) to overcome our blockers (especially our resistance to positive feedback); (2) to develop our strengths through harnessing the power of the growth mindset; (3) to shift our focus away from weakness and what doesn't work; (4) to find our niches and make the most of them; (5) to adopt the right habits but avoid habituation; and ultimately, (6) to practise the art of the possible.

- We are resistant to positive feedback because we may fear becoming complacent or arrogant, or because we don't see the positives ourselves. To have the best chances of sticking, positive feedback needs to be specific, targeted and with evidence.

- We learn best from heroes and role models through effective use of positive upward comparisons, whereby we assimilate into ourselves the aspects of other people that we admire, and to which we aspire.

- When we have a growth mindset, believing that our strengths and abilities can be developed and we can learn more and become better by working at things, we are far better enabled to achieve greater success. People with a growth mindset also tend to have more accurate views of their own strengths and weaknesses.

- We should strive to develop the good habit of using our strengths more and in more and different situations, while guarding against habituation – becoming used to things because we are doing them. We can overcome habituation through varying our contexts, even if the central activity, or strength being used, is the same.

Areas for Reflection and Action

- Can you identify the blockers to you realising strengths in yourself? What can you do about them? Who can you ask to give you positive feedback that is specific, targeted, and with evidence?

- Do you have a growth mindset or a fixed mindset? What are the implications of this for you realising your own strengths, and what can you do about them?

- Who do you most admire, and what do you think you could learn from them? How can understanding and applying the principles of positive upward social comparisons help you to do this?

SIX

Harnessing Strengths at Work

"…one cannot build on weakness. To achieve results, one has to use all the available strengths…These strengths are the true opportunities. To make strength productive is the unique purpose of organization."
Peter Drucker, *The Effective Executive*

WHAT IMAGES COME to mind when you think about 'work?' What does Monday morning (assuming a traditional working week) bring to mind for you? Are you filled with dread - or bursting with energy and ready to go again? The accepted view of work has historically been almost uniquely negative – type 'work' into an online thesaurus and see some of the synonyms that come up: *chore, daily grind, drudgery, obligation, slogging, task, toil, travail.* Even more telling, just look at the antonyms (words meaning the opposite) that are provided: *entertainment, fun, pastime.* Studs Terkel, who conducted 128 interviews with people across America in the early 1970's, asking them about their jobs - with those jobs ranging from bus drivers to gravedig-gers to prostitutes to airline stewardesses, amongst many others – also concluded that people often see work very negatively:

"This book, being about work, is, by its very nature, about violence – to the spirit as well as to the body...To survive the day is triumph enough for the walking wounded among the great many of us."

But, Terkel went on:

"It is about a search, too, for daily meaning as well as daily bread, for recognition as well as cash, for astonishment rather than torpor; in short, for a sort of life rather than a Monday through Friday sort of dying."

In the thirty or so years since Terkel's interviews, work has changed – but not enough.

There is, however, a different way. A different way that pioneering organisations are now beginning to discover and apply. We are still at the beginning of this change curve when it comes to this different way, but companies like Aviva, Norwich Union, and Standard Chartered Bank in financial services; BAE Systems, Cougar Automation and Toyota in engineering; O2 and Yahoo in new media and communica-tions; Accenture and CAPP in management consulting, are all taking committed steps toward applying strengths in their organisations. In fact, CAPP was established as an explicitly strengths-based organisa-tion - but more of that later.

This different way is about organising work in a manner that is predicated on a powerful and important double-win: a win for organi-sations and the bottom line, and a win for individuals and their health, well-being and contribution. This different way is about organising work in a way that realises strengths – in both the individual and the organisation. This chapter is about the why, the what, and the how of realising strengths at work.

The Business Case for Harnessing Strengths at Work

What is the evidence that focusing on employees' strengths is a good thing for organisations to do? There aren't yet hundreds of studies to support it – remember, the strengths approach is still in its infancy, and a body of academic research takes years and years to come to fruition. But the available evidence is compelling – and cannot be ignored by any Chairman, CEO, director, manager or employee within an organisation. For example, in a study of 19,187 employees, drawn from 34 organisations across seven industries and 29 countries, the Corporate Leadership Council (CLC) found that an emphasis on *performance strengths* was linked to a 36.4% *improvement* in performance, while an emphasis on *personality strengths* was linked to a 21.3% *improvement* in performance. In contrast – and this is the kicker – an emphasis on *performance weaknesses* was linked to a 26.8% *decline* in performance, and an emphasis on *personality weaknesses* was linked to a 5.5% *decline* in performance.

The message of this study is both clear and compelling: focusing on strengths enables higher performance, while focusing on weaknesses undermines performance. The reasons for this are likely many and varied: employees whose managers emphasise their strengths feel that they have a good fit with their job and are more committed to the organisation, they are also likely to feel that they are appreciated and are able to make a contribution. For all of these reasons, they apply more discretionary effort to ensure that they get the job done. In contrast, employees whose managers emphasise their weaknesses are more likely to feel that they are in the wrong job, and to withdraw their effort as a result, leading to the falls in performance that were found in the CLC study.

Similarly, Jim Harter, Frank Schmidt, and Barry Hayes, writing in the *Journal of Applied Psychology*, reported that employees who said they were able to use their strengths at work every day were significantly more engaged, and that engagement, in turn, was linked to a number of bottom line business outcomes, including customer satisfaction, productivity and profitability – this based on a sample of 198,514 employees across 7, 939 business units within 36 companies.

As well as academic research, the evidence also comes through loud and clear from the experience of the organisations who are themselves consciously adopting strengths-based approaches. Do you remember Roger at Cougar Automation, who prepares the design briefs in a single day, compared to the 2-3 days it used to take his colleagues to prepare them? As a result of this, and many other instances like it, Cougar Automation is able to demonstrate consistently excellent business results, with a return on investment that is in double figures, compared to an industry average of around 6%, and customer satisfaction ratings consistently running above 90% - again, unheard of in the industry – and no doubt a key reason why they were the Winner of the 2007 Customer Experience Awards.

A similar story comes from Adam Eaton, who is Director of Leadership Development for Aviva, and in charge of the company's 'Leadership Academy' programme. After learning about his own strengths on one of these programmes, a senior manager returned into the business and re-organised his team according to their strengths. Just by doing this, he calculated that he had saved the organisation £250,000 per year. Another senior manager returned to his business with a new knowledge of strengths, and recognised a natural talent in one of his employees that he had not previously identified. As a result, he was able to re-allocate to this employee a project that had had a £100,000 consultancy budget earmarked against it, thereby saving the £100,000!

Norwich Union (part of Aviva) has been using strengths as a central focus of their recruitment for the last two years – with compelling results, as they reported in *Strategic HR Review*. They have consistently attracted more of the right people, recruited them more efficiently, and then put them in roles where they are able to do what they do best and what they love to do. The results? All new recruits from the strengths-based recruitment approach scored above 90% in their performance appraisals, and attrition has halved. At the same time, they have been able to deliver a better recruitment experience both for candidates who were successful and for those who were not – a compelling business need, when potential candidates are equally likely to be potential or actual clients. As one unsuccessful candidate described their recruitment experience: "About half way through the interview, I realised that this wasn't the job for me – I didn't have the right strengths. And strangely enough, that was okay."

For BAE Systems, the strengths work with the board of the £2.5bn Air Support business unit has also delivered enhanced board effectiveness and improved business performance, enabling the team to work more effectively with each other and throughout the wider organisation, delivering a major change programme within tight financial and time constraints, as reported by Tim Smedley in a *People Management* feature article.

Pulling together all of this evidence, the Centre for Applied Positive Psychology (CAPP) developed a 10-point business case for strengths-based organisation. The 10 business benefits they identified for organisations working from people's strengths were extensive:

1. Tap into unused talent throughout the organisation;
2. Attract and retain more of the people it needs;

3. Improve individual performance;

4. Build employee engagement;

5. Develop flexibility;

6. Improve teamwork;

7. Increase diversity and positive inclusion;

8. Increase openness to change and the ability to deal with change;

9. Deal more positively with redundancy;

10. Contribute to the happiness and fulfilment of employees.

This last point might seem like a strange one for organisations to be interested in – except maybe for the John Lewis Partnership, an organisation that has the happiness of its employees as one of the reasons for its existence – but it is an intrinsic part of the double-win promise of realising strengths at work. Using strengths is a powerful way of accessing and harnessing discretionary effort – simply because by working from people's strengths, we are asking them to do more of what they enjoy and do best. And as our research has shown, using strengths more is associated with significantly higher levels of happiness, well-being and fulfilment, as well as a greater degree of authenticity and personal integration, feeling in touch with yourself and acting in ways that are right for you. Further, research has consistently shown that happier, more fulfilled employees are more productive and perform better across a range of organisational metrics. As such, working from strengths is likely enabling better organisational performance through a number of different routes.

Clearly, whether the evidence comes from academic research or practical experience, the findings are consistent and significant: Focusing on employees' strengths drives business outcomes. Given that, how do we go about doing it?

As defined by my CAPP colleagues Nicky Page and Dominic

Carter, "*Strengths-based organization is a term used to describe both the process and the outcome of harnessing individual strengths for joint performance in organizations.*" The question of how a fully fledged strengths-based organisation would look, feel and operate is a huge topic, and one that deserves to be the subject of another book: I hope it shortly will be. For our present purposes, though, I will restrict my attention in this chapter to the simple idea of *working from strengths*, the essence of harnessing strengths at work, and, for the majority of us, the best opportunity to realise strengths in ourselves and others.

Working from strengths is fundamentally about respecting and valuing diversity, difference, and individual contribution, using this as the basis from which performance can be maximized, individually and collectively, across the organisation. Strengths-based working builds on and incorporates many elements of traditional best practice - things like clear objectives, honest performance conversations, and real time feedback – but its fundamental focus is on what people do best, and how they can build on that further, by developing, refining and deploying their strengths to best effect – both for themselves and for the organisation. This approach can be starkly or subtly different from traditional approaches, depending on how the ubiquitous competency framework is applied. Before we get into exploring working from strengths, however, we need to make a quick detour to understand where the strengths approach fits in relation to competencies.

What about Competencies?

For many organisations, the focus of people management and especially development is much more explicitly about 'gap analysis,' then subsequently 'plugging the gaps' through reference to 'areas for development' (read: work on your weaknesses). This perennial 'gap focus' gets far more airtime than building on strengths, which might at best get a cursory mention in a performance review or development assessment. As one recruiting manager described it to me:

> "We spend a fortune on recruiting people for what they do well. Then we spend another fortune trying to fix their weaknesses. You would think that somebody would wake up to this and do something about it."

Indeed. But the negativity bias plays itself out in every walk of life, organisations most especially included, particularly in the context of competency frameworks that dictate that every person who wants to succeed in the organisation must be good at everything that is included within the competency framework. Where is flexibility? Where is originality? Where is respect for difference? Where, above all, is the fact recognised that people go about achieving the same goals in different ways? Not in the way most competency frameworks are applied, for sure.

For example, a senior HR Director described the competency approach as "flatlining" – focused exclusively on trying to get everyone to the same minimum level, ignoring the areas where they could excel. Maybe this was just me, but all I could think of after this comment was the flatline of a heart monitor when somebody has died. How many organisations are dying because of the flatlining of their competency frameworks, I wondered?

David Taylor, author of *The Naked Leader* book series and Honorary Professor at Warwick Business School, seemed to share the same view when he offered this advice to his audience at the CIPD Annual Conference in October 2006:

"How many of you work in organisations that have competency frameworks?"

[Numerous hands go up.]

"Do you know the best thing to do with them?"

[Shaking heads.]

"Take them home, and give them to your children for drawing paper."

Clearly, David is not a big fan of competency frameworks either.

The issue, however, is not with competency frameworks *per se* – in fact, David McClelland's original approach and rationale for developing competencies shares a lot of similarities with the strengths approach today. The issue, rather, is with the ways in which competency frameworks get applied – as generic solutions to specific problems, that, in turn, are used to dictate a rigid behavioural framework to which everyone in the organisation is expected to adhere. Within this framework, there is an inherent focus on gap analysis and plugging the gaps where they are identified, and little, if any focus on exceptional performance and how it can be built on further to ensure future success. This was not how competencies were intended, but it is often how they have been applied.

If, however, competency frameworks seem to be set in stone within your organisation, they can often be realigned in the way in which they are applied – keeping many of the structures and metrics that the competency framework provides, but avoiding the hamstrung effect of requiring that everyone scores well at everything, and thereby missing the greatest opportunities that people have to contribute – through their strengths – which is where we turn next, as we return to exploring strengths-based ways of working.

The Team as the Unit of Strengths-based Working

As Jon Katzenbach and Douglas Smith defined:

"A team is a small number of people with complementary skills who are committed to a common purpose, performance goals, and approach for which they hold themselves mutually accountable."

Every organisation, of any size, is made up of a (larger or smaller) number of (larger or smaller) teams. On this basis, it can be helpful to approach the use of strengths in organisational settings through the lens of the team. Teams exist within every organisation – and outside them – and the team can often provide a microcosm of the organisation itself: how the team interact and relate to each other is ultimately played out in the success or failure of the organisation. Great teams build great organisations that achieve great success: This is the central message of Jim Collins' excellent book, *Good to Great*, as well as a central thesis of Allan Leighton's findings from interviewing 60 top business leaders in his book, *On Leadership*. Average teams build average organisations that – at best – achieve average success. As we found in the opening chapter, nobody wants to be average.

Teams provide the lens for the strengths approach because they possess all the ingredients that are needed for strengths-based working. Teams have their own psychological climate, they are comprised of different people with different collections of natural talents and strengths, they interact with each other, and they are striving to find the optimal way to achieve a mutually desired outcome. As a result, teams provide a way of aligning the building blocks for joint performance that Peter Drucker regarded as the unique purpose of organisation: "To make strength productive is the unique purpose of organization... Its task is to use the strength of each man as a building block for joint performance."

In many areas of life, and especially in large organisations, the demands are simply far too great to be shouldered by any one individual. Given our individual limitations, there is only so much that we can achieve alone. This is why teams, and later, organisations, have been formed since time immemorial: to achieve collectively what could not be achieved individually. As Stephen Miles and Michael Watkins wrote in the *Harvard Business Review*:

> *"Bringing together two or more people with complementary strengths not only compensates for the shortcomings of each but also results in a team in which the whole is much greater than the sum of the parts."*

Making the most of each individual's strengths through leveraging the power of the team can be achieved in at least four ways: role fluidity, role shaping, complementary partnering and strengths-based teamworking.

Role fluidity is about adopting fluid and flexible boundaries – where boundaries even exist – between who does what and when. This can be seen in relation to two similar, but equally quite different team sports: football and water polo. In both, the objective is to score goals against the opposing team, while avoiding conceding any goals yourself, thereby trying to finish the match having scored more goals than your opponents. In football, all the players have a designated position (goalkeeper, defender, midfielder, attacker) and are largely expected to play in that position. In contrast, in water polo, the only distinction is between the goalkeeper and the outfield players. With the (possible) exception of the goalkeeper, everybody attacks, and everybody defends – there is great role fluidity and very little demarcation of who should do what and when. Instead, the focus is on the shared objective of the team as a whole, and the team therefore functions as an amorphous single unit. In this way, every player flexes their position according to what the situation demands and what the team needs. There is no rigid demarcation of roles, with players covering only their own nominated positions, but instead a fully shared and collective responsibility for achieving the outcome for which the team is aiming. Every single player in a water polo team does whatever is required of them for the team to win. Like *The Three Musketeers*, it really is "All for one and one for all."

For role fluidity to be effective, team members need to have a shared understanding of the objective they are all trying to achieve, and not be precious about who does what to achieve it. In contrast, they will flex and bend, chop and change, as the task requires and as they are best able to contribute. Whoever is best qualified, whoever has time available, whoever has the energy to give – these are just some of the factors that influence the seemingly chaotic – but highly effective – practice of role fluidity.

The defining characteristic of this approach is that everyone is clear about what the team is trying to achieve, and everyone is committed to achieving it. In this way, weakness is made irrelevant because whenever a weakness-inducing element comes up for somebody, a colleague can readily be asked to step in and take over if they are better equipped to do so. And when role fluidity is functioning at its most efficient, even the invitation is superfluous: people simply know what needs to be done and how to work together, and they do it.

Role shaping takes this a step further by defining the role around the person, rather than trying (and all too often, failing) to define the person around the role – do you remember Alastair Ham's experience, which we discussed in Chapter 5: "I have never had a pre-defined job. In every role that I have held, I have crafted that role, and the responsibilities within it, according to the strengths that I bring." Alastair's experience is a great – but all too rare – example of role shaping in practice, and the benefits it can bring to both the individual and the organisation.

Too often, it's the case that the requirements and responsibilities of any given role were set by somebody - with the best of intentions - on the basis of establishing what a previous role holder did, and then assuming that whoever did the job in the future would have to do the same things. But roles are never set in stone – especially in an organisational climate as fast-moving and constantly changing as it is today. Recognising the rapid shift of the organisational climate, we should also recognise that roles within organisations can be shifted too. Of course, there are elements to any role that define it centrally, that are non-negotiable: one would not want to work with an accountant who was no good at maths, or with a therapist devoid of empathy. But outside these core role requirements, there is much more that can be flexed and negotiated – to everyone's benefit, including that of the organisation. Remember, for example, what happened at Cougar Automation, when Roger started working exclusively on the design briefs, which he did best, leaving his colleagues to work on writing the software – which they did best. And all because the Cougar team were prepared to recognise that roles are not set in stone, and can be flexed as the requirements of the organisation and the people in the organisation flex.

Complementary partnering is about the idea of working with someone who compensates for your weaknesses and simultaneously plays off your strengths. Richard Branson describes it perfectly in his autobiography *Losing my Virginity*, when he is talking about the *Student* magazine:

> *"Throughout my life, I've always needed somebody as a counterbalance, to compensate for my weaknesses, and work off my strengths. Jonny and I were a good team. He knew who we should interview, and why. I had the ability to persuade them to say yes, and the obstinacy never to accept no for an answer."*

The corporate world provides ready examples of these highly successful double acts, including, for example, Lord (James) Hanson and his business partner Lord (Gordon) White (sadly both now deceased), of Hanson plc, and Archie Norman and Allan Leighton who turned round the ailing supermarket retailer, Asda. Archie Norman provided the vision and people focus, while Allan Leighton concentrated on operational excellence.

Yet perhaps the most important – but uncelebrated – double act throughout any organisation are the directors and their PAs: I have met many directors who admitted quite openly that they would not know what they needed to be doing, or where they needed to be, if it wasn't for their PAs organising their diaries and their lives for them: complementary partnering in practice. But the role of the PA often also goes beyond this administrative caretaking. For example, Rebekah Wade, editor of *The Sun* newspaper, is particularly proud of her PA, Cheryl Carter, recognising her as integral to the business:

> *"Cheryl is one of my best assets…She's not the person who sorts out my diary; she's very much part of the business."*

All of us could likely do this more, but unfortunately there tend to be organisational and cultural 'norms' that get in the way and stop us. I have often heard people express the concern that working like this leads to social loafing – the idea that people ride on the back of other people's efforts without doing anything themselves. And while this can happen, it is always more reflective of the culture of the organisation and attitude of the people within it, far more than it is of the nature of the strengths approach to working itself.

When people are committed to achieving a common purpose, they are most effective when their contributions are aligned with what they do best and what they love to do. This can happen most efficiently when we are able to work in complementary ways with the people around us, something described by Roy White, Vice President, Human Resources, Sony Europe:

"I have a colleague who is very structured and really detailed, and she is always wanting to make sure that things are done properly. I think that for around 30-40% of the time I drive her mad, because she would see me as taking things too lightly and not going into enough depth. That works the other way too, in that I get frustrated because it can take so long to do the analysis for something, and yet you already know what the answer is going to be – so why be concerned with doing the analysis in the first place when it will only slow things down, especially when we need to do things a lot faster? We have talked about this a lot, about how we frustrate each other, but also about how we help each other. Now we smile about it, because we recognise that we both need each other. I really appreciate her, because she goes into that depth of analysis and I can trust that whatever she does will be of the highest quality. She appreciates me, because she is able to recognise that I make things happen and push them through faster than would have happened otherwise. Through being able to work with each other like this, we have found a way of working together that is very complementary, that means we can get the best out of each other by both doing what we do best."

Strengths-based teamworking follows exactly the same principles as complementary partnering, it just chunks up a level and applies the approach to a team, rather than to a pair of individuals. The fundamental principle of team working is that the team can achieve more collectively than they could as a group of individuals. Through the lens of the strengths approach, this is about allocating tasks, roles and responsibilities according to strengths: Who has the strengths most appropriate for delivering the goals we are striving to achieve in this area?

We can trace historical examples of strengths-based teamworking as far back as at least the Trojan War. Led by the powerful King Agamemnon, the Greeks still had much need for, and made great play of, the strengths of other major characters in the Greek high command: the battle prowess of Achilles; the cunning of Odysseus; the counsel of Mentor; and the wisdom of Nestor, to name but a few. It is likely that, explicitly or otherwise, Agamemnon was following the edict of the ancient Greek principle of *kratisto* in organising his troops for the campaign. *Kratisto* means to the strongest, to the best, or to the most able. It is a term made famous by Alexander the Great, who is believed to have uttered the word with his final dying breath. When asked by his generals to whom he bequeathed his kingdom, Alexander is said to have replied: "*Kratisto.*"

The principle of *kratisto* is about understanding the different strengths available from the individuals in a team, and then aligning those strengths in the team in such a way that performance is maximised by having people doing the things that they do best. As the Scottish millionaire entrepreneur, Sir Tom Hunter, describes it:

> "*Entrepreneurs who want to build businesses of substance and size need to understand what they are good at. Then they can recruit to their weaknesses and build a balanced team.*"

Sir Tom's advice is the basis of strengths-based teamworking, that we should strive to build teams with the right mix of complementary strengths that are needed to deliver the performance outcomes required. Sometimes we might be fortunate enough to get the right balance of strengths just by being able to recruit the right people into the team. Most of the time, however, we will need to be prepared to be fluid and flexible, shaping roles and responsibilities according to the strengths of the team and the dynamic requirements of the situation.

For example, in a consulting assignment with the board of the Air Support business unit of BAE Systems, I applied strengths-based team-working as a way of approaching a number of business imperative challenges that the organisation was facing, and which were not being progressed as rapidly as they needed to be. Rather than allocating roles and responsibilities on the basis of traditional functional or operational lines of responsibility (e.g., the Employee Opinion Survey being given to the HR Director because it was an HR matter), we allocated roles and responsibilities on the basis of the strengths of the board members, as had been established through strengths identification work previous to the session. This process threw up some unusual pairings – with people working on projects they would not typically work on, and with people with whom they would not usually work.

The brief was simple: Report back in one month, and if the strengths approach works, then we will see movement across the project areas iden-tified. One month later, the strengths approach clearly had worked. The review of the project deliverables was like receiving a Grade A+ school report: ticks all the way down the page. Projects had moved, and actions had been taken, because people were being asked to do things that explic-itly played to their strengths, that they were naturally drawn to do, and that energised them, just as the research evidence indicates. They did not suddenly have more time, but they did have a greater alignment between the projects they were being asked to work on and the work they naturally wanted to do. For example, one board member was tasked with devel-oping a strategic vision for an area where he would not traditionally have had responsibility – and yet, developing strategic vision was one of the things that he did best and that he loved to do. Simply put, he didn't need to be asked twice to do it, a finding that I have seen replicated hundreds of times across hundreds of different situations.

With this shared understanding established, one is able to begin to create a culture of strengths-based organising that is committed to enabling people to use and deliver through their strengths wherever that is possible, but still recognising fully that we don't live in an ideal or utopian world. From that basis, here are some typical questions that a leader or manager may ask to establish how best to deploy *kratisto* in practice:

- What can I count on you for the most?
- In what roles or activities can I expect to see your best performance?
- Given our organisational objectives, where do you think you could make your greatest contribution?
- What should I try and avoid asking you to do?

Creating the team environment that can make *kratisto* a reality does require an understanding of what the strengths approach is about – and equally, what it is not about. I have sometimes heard the complaint that adopting this approach is a shirker's charter that can lead to the excuse of "I'm not doing that because it doesn't play to my strengths." In my experience, this is usually a reflection of the organisational culture and its lack of engagement and accountability, far more than it is a reflection of the strengths way of working. As we touched on above, working from the strengths perspective is about doing more – and doing it wherever possible – that plays to and harnesses what people naturally want to do and do best, but it *does not* provide the excuse for inaction when that opportunity is not there.

In contrast, working from strengths assumes and expects a level of basic maturity whereby people are able to accept that not everything they do will be allowing them to use their strengths, and that they sometimes need to knuckle down and get on with things that aren't making full use of their strengths. This I know from my experiences of working with strengths-based organisation in practice, but it should not undermine our commitment to enabling people to work from their strengths wherever and whenever they possibly can – and for the modern organisation, this is becoming a business imperative. As Noel Tichy describes it in *The Leadership Engine*:

> *"It is only by combining the strengths of everyone in the organiza-tion and helping them to work to his or her best ability that organi-zations can win in the marketplace today."*

Possible Objections to Strengths-based Teamworking. In the modern organisational climate, Tichy's advice is even more compelling – and yet strengths-based approaches to work can still come up against objections. One reasonable objection to both complementary partnering and strengths-based teamworking is that there may not be a person in the pair or in the team who has the strengths that are required for a particular task. Indeed, there may not, and the challenge then is what we do about it. The first solution, though not always possible, is to find someone who can fill the gap and take on the task that is not welcomed by anybody else. Assuming this can't be done, the next approach would be to find the person who is best equipped to take it on, recognising that it is not playing to their strengths. They should not be expected to do it all the time, and they should have the opportunity to recharge properly when they have been working on it. Working in our areas of weakness can drain us, and lead to burnout more quickly, with that burnout being more severe. As such, we need to build re-charging, energising activi-ties into our schedules that will compensate for when we do need to engage in the weakness-inducing tasks that are, for whatever reason, inescapable.

For example, when I started working with my team at CAPP, there were certain responsibilities that fell to me and that couldn't be shifted – for a while, at least. These responsibilities did not play to my strengths, but they still had to be done – completing the quarterly VAT tax return being one of the best examples of that time. Recognising this, first, we ensured that I had other more fulfilling things to do either side of the time that I was working on the VAT return. Second, as soon as was possible, we moved the responsibility for this to our external accountant – who loves to do the VAT returns!

This example illustrates two important points. First, adopting the strengths approach is fundamentally not a charter that permits people to refuse to do things on the basis that "It isn't playing to my strengths." Such complaints reflect an immaturity of understanding and application in relation to strengths. Second, it illuminates the core point about respecting and valuing diversity and difference. While I would not enjoy completing the VAT return, I was able to recognise that there is someone else who would, rather than judging it as being fundamentally a task without merit or attraction to anyone, simply on the basis that it felt that way to me.

As a partner at one of the Big Four professional services firms once said to me: "I really get the strengths approach and think it has a lot of merits. But the fact of the matter, in our business, is that nobody likes auditing, yet it still has to be done." My rejoinder was twofold. First, just because *you* don't like auditing, it doesn't mean that nobody else does. (Remember the fundamental of the strengths approach about recognising, respecting and valuing difference and diversity). Second, it may be the case that there are not enough people who love to audit as there is auditing work that needs to be done. But that is an issue of scale rather than an issue of absolute principle.

People who love to do auditing do exist – I met one of them when I asked Kerry Thorley of Baker Tilly, who was auditing our company accounts, what she thought about her job:

"I love it," she replied. *"I love auditing and following down the paper trails, the checking and cross-checking that it requires. I feel like a detective putting all the pieces of the jigsaw together."*

Hence, people who love auditing certainly do exist – and I would argue, from principle, that the same would apply to any role. Recognising this kind of diversity is not only a matter of respect. It also makes good business sense to find the people who love to do the things that need doing.

Sometimes – but just sometimes – however, weaknesses cannot be made irrelevant through role fluidity, role shaping, complementary partnering or strengths-based teamworking. Sometimes there are things in a person's role that they just have to be able to do – to a level of competence, if not a level of excellence. When this is the case, we are faced with an *inescapable weakness* (assuming that the person is not better being redeployed into another role, whether inside the organisation or external to it).

Inescapable weaknesses refer to those elements of a person's role that are so central to the position that they have to be delivered by the role holder, but for which the role holder has no natural ability – or affinity. Instead, they just manage to find a way around it. Arvinder Dhesi and his lack of ability in project planning – we met Arvi in Chapter 5 – provides a wonderful example of this. As you will remember, Arvi was simply no good at project planning, and suddenly found himself in a situation where he needed to do it – and well, and quickly. His solution – he simply learned how to do it *well enough*, achieving a level of competence that allowed him to do the job effectively, but without seeking to retrain as a project manager or striving to develop his project planning skills to be an A+.

The secret is in how he – and in turn, how we – deal with situations like this. Where these circumstances arise, our attention is legitimately focused on what can be done to develop the weakness, to achieve a level of competence, while accepting that excellence is not a realistic expectation. To this end, traditional training and development activities can often be applied: behavioural feedback, skills development, executive training courses, performance coaching – even the most basic of project planning courses! Any or all of them may be effective at mitigating the negative impacts of the weakness, and developing it to a level that is 'good enough,' rather than A+. When this is done, the weakness has been made irrelevant in another important way: it has been prevented from undermining performance, while we remain aware that it has not suddenly become a strength on which we can build future success.

Overall, strengths-based teamworking is about people working together to achieve a common purpose in ways that maximise and harness each of their individual contributions. This teamworking is synergistic, in that it takes the best of what everyone has to offer, and combines it in such a way that people individually delivering their best performances are collectively delivering an outcome which is far greater than the sum of its parts. Strengths-based teamworking is the most effective way to make strength productive, which as Peter Drucker described in the opening quote for this chapter, is *"the unique purpose of organization."* Figure 6.1 gives a graphical representation of how organisational teams can co-operate to make strength productive and make weaknesses irrelevant.

Strong Managers and Strong Leaders Create Strong Teams

Managers and leaders have a centrally important role in making strength productive and rendering weaknesses irrelevant - both in their

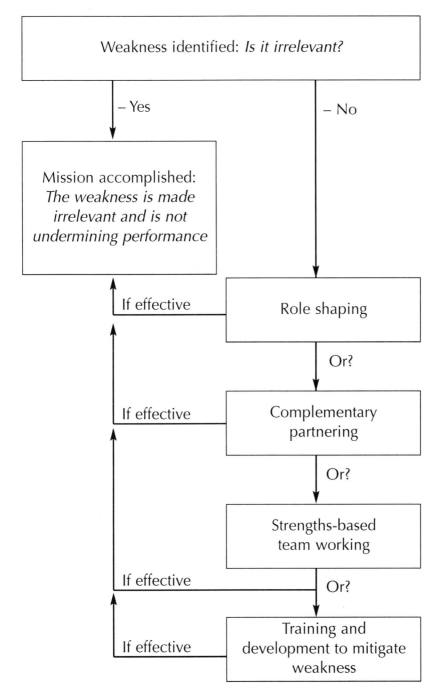

Figure 6.1 Making Weaknesses Irrelevant

teams specifically, and in their organisations more broadly. As Deborah Ancona and colleagues argued in the *Harvard Business Review*, traditionally, the view has existed that the leader should be all things to all people. According to this view, leaders:

> "...should have the intellectual capacity to make sense of unfathomably complex issues, the imaginative powers to paint a vision of the future that generates everyone's enthusiasm, the operational know-how to translate strategy into concrete plans, and the interpersonal skills to foster commitment to undertakings that could cost people's jobs should they fail."

When the complexity of the modern organisation is recognised like this, it is clear that no single person could be expected to do everything – they would be unlikely to have the depth and breadth of strengths required, let alone the time! As Ancona and colleagues further describe:

> "Only when leaders come to see themselves as incomplete – as having both strengths and weaknesses – will they be able to make up for their missing skills by relying on others."

To do this effectively, leaders should practice the seven elements of strengths-based leadership:

(1) Know your own strengths and weaknesses, accepting them both with humility;

(2) Know the strengths and weaknesses of your teams, respecting team members for whatever they bring to the mix;

(3) Arrange your work teams and organisations according to the principle of *kratisto* – allocating tasks to the person who is strongest or best suited to deliver them;

(4) Give and receive positive feedback, acknowledging your powerful responsibility for this as a leader;

(5) Reveal weaknesses – appropriately and authentically. Revealing weakness authentically shows both that we, as leaders, are human; it also offers an invitation to others to step up and contribute;

(6) Calibrate strengths effectively, by learning how to dial strengths up or dial strengths down, according to the need of the situation and the principle of the golden mean;

(7) Recognise your role as a "climate engineer" through celebrating success and rectifying failure – with this last responsibility being the specific domain of the manager (in relation to the team) or the leader (in relation to the organisation).

Influenced greatly by the leaders – described by Stefanie Naumann and Nathan Bennett as "climate engineers" – the psychological climate of a team is the product of the interactions between that team. Positive, healthy interactions create positive, healthy teams. At the heart of any positive, healthy interaction is respect. As Alastair Ham, Group Organisational Development Director of Aviva describes it:

> *"Respect is so fundamental that without it, nothing else really matters."*

The strengths approach can only flourish when we recognise and respect difference and diversity: we all have different strengths, and achieve our greatest successes by combining our strengths with the strengths of others.

Respect can be powerfully demonstrated by the leader or manager through the way in which they identify strengths in a person and communicate those strengths to them. As climate engineers, the impact of this identification reverberates right across the team, sending a message that *"This is the way we do things around here."* Second, any leader worthy of the name will be respected by their staff, and their opinions valued, even revered. If a leader identifies, recognises, and feeds back to you the strengths that they see in you as an employee, the impact is profound. One of validation, recognition, encouragement, even inspiration. We all need to be recognised, and being recognised for what we do best and most enjoy can be the most rewarding recognition of all – especially from the boss.

Sadly though, our experiences in organisations are perhaps the sources we are least likely to credit with being the inspiration of a "golden seed" - an encouraging word, a talent identified, a strength supported (we will learn more about golden seeds in Chapter 7, *Golden Seeds and Flourishing Children*). As you might remember from Chapter 5, Mike Westcott, Group HR Director for National Grid, makes the case that all too often, golden seeds are planted in us by partners, parents, relatives, teachers – and not by our managers at work. This is something which we, as managers and leaders, should strive to change.

When teams are working together in ways that are respectful and valuing, and that recognise, support and celebrate each other's strengths, they are likely to be highly effective. Equally, they are likely to create a psychological climate that is conducive to optimal performance, where people want to give of their best on a daily basis.

As research by Marcial Losada and Emily Heaphy shows, the most productive teams have the right balance of positive interactions to negative ones: at least six positive to every negative. Positive interactions are characterised by a sense of inquiry, of valuing the other person's perspective, of wanting to understand. For example:

"That's interesting, can you tell me more about that – I hadn't seen that angle to it before."

"I can see where you're coming from there, that's a really good point. Another way in which we could build on that would be to..."

In contrast, negative interactions are characterised by a sense of advocacy, of presenting your own view and shutting out the views of other people, not being interested in their opinions or perspectives, and dismissing their inputs. For example:

"I don't agree with that, and we're not going to do it that way – you just don't understand."

"But that's utter rubbish. This is my decision and it's final. I really wonder sometimes if you know what you're talking about, or why I hired you in the first place."

Looking at the nature of these interactions, it seems pretty easy to see why we would need more positive ones than negative! But equally, as Barbara Fredrickson and Marcial Losada subsequently demonstrated, it *is* possible to have too much of a good thing. Interactions where everything is happy-clappy and sugar-coated are no good either – they also lead to break downs in performance. Fredrickson and Losada showed that when the ratio went above 11:1 positive to negative interactions, then teams simply go round in circles without anything being achieved. This is an excellent empirical demonstration of the golden mean that we discussed in Chapter 4: the optimal lies between deficit and excess, in this case, between 3 and 11 positive interactions for every negative interaction. As interactions go, there are perhaps none more maligned than performance appraisals – and it is to these that we turn next.

Strengths-based Performance Appraisals

If you have worked with an organisation for six years, and had half a dozen annual performance appraisals, the chances are that you will have come up against the same 'areas for development' each of those six times. When I have asked this question of conference audiences, there have been shrieks of recognition as the realisation hits: weaknesses don't shift that much, so it tends to be the same things that come up year after year. As the famous saying goes, *"The definition of insanity is doing the same thing and expecting a different result."* And yet, that's exactly what a lot of performance appraisals seem to be set up to do. But the good news is, just as with traditional means of organisation more generally, there is a different way. A way of talking about performance that is not constrained by focusing on the past, or handicapped by covering only the things that didn't work.

Historically, we were taught to begin a performance appraisal with something positive, then cover the negative feedback that was the meat of the process, then end with something positive so that the person left feeling good about themselves. This process was, without doubt, well-intentioned. But in practice, it led to a five-minute warm-up, a fifty minute punch-up, and a five-minute cool down in the traditional feedback hour. Of course, the 'punch-up' is metaphorical rather than actual (most of the time, anyway!), but it does serve to illustrate the key point that the recipient of this process often felt defensive, closed and withdrawn as a result. It is not at all uncommon for people in organisations to talk about 'the performance review season,' using this as a euphemism to explain why it is that everyone is walking around feeling touchy and preoccupied. According to one of my colleagues in a major blue-chip corporation, this lasts for about a month either side of the process!

In contrast, strengths-based performance appraisals have a quite different feel to them. At its most basic, the conversation can be structured around two beautifully simple but informative questions:

- *What would you like to do more of?*
- *What would you like to do less of?*

And these questions, in turn, can readily be supplemented by two more:

- *What are you doing when you are at your best?*
- *What are you doing when you are at your worst?*

And then directed towards the future with:

- *What are you going to be doing when you are at your best in the next 6-12 months?*
- *How can I help you to do that?*

The answers to these questions – and the conversations that follow – take on a remarkably different hue to the nature of more traditional performance review conversations – as long as the process is being informed by the strengths approach, and not being used as yet another excuse to drill down into what it is that people don't do well. As a result, the outcomes of the performance conversation are quite markedly different: people feel open, involved, engaged, excited about what their future holds, and keen to get out there to get on with it again.

At CAPP, we use these questions and this approach – but we also take it a step further, by using it as part of face-to-face 360's within the team. A 360 approach involves asking the people around any given individual – their superiors, their peers, their subordinates – what they have observed about the individual, either according to a number of pre-established areas or in an open-ended way. This is almost always done confidentially and anonymously, so nobody knows who has said what about them – holding 360's face to face with the entire team is what makes the CAPP approach so different. The effects of doing so, however, are momentous: very open communication, clear understanding of what each person can contribute and where they struggle, appreciation and valuing of difference and diversity, and, most important of all, the establishment of a clear platform for exceptional team-working.

Face to face 360s can be an immensely powerful practice. For this reason, it is very important to recognise that the effects on people can be equally powerful – whether those effects are positive or negative. Being aware of this, it is imperative that the process is properly established and managed to ensure that people behave appropriately and professionally in relation to one other. It requires a level of trust, honesty, and openness across the team, as well as a degree of emotional intelligence and sensitivity about how both to deliver and to receive feedback, together with a clear eye on the overall objectives that the process is designed to achieve. If any of these elements are missing, the team face-to-face process should not be used. It is exactly to guard against these concerns that traditional 360s are confidential and anonymous – and yet still the anecdotal evidence abounds of 360 feedback recipients needing a bottle of 'something strong' to hand before they read their reports. Thankfully, with more of an explicit focus on strengths, the prospect of feedback is more appealing. There is a different way. There is a better way.

Strengths-based performance appraisals – and 360 processes – are much more focused on understanding the questions of "*What worked?*" and "*What has gone well?*" than they are interested in holding inquests into what didn't. For sure, there may be lessons to be learned, but just as Jerry Porras and colleagues described in their study of highly effective individuals:

> *"Builders harvest failure...Sure, they focus most of their energy on passions and strengths, but they don't waste their mistakes by dismissing them."*

As ever, the question is one of balance: how to learn from mistakes without being consumed by them, and how to build on success without becoming complacent.

Strengths-based performance appraisals place their focus squarely on performance, understanding that enduring success is only achieved through building on strengths. The lessons to be learned from failures should be harvested, but should never get in the way. Drawing from Fredrickson and Losada's ratio, performance reviews should give at least three times the amount of focus to strengths and success that they give to weakness and failure. After all, performance reviews should be all about helping people to deliver their best performances. When the organisational bottom line comes into it, it's all about performance.

It's All About Performance – But There Is (and Should be) the Double-Win: A Vision for People in Organisations

Just as the optimal lies between enough positivity and too much positivity, so the focus of strengths use should always be optimal performance. As we discussed in Chapter 4, the strengths approach is not an excuse for a happy-clappy, sugar-coated way of working that neglects the often harsh realities of the commercial world. Rather, the strengths approach is about enabling people to do more of what they do best, while managing and working around the things they don't do well. But above all, when applied to the world of work, it's about performance – and we need make no excuses for that.

As the evidence – both academic and anecdotal – clearly demonstrates, people deliver their best performances when they are working from their strengths. As such, organisations have an incumbent responsibility – and a major competitive opportunity – to realise the potential of harnessing their people's strengths at work. Perhaps the unique value of the strengths approach at work is the powerful double-win that it delivers both for organisations and for individual employees.

When individuals are working from their strengths, they are doing the things that they do best and that they love to do. They are following the direction of their actualising tendency and are more authentic and in tune with themselves. They achieve their goals better. They are more engaged and effective. They are happier and more fulfilled. They work harder as well as smarter.

All of these *individual* benefits help to deliver *organisational* benefits that impact bottom line performance directly. It is this that makes for the unique value of the strengths approach. To extend what we have seen in other contexts, *harnessing strengths at work is the smallest thing to make the biggest difference.*

The strengths approach provides a rare opportunity for a way of working that makes the best of what people have to offer, while also enabling them to make the best of themselves. It provides an opportunity for forming a true partnership between organisations and their employees that it is fit for the rapidly changing 21st century world of work. With the growing challenges of globalisation, a knowledge economy, retiring Baby Boomers, and a new Generation Y of workforce entrants who want to renegotiate the traditional organisational contract, organisations are increasingly recognising that there needs to be a different way.

There is a different way. It is the way of the strengths approach, as we have been exploring throughout this book. Whether as individuals, a small team, a function, a business unit, or an entire organisation, we can start to redefine what work is. We can begin to offer a new vision for employment and organisational life that is fit for purpose for the challenges of the 21st century workplace. When we recognise just what a huge proportion of people's waking hours are spent at work, and the amount of their energy that is expended in pursuit of what the organisation demands of them – we need to. We need to find a new vision for employment and organisational life that will inspire and engage. Quite simply, the organisations that do this will become the success stories of the 21st century. Those who don't will become its historical footnotes.

The potential of people is our last great untapped resource and yet so often we still seem relatively unable to do anything systematic about it. Organisations spend millions upon millions of pounds each and every year to release more from what they *believe* to be their greatest asset – their people. Yet they fail to take the necessary and vital step of realising that their genuinely greatest asset is their *people's strengths*. In this chapter – and in this book more broadly – I hope that I have inspired you with the possibilities for harnessing strengths at work, so that the strengths approach can deliver the double-win of the individual and organisational benefits it promises. After all, money talks, and when it does, organisations listen.

Key Points

- When managers focus on the strengths of their employees, they deliver significantly better performance. When managers focus on the weaknesses of their employees, performance declines. The reasons for this include employees feeling appreciated and that they have a good fit with their role, and that they are able to make a positive contribution and so give more discretionary effort as a result.

- Working from strengths can best be understood in the context of teamworking, through role fluidity (being flexible about the boundaries of roles and responsibilities); role shaping (redesigning roles so that they fit better with individuals); complementary partnering (people working off each other's strengths in mutually beneficial ways); and strengths-based teamworking more generally, following the principle of *kratisto* (allocating tasks to the person who is strongest or best suited to deliver them).

- Inescapable weaknesses are those elements of a role that cannot be covered off through working from strengths, and so require the person to develop the weakness so that it is 'good enough,' and does not undermine performance – but nothing more.

- High performing business teams are characterised by ratios of positive to negative interactions of between 6:1 and 11:1, as well as interactions that move freely between inquiry (seeking to understand) and advocacy (promoting one's own perspective).

- Working from strengths provides a new paradigm for the world of work and people's experience of organisational life. It delivers the powerful double-win of enhanced organisational performance and improved individual contribution, well-being, and fulfilment. As such, harnessing strengths at work is another manifestation of the smallest thing to make the biggest difference.

Areas for Reflection and Action

- Think about your current role. To what extent does it allow you to work from your strengths? How could you shape it, or co-operate with others, in order to spend more time working from your strengths?

- Do you have strengths that you are not currently using at work? Why? Can you identify opportunities where you could contribute at work through using these strengths more? Discuss with your manager and your work colleagues.

- What did you discuss in your last performance appraisal? Do the same 'areas for development' keep coming up over time? What can you do to have a conversation with your manager about this, in order to re-orient your work focus – and your performance appraisal – to how you can better contribute in the future?

SEVEN

Golden Seeds and Flourishing Children

"All children are gifted, some open their presents later."
Motto painted on the wall of Eshe's Learning Centre, Arapita
Avenue, Port of Spain, Trinidad, West Indies

S O FAR IN this book, our focus has been primarily on realising strengths in adults. In this chapter, we now change
tack very slightly, and turn our attention to looking at strengths in children. Our focus here is particularly on what significant adults –
whether parents, teachers, or others – can do to realise and develop children's strengths as a core means of raising flourishing children. Raising
children successfully is legitimately recognised as one of the hardest,
but equally one of the most important jobs in the world. There is
nothing necessary to qualify one for becoming a parent – and yet the
implications of this task are immense, the responsibilities great.

My aim in this chapter is to introduce you to the core aspects of what realising strengths in children involves, and how we might go about doing it. As I do so, we should remember two important points. First, all adults are different, with different strengths, experiences, personalities, talents and aptitudes. Second, all children are different, with different strengths, experiences, personalities, talents and aptitudes. As a result, there are as many combinations of parent and child, or teacher and child, as there are adults and children in the world. While we could turn to any number of sources that purport to explain and navigate these, we actually do not need to. The strengths approach provides the compass that we need in seeking to explore and navigate these relationships, and that compass sits at the heart of what the strengths approach is about: *value people for who and what they are, rather than lamenting what they are not and trying to change them*. This applies most especially to children, who are most receptive (or most vulnerable, depending on one's stance) to the messages that we convey.

In the course of this chapter, we will go on to explore what is achieved by valuing children for who they are, and why – and most importantly, how we can do this most effectively. This involves creating the environments that best nurture the golden seeds that we may plant in order to create flourishing children. It is about treating each child as an individual, allowing children to have their own voice, and ensuring they take on board the positive messages of the growth mindset that we would want them to receive from us. It is about allowing children room to experiment and explore – and make mistakes - while at the same time *ourselves* behaving in the ways that will role model how we would like *them* to behave in the future: there is no mirror to oneself so accurate as seeing how your children develop and grow up. Through each of these important ways of being with children, we create the environment that enables them best to realise their strengths, as Figure 7.1 represents. To begin, though, let's look at the question that is probably uppermost in the minds of many of you as you think about your own potential for realising your children's strengths: how soon can we spot strengths in children?

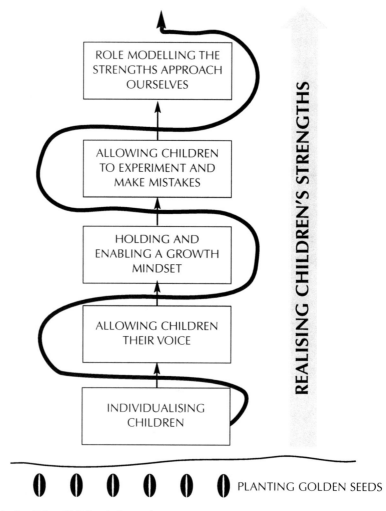

Figure 7.1 Realising Children's Strengths

How Soon Can We Spot Strengths in Children?

As anyone who has spent any length of time with very young children will know, even at the youngest ages, it is possible to identify differences in character between them. Some children are predisposed to be kind and caring, others demonstrate greater strengths in curiosity or bravery. It is impractical, if not impossible, to attempt to stipulate an age below which children 'do not have' strengths, or indeed, to stipulate an age at which strengths suddenly become apparent. The development of strengths will vary according to the nature and nurture of the child, just as it will vary according to the nature of the strengths themselves. We explored the origins of strengths in Chapter 2, and seeing strengths emerge in children is perhaps one of the most powerful examples of these origins that we are able to witness.

Given that strengths represent pre-existing capacities, we might expect that they would be evident in children from a very young age –and the research does bear this out. For example, Hoffman describes the case of a 15-month old boy who brought his own teddy bear and gave him to a friend who was crying in order to comfort him, and Dunn and colleagues found that a quarter of 2-4 year olds frequently comforted younger siblings who were upset. I have seen these patterns – and these individual differences – across my own children, and I am sure that readers who have children of their own, or who have spent time with children in other ways, will share these experiences. From very early ages, certainly from the first year and beyond, it is possible to start to know the character of a child. My daughter Lucy might want to spend her time peacefully alone, whereas Sophie revels in being the centre of everyone's attention – a strength that we call *Spotlight*. "Look at me!" is her catchphrase, and at the same time being "interested in ***everything***" (from her school report – italics and bold in the original) – and clearly reflecting the genetic influence of nature from her father's curiosity!

Nansook Park and Christopher Peterson were interested in what strengths parents would be able to identify in their young children – and particularly if these strengths would be consistent with the 24 character strengths of the VIA Classification. To explore this, they asked parents of children aged between 3 and 9 years to write about their child's personal characteristics and individual qualities. They then analysed the 680 written descriptions that they received from parents, to see what character strengths were identifiable in the descriptions. The most frequently reported character strengths identified were love (56%), kindness (38%), and creativity (34%). Next in the ranking were humour (26%), curiosity (22%), love of learning (20%), and perseverance (20%). Children who were reported by their parents as having strengths of love, vitality and hope were also reported as having greater happiness.

From Park and Peterson's work, the other evidence reviewed – and I expect, your own experience as parents or observers of young people - it is eminently clear that character strengths can be identified readily in children as young as 3 years of age. It is also clear that certain character strengths – typically strengths of mind (for example, open-mindedness, perspective), rather than strengths of the heart (for example, love, kindness) - tend to be less prevalent. The reason for this seems to be some combination of the fact that these strengths of mind require a certain level of cognitive capacity for children to be able to demonstrate them, together with children's limited cognitive development: without the cognitive capacity to do so, we could not expect young children to be able to demonstrate these strengths. While strengths assessments for older children do exist (for example the VIA-Youth and the Clifton Youth Strengths Explorer), it is clear that strengthspotting is fundamental for identifying strengths in children, and has a hugely important role to play in their development - as we go on to explore with the "golden seed."

Planting Golden Seeds

A golden seed refers to the way in which someone can notice and commend an ability or talent in us, identify its significance, and reinforce it with us, so that we start to internalise it and begin to think "I can do it! I might be good at this." In Chapter 4 we talked about this as strengthspotting, but the memorable phrase "golden seed" was popularised by Charles Handy, who in turn attributes it to Freud (although I have been unable to find anywhere where Freud actually uses this term). As Handy describes it, a *"golden seed…refers to the way someone can often, in our formative years, notice an aptitude or a talent in us and pick it out, comment on it, often just in a chance remark. We tuck away this expression of confidence in us and, when the time comes, we dig up this seed, water it and prove it true. Often, the most memorable thing a teacher can do is to give us our golden seed."*

At the primary school attended by two of my children, golden seeds are abundant – led in large part by the belief and passion of the Headteacher, Bill Hedges. If you are a pupil at Templars Primary School, and you have to wear glasses, you are made a member of the Spectacular Spectacle Club, joining the ranks of both pupils and staff alike who wear glasses and are celebrated for it with their photograph on the Spectacular Spectacle Club membership board. Instead of getting caught doing something naughty, Templars has 'Caught You Being Good' slips. On Friday each week they are entered into the prize draw at the Caught You Being Good Assembly, and the lucky child from each year group whose ticket is drawn wins a prize. The positive, seemingly strengths-based philosophy permeates the school. I was shot through with affirmation and agreement when Lucy, who was 6 years old at the time, came home one day and announced that her teacher, Mr. Harris (as it happens, a member of the Spectacular Spectacle Club), had said, "Do more of what you're best at" – a strengths philosophy in action -

and one which she had clearly internalised. I hope she will carry this with her as a golden seed for the rest of her life.

In contrast to golden seeds, we might also have experienced what I refer to as "leaden seeds" at some time during our lives. Whereas a golden seed is focused on enabling what we *can* do, a leaden seed has the effect – initially, at least – of disabling us in relation to what others judge we can't do. Leaden seeds are those negative remarks that sear themselves deep into our identity, serving as the root cause of that little voice that gets in the way, undermining our belief in our own potential and possibility by telling us that we can't do something – and yet when, buried somewhere deep inside us, we really believe that we can. These leaden seeds are often not intentional, but may often reflect someone else's frustration or passing bad mood. But, like the Velcro of negative feedback, they stick, and their effects can be to poison what otherwise we saw as being best in us, as Figure 7.2 illustrates.

How we respond to leaden seeds will often shape the directions of our lives, for better or for worse. For some, the weight of the leaden seed can be something that holds them back, especially when other enabling factors (such as feeling individualised, having their own voice, and holding a growth mindset) are missing, which would otherwise help enable them to overcome this weight. For others, the weight of the leaden seed can be transformed into the ballast for the catapult that they use to propel themselves through life and to prove the leaden seed wrong. I know many people who take great pleasure and find deep fulfilment from doing the things that other people told them they could not do – and I am one of them – do you remember John Tooby and Leda Cosmides who opened Chapter 5: "*Everything that every individual has ever done in all of human history and prehistory establishes the minimum boundary of the possible. The maximum, if any, is completely unknown.*" This being so, we should never accept – as children or as adults – that there are things that cannot be done.

Figure 7.2 Golden Seeds and Leaden Seeds

This drive to turn the leaden seed into gold can be kindled and enabled through having the right conditions and supporting environment – at any stage in life, but the sooner the better. Almost always, though, this drive comes from a person's deep and unquenchable sense of their own possibility and potential – no matter what others have said to them, they have held onto this fundamental view of themselves. At base, I hold absolutely that we all have this belief – for some people, sadly, it is just buried much more deeply than for others. To be clear, though, the fact that many of us have turned leaden seeds into gold - and the fact that many more of us will continue to do so – does not excuse these leaden seeds being given in the first place, nor does it lessen the importance and value of our responsibility as adults to give golden seeds wherever we can do so.

The Celebrating Strengths work initiated by Jenny Fox Eades, with primary schools in the South Leys Cluster, in Scunthorpe, North

East Lincolnshire, UK, has institutionalised the giving of golden seeds. Jenny's work on Celebrating Strengths is all about building strengths-based schools – schools where the focus is primarily on strengths, not weaknesses, and where teachers and pupils aim not at being 'ok' but at being excellent. One of the core ways through which this is achieved is through teachers and children themselves identifying and naming strengths in each other – giving golden seeds is a matter of course. The methodology that Jenny uses is based around her idea of a Strengths Gym, a programme for helping adults and children identify and use their strengths in and out of the classroom. It embeds these strengths into a cycle of festivals and storytelling, including new versions of ancient stories, to create long lasting change. Celebrating Strengths has the aim of enhancing, developing and celebrating the strengths of the school, its staff and its pupils – and thereby helping all members of the school to flourish. You can read more about Jenny's work in her excellent book: *Celebrating Strengths: Building Strengths-based Schools.*

In another example of the planting of golden seeds, Vernon Bryce, Operations Director, Kenexa Europe, a recruitment and retention solutions company, tells the story of how his grandfather planted golden seeds in him as a young boy:

> *"I first met my granddad when I was five years old, when I came back from living in Singapore. I always remember him saying 'Well done' to people, and I quickly cottoned on that if I did something well, I would get another 'Well done.' So if I knocked a nail into a piece of wood in a particular way, I'd get 'Well done.' If I read my book nicely, 'Well done' again. Over time all of these 'well dones' became hugely reinforcing, and have paid off at numerous moments in time ever since."*

Whether it is Charles Handy, Bill Hedges, Mr. Harris, Vernon Bryce's grandfather, or the impact of *Celebrating Strengths*, these are all instances of where parents, teachers, and even institutions as a whole have taken on the role of planting golden seeds. It is one of the most important things that we can do for children and adolescents throughout their formative years. Recognising an activity done well, rewarding an area where a child shows promise, offering encouragement as a youngster works to master a task – all these can be single instances of recognition and validation, but single instances that can have a profoundly positive impact that resonates throughout the rest of their lives.

Having a golden seed planted in us during our formative years can be one of the most powerful ways of realising the magic that resides in each of us, and starting on the path of realising our strengths as children. As adults, planting the golden seeds of strengths in our children is not just a deeply fulfilling and rewarding thing to do: it is also a fundamental responsibility. As the personal stories told here attest - and as I expect reflections on your own experience will also show - the enduring value of a golden seed is likely beyond gold.

As a way of exploring this for yourself, take a moment to think about who may have planted the golden seeds in your life. Who are the people who you think back to when times are tough? Who gave you a belief in yourself that enables you to drive forward to this day? Who spotted the strengths around which you may now be building your life? These are likely to have been powerfully emotive experiences that still seem as vivid and impactful today as on the day they were made. If, having thought about the origins of your own golden seeds, you would like to share their story, please visit us at **www.averagetoaplus.org**

Environments in which Strengths can Flourish: It's all about Golden Seeds

Given the impact of developing golden seeds, what can we do to create environments that nurture and support them? First, we should ensure that we recognise, respect and value each child as an individual. We are constantly under pressure to take short cuts, to stereotype, to treat people as groups rather than as individuals, because it is less complicated, quicker and more efficient that way. These are all understandable and defensible reasons not to individualise, but unfortunately they do not create the environments where golden seeds will flourish. Just as we need to counter our evolutionary bias to attend to the negative (see Chapter 3), so we also need to counter our cognitive bias to *stereotype* rather than to *individualise*. Vernon Bryce, himself a father of five children, including twin daughters, was always at great pains to emphasise that they were sisters, rather than twins, each with their own unique individual differences. As Vernon described it:

*"People would say 'Look at these lovely twins,' and my wife and I would always stop them and say, 'No, they're **sisters**.' Little decisions like that are hugely important, since they allowed the small tendencies, that each of these girls had, to develop as it was right for them to develop. With those small tendencies, we can reinforce them or we can kill them. We make gross oversimplifications and assumptions that crush the little signals that great teachers - and others who are great with children – will spot and nurture. If we are able to just pay more attention to people's individuality, they will do so much better."*

The second factor in creating these environments that will nurture golden seeds is to allow children their voice: without children having a voice, their strengths are unlikely to peek through, and the opportunity to plant the golden seed is all the more difficult.

Third, we need to be mindful of the growth mindset messages that we convey to children, ensuring that they are received as we intended them to be, and that they have the effect that we wanted the messages to have – as we will see, this is not as easy as we might at first think. We turn to each of these topics next.

Individualising Children

Individualising children is about recognising and valuing children for who they are. This rests on understanding them as independent beings with their own directions, strengths, desires, values, preferences, hopes and fears. Sometimes we can fall into the trap of trying to live the lives through our children that we missed out on ourselves. We do this by projecting on to them our own aspirations, hopes and fears, rather than leaving them free to feel their own. We can overcome this by recognising that children are not empty vessels waiting to be filled with the things that we wished we had done in our lives, or with the things that we know characterise someone else in our family, our classroom, or our social circle. Instead, they are their own unique person, and should be treated as such. Individualising children is about recognising and valuing the diversity of children's existence and experience. As Bill Hedges, Headteacher of Templars Primary School describes:

> *"Every child is unique and has to be treated uniquely. Our focus is on helping every single child to achieve their potential…We are very good at working with children with special needs – whatever those needs are, and at both ends of the ability spectrum. But the important thing is that as soon as we start addressing children with special needs, we are forced then to start addressing children who don't have special needs in that context, but who have their own unique needs as individual children."*

Individualising children is about striving to see things through their eyes, to understand the world from their perspective, and while doing so, being able to convey naturally to them that they are understood, that they are valued and appreciated for who they are and what they bring. Again, as Bill Hedges puts it, *"You do not get children to respect you unless you can demonstrate your respect for them."* With that individualised validation, children start to feel permission to be the authors of their own lives, to find the directions that are right for them, and to become who they are capable of becoming. This mindset in a child is fertile ground for sowing golden seeds, since they are ready to receive them, believing in themselves and their belief in their own abilities to carry through and deliver against the belief that others have shown in them.

There are, however, a number of things that can get in the way of us individualising children – a lot of which can be traced back to stereotyping and the – often very legitimate - mental shortcuts that we need to take. Think of it this way: at any moment in time, our senses are assailed by a vast array of different sensory information. As I sit and write this chapter, and attend to what my senses are telling me, I am conscious of the touch of my fingers on the keyboard, the music from the CD player, the feel of the chair against my back and legs, the temperature around my sock-less ankles, the fresh smell of the light breeze from the window, the intense focus of my mind as I think about what I am writing and how it all fits together, the itch just behind my ear that needs a quick scratch. And then I look up, and see, hear, smell, and can touch so much more – so much more of which I wasn't previously aware, because I was focused on the task at hand: writing this paragraph. Assailed by this vast array of information, I focus only on what is most immediately important to me, and, hopefully safely, ignore the rest. The same principles apply to stereotyping – and despite the negative connotations of the word 'stereotype' – we all do it, and probably far more than we actually recognise.

Stereotyping provides us with a means of making sense of this vast array of information with which we are presented, sorting and sifting it rapidly and efficiently, and making quick-fire judgements based on limited information and experience – what psychologists call heuristics, or short cuts, in our mental processes. Usually, these judgements are fairly accurate, or at least accurate enough – and this is why we have evolved the ability to stereotype and categorise information in this way: because it works. It works, that is, until we attribute characteristics to a person on the basis of including them in a particular group, when actually, those characteristics don't apply to them as much as we think, and sometimes not at all. Most of the work on stereotyping has, for important reasons, been focused on discrimination and prejudice, particularly around race and gender. But the lessons we can learn from where stereotyping falls down are equally and particularly appropriate for the ways in which we individualise children.

When we fall into the stereotyping trap with children, we are making judgements and assessments about a specific child that are based on our general experience of many different children. Individualising children requires that we do the opposite: instead of treating all children as examples of that wider group, "children," we should be treating each child as just what they are – an individual, with their own experiences, interests, aptitudes, talents and strengths, a unique person with a unique place in the world. When we are able to do so, we see children for who they really are and for what they really have to offer. And when we do this, we are on the way to creating an optimal environment for children to realise their strengths. To build on this further, children need to be given permission to be who they uniquely are. They need to be given permission to find their own voice.

Allowing Children their Voice

Allowing children their voice is fundamental in creating environments that will nurture golden seeds and thereby allow children to realise their strengths. As we discussed in Chapter 2, strengths evolve and emerge in us according to our actualising tendency, our inner growth force that indicates the directions that are right for us to follow, to grow and develop as individuals, and to become what we are capable of becoming. A particular aspect of how the actualising tendency shows itself is in how we develop and then deploy our strengths - and this is probably nowhere more salient than in children. If we convey the message that we want our children to grow up as an image of ourselves, or as any image that *we* might want them to be, rather than allowing and enabling them to become who *they* naturally are, then we inevitably distort the directions of their growth, limit their potential, and undermine their happiness. I doubt that any parent or teacher would intentionally set out to do this, so it's worth us looking at some of the evidence for how we can best allow children their voice.

Susan Harter, a developmental psychologist at the University of Denver, examined how the positive regard of parents and peers influenced the degree to which adolescents felt that they were able to 'be themselves.' Their findings were unequivocal: adolescents who reported the most *unconditional* support from parents and peers also reported the highest levels of behaviour that was true to themselves. In contrast, adolescents who reported the most *conditional* support from their parents and peers similarly reported the lowest levels of true-self behaviour, attributing this directly to the fact that their parents and peers did not value them for their true self. As a result, these conditionally-valued adolescents were suppressing their true selves in order to gain support and acceptance from the significant others in their lives – but at the cost of their authenticity. In essence, they were distorting the ways in which they lived their lives in order to gain the approval of their parents or significant others. And the more they moved away from the directions that were right for them, the less in touch with their true selves they became, and so, by extension, less able to realise their strengths.

This is just one of many studies that points to the central idea that when people – in this case, children and adolescents – are deflected from the directions in life that are right for them, they suffer as a result. Numerous studies have now shown that inauthenticity is a key predictor of unhappiness, anxiety and depression. My colleagues and I have found strong evidence that people who are more in touch with their true selves are more likely to be using their strengths, and also report higher levels of happiness, fulfilment and vitality. And of real interest to us were the unanticipated and spontaneous reactions of the many people who said that just taking the opportunity to think about when they used their strengths had led them to think more carefully about their future career choices and the directions they took in their lives.

If, as the evidence seems to point to, the most important thing in raising flourishing children is about enabling and allowing them to be who they naturally are and to follow their own directions, how do we go about doing it, and what does this mean for growing children's strengths? The first question informs the second, and we can consider each in turn.

In her excellent chapter on authenticity in the *Handbook of Positive Psychology*, Susan Harter describes a number of approaches for fostering true-self behaviour in children. These include:

- Encouraging adults to talk about the *child's* reality, and see things through the child's eyes, rather than forcing their own interpretation, perspective, or agenda onto events;

- Actively valuing and respecting the child's experience for what it *means to the child*. For example, rather than dismissing the loss of a favourite doll or teddy with "Don't be silly, it's only a toy" (an adult perspective), adults should accept and acknowledge the real sense of loss that the child may be experiencing, even using this as an opportunity to explore the nature and inevitability of loss throughout human life;
- Allowing children to develop their own narratives and stories about their life, rather than requiring them to tell their life story in a way that fits with what we want to hear as adults, conveys to the child that they are authors of their own life experience and are instrumental actors in their own life, rather than leaving them with a feeling of being puppets in someone else's (e.g., the adult's) life;
- Listening to children and genuinely hearing what they have to say are also powerful means to convey our respect and valuing of them as individuals. In turn, children are able to express themselves effectively and authentically, knowing that their voices will be heard;
- And finally, "...children and adolescents need to be actively validated for who they are as a person; they need to be told that they are valued for their personal strengths."

It is just as important for children to internalise strengths to ensure that they are carried forward and deployed effectively, as it is for adults. Again *Know thyself* and *To thine own self be true* equally apply. Thus, when, as adults, we are giving children positive feedback, we should strive to do so in a way that enables the child to internalise and actively own the positive messages. Enabling the child to internalise the feedback for themselves is vitally important for their own growth and authenticity, and for enabling them to follow the directions in life that are right for them. When feedback is always conditionally given, it leaves the child dependent on external praise from others, and so always looking for conditional approval, rather than having their own sense of what they can do, and can do well.

For example, conveying to a child *"Well done, you should be very proud of yourself for learning to swim 10 metres without armbands"* is much more likely to be internalized than *"Well done, I am very proud of you for learning to swim 10 metres without armbands."* The first message conveys that the child should be proud of their own effort and achievements (an internalised message); the second conveys that the child should seek the praise of their parents or significant others in order to feel rewarded (an externalised message).

Holding and Enabling a Growth Mindset

Enabling children to hold a growth mindset, as well as holding a growth mindset ourselves, is the third element of creating environments that will enable children to realise their strengths. Carol Dweck, who we met in Chapter 5, emphasises the importance of whether we convey a fixed mindset or a growth mindset to a child. Remember, a fixed mindset is where we believe that we have a fixed amount of intelligence or ability for something, and a growth mindset is where we believe we can grow and develop ourselves through our own efforts. Further, the mindset we hold has extremely important implications for how much effort we put in and how we deal with failure. For fixed mindset people, effort doesn't really come into it: you can either do it or you can't, and if they can't, they stop trying. In contrast, for growth mindset people, you can do it if you put in the necessary effort, and so they work harder to achieve what they want. When it comes to dealing with failure, these lessons play out even more. Fixed mindset people dismiss the task as meaningless or unimportant and give up on it when they fail. Growth mindset people learn the lessons of failure and work harder to incorporate them next time, with the result that they typically succeed in the end.

Giving the right messages to children is a key way in which we can steer them towards a fixed mindset or a growth mindset, with all the consequences that follow for each. For example, in one of her studies, Dweck told children who were studying maths about great mathematicians. One group were told that the great mathematicians were geniuses who easily came up with their mathematical discoveries. This alone was enough to put the children into a fixed mindset, since it implied that maths is about 'you can either do it or you can't' – just the message of a fixed mindset person. The second group were told that the mathematicians were passionate about maths and ended up making their great discoveries as a result – which propelled them into the growth mindset of thinking that skills and achievement come through commitment, effort and hard work.

These simple differences in message had a profound impact on the messages that the children internalised – and as a result, the messages that they would take forward with them in their lives. (Of course, in case you were concerned, Dweck and her colleagues undid the fixed mindset intervention before the children left the experiment.) When children are enabled to have a growth mindset, they are more likely see their strengths as able to be developed, and therefore to expend the effort needed to develop them. Without a growth mindset, children are unlikely to have any realistic chance of realising their strengths or their life's potential.

As such, in terms of giving the right messages to children, we need to ensure that what we are helping children to hear is the growth mindset messages about how it is effort, commitment and hard work that count, and that failure can be learned from, rather than being

absolute. At the same time, these messages need to convey our unconditional acceptance and individual valuing of the child, just as we
discussed above. Consider the following examples of how well-intentioned comments can be interpreted quite differently by the child:

- What the parent / teacher says is:

"Wow, you did that really quickly! You're so clever!"

What the child hears is:

If I don't do something quickly, then I'm not clever.

So, to develop the growth mindset, we might say:

*"Wow, you did that really quickly. I'm sorry that it was too easy for you
and that I have wasted your time. Let's do something that you can really
learn from."*

- What the parent / teacher says is:

"You got an A grade. Well done, I am so proud of you!"

What the child hears is:

If I don't get an A grade, you won't be proud of me.

So, to develop the growth mindset, we might say:

*"Wow, you got an A grade. You must have worked really hard to achieve
that, and your effort and commitment really paid off, well done."*

- What the parent / teacher says is:

"If you want to get a good job, you need to get good grades."

What the child hears is:

*My parents / teacher want me to get a good job, and they will only
love / value me if I do.*

So, to develop the growth mindset, we might say:

*"If you want to get a good job, you need to work hard and try your
best. But different people have different aptitudes and abilities. The
important thing is for you to do the things that are right for you."*

As you can see, giving the right message also involves ensuring that children hear what we intend for them to hear. This comes through being aware of how the way in which we present that message influences what it is that children hear and take from the message. As you strive to create an environment where you can nurture golden seeds in your children, it's worth noting that, according to Dweck, the thread that unifies all great parents, teachers and coaches is that they believe in people's ability to grow and develop. As well as having this growth mindset themselves, they also infuse it into others. Thus, holding a growth mindset is one of the key ways in which we can realise strengths through nurturing golden seeds and raising flourishing children, as Figure 7.3 shows. And, as you might have now come to expect, there can be certain strengths that predispose people to do this much more naturally, as we go on to explore.

Strengths of Parenting?

Given the understanding of strengths that I hope you are now developing as you read this book, I suspect it won't come as a surprise to you to hear that there are certain strengths that may predispose people to be naturally good at creating these optimal environments for children to realise their strengths – and there are. Probably the most important of these strengths is one that we call *Unconditionality*, which is about valuing and accepting people for who they are, without attaching any conditions to that valuing and acceptance. Of course, if you don't have *Unconditionality* as one of your own strengths (and the vast majority of us don't), it is not the end of the world – it just means that you might have to work that bit harder, and be that bit more conscientious, in creating these optimal environments.

It is also very important to recognise that there are many different

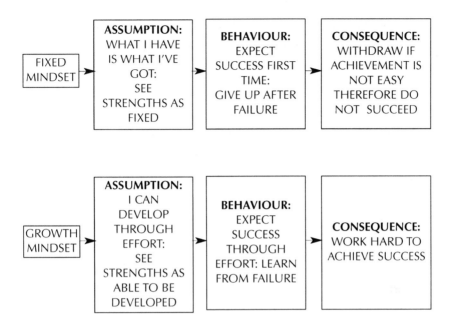

Figure 7.3 The Effects of Fixed Mindsets and Growth Mindsets

ways in which we can achieve the same outcomes – and just as we talked about in Chapter 6 about harnessing strengths at work, we should remember to be focused on the outcome rather than necessarily the process through which that outcome is achieved (the strengths approach is remarkably consistent across many different contexts!). Some parents may create optimal environments for children to realise their strengths through the parent's own strength of *Unconditionality*, for others it may be about being an *Esteem Builder*, for others using their strength as an *Enabler* could be key, and for yet others, it might all come back to *Nurture*.

In practice, this means that if you don't happen to have *Unconditionality* as a core strength, then in no way does it automatically make you a bad parent, and it's worth recapping on the two major reasons why that is so. First, just because we don't have a strength for something, it doesn't mean, by default, that it is a weakness – there are many gradations in between, and the characteristic in question may well be one of them. Second, strengths are not linear or unidimensional, just as we discussed in relation to particular strengths and particular occupations: there is more than one way to get the job done, and to get the job done well. There are many different ways through which people achieve the same overall outcomes, and strengths of parenting and raising flourishing children are most especially included here. We can still do many things, even though we may not find that they come naturally or that they are energising. Where this is the case, we simply need to do them *well enough*. This may mean that we need to work a little harder at them, but our efforts will pay off – especially if we hold a growth mindset! As ever, there are lessons – little tricks and techniques – that we can pick up and learn from others for whom it does come naturally. I am extremely fortunate to have one such role model in my life: my mother.

Hilary is the model of *Unconditionality*. A mother to four children, and grandmother to nine (and counting), she embodies the trust and belief in the right directions of every individual, and especially every child, that she knows. Whatever you had done, right or wrong, good or bad, you would be accepted and loved. *"There might be some times when I don't like you, but I always, always love you"* is a phrase that she would often use at the difficult times in her growing children's lives, when they tested the boundaries and pushed too far. *"I don't mind what you do, as long as you are happy and you don't break the law"* was the creed on which her children were raised, giving them a foundation of autonomy to explore their own paths through life, while still being located within a framework of moral integrity. And whoever arrived at the door of her home, they were welcomed no matter what their background or history: people were not judged by their past misdemeanours, but were instead encouraged on the basis of their future possibility and potential, and her unshakeable belief that, given the right support and under-standing, everyone is at heart a good person.

Cynics might present this view as naïve, but the alternative is to see the bad in everyone, rather than the good – just as we considered in relation to views of human nature in Chapter 2. Throughout her life, Hilary will tell you that this view has reaped many more dividends than disappointments. Hilary is the best model of unconditionality for which one could hope, enabling children to find their voice and follow their own directions in a way that provides lessons for us all, in what-ever capacity, for developing the next generations and guiding others as they find the directions in life that are right for them

Whatever the strength that we can best deploy in our interactions with children, having a passion for them and their development, and a focus on building and harnessing what they can do best, provides a recipe for the effective realisation of children's strengths. Jill Garrett, formerly a school headteacher at 31 years of age, but now a Director of Caret Consulting, an organisation that develops leaders through their strengths, describes it in this way:

> "When I was a teacher, I began to realise that my youngsters were getting really good results. Different people would teach the same children, but they wouldn't get the same results – and I think this was because they didn't have the same passion for the children. It seemed to me that I could naturally see the things that the children were doing well, and so I began to think much more about the idea that everybody is good at something, and that you just have to find what that is. When you can tap into what it is that excites people, you get so much more from them – and that is true for both children and adults alike."

Allow Children to Experiment – and Make Mistakes

Perhaps one of the most important ways in which we can help children to identify and grow their strengths is through experimentation – trying things out, sometimes making mistakes, sometimes succeeding, taking two steps forward and one step back as they add to their understanding of how the world works and their place in it. Of course, much of this is intrinsic to what it means to be a child – children's lives are - and should be - characterised by this sense of boundless curiosity and ceaseless wonder. But as adults, there is much that we can do that will either *enhance* that propensity for exploration and growth, or that will *undermine* these natural developmental trajectories. As adults, we have a responsibility to ensure that children have the opportunity to stretch their wings, to test themselves against the outer reaches of possibility. As adults, our role is to educate them in relation to their options and opportunities, recognising that there is a vast and ever-changing world 'out there,' that permits of new possibilities that didn't exist even yesterday. Sadly, a lot of this freedom for experimentation is being lost in our over-concerned society – but we need to reclaim it. There is hope: the fact that Conn and Hal Iggulden's *The Dangerous Book for Boys* was a runaway bestseller attests to the re-kindling of our interest in the joy and necessity of experimentation, exploration, and adventure for our children.

Providing children with opportunities to try new things and experience new places, sights, sounds, smells, and tastes is an important part of what parenthood – as well as teaching – is about. When children are empowered and valued for who they are, they feel the permission they need to explore the natural world around them – as well as being able to explore more of who they are. In contrast, children who are brought up in environments of excessive control, or restrained by the conditional approval of the significant others in their lives, will be distorted from following the paths that are right for them. Instead, they will live half-lives in a cocoon of constraint, always wondering, often fearfully, what the world might really hold for them, if only they could break free and have the confidence to step forth and explore it.

This confidence to step forth and explore the world comes from having a secure attachment base – something established and later popularised through the groundbreaking work of psychologist John Bowlby. As parents, as teachers, or as significant others in children's lives, one of our fundamental responsibilities to the child is to provide them with this secure base of attachment from which to venture out into the world. Having this secure base, the child feels safe to explore, to test the limits, to discover themselves and rest safe in the knowledge that the safety net of a caring parent, teacher, or other important person in their lives is there for them to turn to when the need arises. And it is this process of exploration, leading to discovery of the external world, and through it discovery of the internal world – who I am, what I believe, what my talents are – that enables the child first to identify and then build on their strengths.

As a young boy at primary school, I signed up for lessons on how to play the recorder. Not because I had a particular musical bent, you understand, or even because I wanted to learn to play the recorder, but just because a lot of my friends had (and notably, too, a girl in whom I had more than a passing interest). My parents paid the requisite fees, including buying the recorder itself and the music book to accompany it. My passion for the recorder lasted about three weeks, when the pain of trying to fit in with something that I didn't enjoy and wasn't good at got to the point where it outweighed my desire to fit in and be part of the in-crowd! But this is not the significance of this story. The significance was my parents' reaction. They had paid for the equipment, and expected me to show a commitment to the lessons. Yet, because I was able to give the reason as to why I didn't want to continue (I didn't enjoy it and wasn't any good at it), they were freely unconditional in their acceptance of my decision.

As a result, I learned that what *I* thought was important (and it was important to my parents, as well as being important to me), that how *I* felt was important (again, it was important to my parents as well as to me), and that, actually, what *they* wanted for me was to do the things that were right for *me*, and that would enable me to become the person *I* was capable of becoming. Obviously, I was not likely to become a recorder-playing maestro, and so, leaving the monetary cost of the experience to one side, the more important lesson was that I had taken another step in the long journey of understanding who I was and what I was best at – and it wasn't playing the recorder!

Of course, we all have to recognise that there are limitations (of both time and money) on the different activities that our children, or the children for whom we are responsible, are able to take on in order to discover more about themselves. But these limitations need not be in any way an excuse for inactivity. By far the more valuable currency is the base that we give children from which to explore, and the reactions we convey when they return to us - whether successfully with a new skill mastered and an area of strength discovered, or with a lesson to be consigned to the box marked 'put it down to experience' – because after all, experience is often the best teacher. Just think of the child – like my youngest son, Ben – who doesn't want to take your word for it that the oven is hot, and so finds out for themselves! (Yes – like his sister and his dad, he's big on *Curiosity* too!)

Recognising this need for children to experiment and explore to find their strengths, what can we as adults do to support that process? As we discussed above, one of the most important things we can do is to provide them with a secure base to which to return – both in a physical and psychological sense. We can also try to provide opportunities, structured or spontaneous, that enable them to explore. And beyond that, we can do something which can be both the simplest but also the hardest thing to do – *to just get out of the way and let them find out for themselves.* This is not about not caring, even though it may seem simple to do because it requires us to do precisely nothing. It is hard to do because our parental and nurturing instincts prompt us to step in and help. But, as is so often the case, the solution here lies in the golden mean: doing the right thing, to the right amount, at the right time, in the right way. Sadly, there is no hard and fast formula for how to achieve this – Aristotle concluded that the only way was through the exercise of *phronesis*, or practical wisdom – but the first step is, at the least, to be aware of what is at stake and to try to follow our best instincts accordingly.

Role Model What You Want to See in Children

The phrase "climate engineers" applies as much to parents and teachers – indeed to any significant person in a child's life – as it does to the leaders of organisations for whom it was intended. Climate engineers are the people in any social setting who set the psychological or cultural climate for that setting. In organisations, this is often the CEO, board, or senior leadership team. In schools, it is likely to be the headteacher. In a classroom, it is the class teacher. And in a family, it will likely be the parents, as well as older siblings – and getting them to understand and recognise their role as climate engineers can be key – especially in large families! The climate engineers are responsible, whether they realise it or not, for the climate that is created within their sphere of influence. And it is quite a responsibility to hold. How you act, how you behave, the views you hold and the attitudes you convey – all are carefully scrutinised and followed by the people in your sphere of influence when you are a climate engineer.

For children, this is doubly the case, because they are looking up to us as adults, and especially as significant figures in their lives, in order to learn how to behave, what to think, and what to believe. Children learn behaviour predominantly through copying others around them, and hence we are role models for the development of young minds. It is a role of which we should be very mindful for the impact that it can create – whether positive or negative. Applied to strengths, children will – without even being aware of it themselves – look to us for validation of what they are good at, the directions they should pursue, and the attributes and aptitudes they possess. Words of praise and golden seeds, just like leaden seeds and words of admonition, can be seared into a child's memory for a lifetime. Knowing this, we should choose our words carefully and strive to role model the people we would like them to become. We can do this very powerfully through giving praise and positive feedback, since by receiving our encouragement, children will learn to encourage themselves – and will also pass on the wisdom that they have learned to other children around them.

For example, Carol Dweck described this response from a child with a growth mindset who was helping another child with a maths problem:

> *"Do you quit a lot? Do you think for a minute and then stop? If you do, you should think for a long time – two minutes maybe and if you can't get it you should read the problem again. If you can't get it then, you should raise your hand and ask the teacher."*

And this was two young children talking to each other. Imagine how much more powerful those messages are when they come from significant adults. We all need encouragement at different times, so having internalised the voice of encouragement from childhood can become a mast of certitude in challenging and uncertain times. As we discussed in Chapter 5, we seem to have a bullet-proof skin that makes us impervious to praise and positive feedback, but this problem applies less to children than to adults. As such, this means that the most opportune moments we have for delivering positive feedback are with our children.

I was brought up on the belief *"There's no such word as 'can't'"* – and I have no doubt that the confidence and belief in my abilities that I have now stems largely from that consistent, repeated encouragement. Tracy Wood, one of the youngest women ever to be made a Partner at Ernst & Young, tells a very similar story:

> *"I was brought up to believe that I could achieve anything I wanted to, as long as I put my mind to it and worked hard enough. My mum instilled in me a belief that I could achieve anything, and so it never really occurred to me that I couldn't. That has been with me all through my life, and I just can't turn it off – it's who I am."*

Children crave our attention and approval, and giving them praise and positive feedback for something done well meets both of these powerful needs. Importantly, it also provides a role model for them in their behaviour with others. Through social learning, children rapidly pick up the ways in which adults interact with them, and indeed the ways in which children interact with each other. This social learning drives their behaviour, attitudes, and interactions, meaning that if we can model positive approaches to them that are built on recognising and validating strengths, then they are likely to take on this language and approach in the ways in which they relate to others.

This is exactly what Jenny Fox Eades has observed in her work with primary schools in Scunthorpe. Once introduced to the language of strengths and an understanding of what those strengths are, and what they look like when they are being used, children start – naturally and spontaneously – to use that language and those affirmations in the ways in which they talk and interact with others. *"That was a very kind thing to do, Johnny"* may not seem like much of a sea change, but it is when you recognise the absence of positives that existed before. Anything that can be taken on board to create more genuinely affirmative ways of interacting has to be a right step in a positive and constructive direction – especially when we remember that we need at least three positive interactions for every negative interaction if we are to create flourishing individuals and thriving teams.

Similarly, how we as adults lead our own lives has a powerful effect on what children perceive of us, and then what they internalise about themselves and about 'the way things are.' If we spend our lives in the drudgery of jobs that we at best don't enjoy, and at worst, actively hate, then we send out a message to our children that that is the way life is. But it doesn't have to be that way: there is a different way. When we are able to find our own niche in life, to have work that we love and hobbies that enable us to become more fully who we are, then we send a very different message: *"This is how it can be – for you, too."*

Recognising this, we should be mindful of our own authenticity and our own quest to use our strengths to make positive contributions to the lives of others, and to find our own fulfilment through the process. We have one chance at life, and it is up to us to make the most of that chance. The chances that we convey to our children, or the children we teach or otherwise influence, are equally important. If we make the most of our lives, we are inviting them to do the same. If we fail to do so, we run the risk of condemning them to that same failure of expectation and realisation, of potential lost and chances for happiness missed. Surely no parent would want that for their child, because as Richard Branson puts it – and he has more opportunities than most to provide a variety of experiences for his children – "I look over at Holly and Sam and realise that I don't want to plan their lives for them. I just want them to be happy."

The Swords Master who we will meet next is another parent who clearly wanted his children to flourish – and he had a remarkable way of demonstrating it. While I was working on this chapter, a friend sent me a copy of this magical story, saying "I heard this and I thought of you, because I think it is fundamentally about strengths." The story was *The Samurai in the Teashop*, and I would like to retell you this as a closing thought for this chapter. I trust you will be able to see why, and that you will take on the Swords Master's wisdom in your own parenting and interactions with children.

We should be ever mindful of the enormous responsibility we bear in our interactions with children, in that we are raising the next generation of adults – the generation of people who, ultimately, will be the ones who take our place. Who will, hopefully, care for us in our old age, protect our natural environment, and build a better world for the future. Our legacy is seen most vividly in the children who follow us and the society they create. Enabling children to become who they are capable of becoming, realising themselves and their strengths through the process, and in turn enabling others to do the same – this is one of the ways in which we can make our greatest contributions.

The Samurai in the Teashop
by Pamela Gawler-Wright

Once upon a time there was a Swords Master who lived in Japan, many hundreds of years ago. And not only was he famous for his skills at the sword, he was also famous for his skills as a teacher of the sword. He was fascinated with the many different ways that different people learn different things. And each one of his sons learned how to master the sword, and in turn became Swords Masters.

But there was one son who was different from his brothers. For while the others could be seen wrestling and playing with wooden swords, eager for the day that their first lesson would begin, this boy could be seen walking in the fields and the woods, collecting flowers. He would gather whole heaps of flowers, as many as he could carry, and he would come back into town with such a burden of flowers, that you couldn't even see his face.

And he would lay out his great store of blooms and foliage before him, and silently he would start to sort, and select. He would discard what was not needed, and he would put together the choicest of blooms. In that moment of perfection, and when he had only the best before him, he would sit, and he would wait. And then, with a flash of his hands, the flowers would be in a vase in an arrangement so exquisite, that all would gasp who laid eyes on it.

And there was something else at which this boy excelled, and that was the writing of the *haiku*. Now, the *haiku* is a form of Japanese poetry, consisting of seventeen syllables, arranged in three lines. And the first line presents an idea, or an object, or a concept. And the second line introduces a contrasting or even conflicting idea, concept, or object. And the third line brings together these contrasting entities into something harmonious, relating, synthesised. And the boy wrote such poetry that it would put to rest the minds of all those who heard it.

And there was one thing at which this boy excelled above all others, and that was the performance of the tea ceremony.

Now the time came for the young man to join his brothers and take up the sword. And, with a stone in his heart, he went to his father and he said:

"Father, I was not made to use the sword. I was made to arrange flowers, to write poetry, and above all, father, I was made for the performance of the tea ceremony."

And to his surprise, his father turned, and looked at the boy, and he said:

"Son, do that which you do best, and which you love to do."

And the boy grew up and it wasn't long before he gathered his friends together, and they built a tea house in the middle of town. And he became a Tea Master of great repute. Far and wide, people would come from miles to enjoy the exquisite arrangements of flowers, to enjoy listening to and writing poetry, and above all, they would come to enjoy the tea ceremony.

Until one day a gang of thugs rode into town. They tied their horses in the square, and they kicked their way into the tea house, and they ordered *sake*. And within an hour they were rowdy, disturbing people, aggressive. Until finally, the Tea Master had to ask them to leave.

And the leader of the thugs drew himself up to his full height, and he looked at this little Tea Master, and he saw that this little man had the audacity to wear around his waist a Samurai sword. For the Tea Master had always worn with pride his heritage, his family honour. For he was the son of a Samurai.

And the thug mocked and he jeered. And he challenged the Tea Master to a duel, at dawn, by sword.

And that night the young Tea Master closed up his tea shop for maybe the very last time. And he made his way across town to his father's house. And well was the Swords Master surprised, to find his youngest son standing there, saying:

"Father, teach me how to use my sword, for tomorrow I must face my enemy."

"Very well," replied the Swords Master. *"First, stand in front of me, and what I want you to do, is to just draw your sword and present it."*

So the Tea Master fumbled, and discovered how to undo his scabbard, and removed his sword, and held it in front of him, hands trembling.

And the Swords Master took one look at the manner in which this had been done, and he said:

"Son, tomorrow, when you face your enemy, when you draw your sword and present it to the man opposite you, it will be the last thing that you do on this earth."

And the Tea Master said:

"Father, what can I give you as one last gift, to thank you for the life that you gave me and all that you have taught me?"

And the Swords Master said:

"You know, everywhere I hear about your performance of the tea ceremony, and yet never have you done it for me. Do it now, as one last parting gift."

And the Tea Master forgot his fear, and with delight, he opened the tea chest that he always brought with him. And he took out the flask of clear spring water, and he skilfully lit his tinder, and put the water to the flame. He took a bag from the chest, and into his hand he poured from it choice leaves of tea. And he began to select and discard, until he had in his hand the very best.

And he poured these leaves of tea into the pot. And at that moment, the water came to the boil, and he brought the tea and the water together. And then he waited. And he waited. And he waited. Until the moment was just right. And then, with peace, grace, and joy, he poured the tea from the pot, gave the cup exactly three and a quarter turns, and presented it to the man opposite him. And his father drank.

The Tea Master packed up his things, and just as he was at the door, his father called to him, and said:

"Son, one last thing. Tomorrow, when you draw your sword, and present it to your enemy, do it in the manner that you perform the tea ceremony. Do it in the manner that you do that, which you do best, and which you love to do."

And that night the Tea Master dreamed of all the things that he had done in his life. He dreamed of all the tiny buds that he had watched push their way through the soil in spring, to open their delicate faces to the summer sun. And he dreamed of all the things that he had not yet done.

And he remembered. He remembered. *"Do it in the manner...do it in the manner...the manner of that which you do best, and which you love to do. That which you do best, and which you love to do. Do it in the manner that you do that, which you do best, and which you love to do."*

Dawn came and the first strands of light fingered their way over the fields to the agreed place of the duel by sword. And the Tea Master stood there.

And the thugs turned up on their horses, not a little surprised to see him standing there alone. And the leader of the thugs jumped off his horse and squared up to his opponent. And then he whipped his sword from its scabbard and sent it swirling, circling, singing through the air. And he brought it down in front of him, presenting to the man opposite him.

And the Tea Master waited. And he waited. And he waited until the moment was just right. And then he drew his sword from its scabbard, gave it exactly three and a quarter turns, and with peace, grace, and even a hint of joy, he presented his sword to the man opposite him.

And the thug looked at the manner in which this had been done. He saw the peace on the face of this man who held the sword in his hand, drawn with grace, presented with joy. And he realised that he must be in the presence of a true Master of the Sword.

And his own sword began to tremble, until he dropped it into the sand as a sign of defeat. He got back on his horse, and he rode away.

And the Tea Master made his way back to town. And he found that his sword was an excellent tool for cutting flowers. And he arrived back with a great heap of colour in his arms. And he opened the Tea Shop, ready for the new day.

Key Points

- Children demonstrate some strengths from a very early age, indicating the role of nature and genetic inheritance in the origins of strengths. Other strengths may not be apparent until later in children, likely reflecting their limited cognitive development, and the level of cognitive development necessary for some strengths to be shown.

- A golden seed refers to a positive comment that someone makes to us, and that helps us to believe in and internalise our view of the strengths that we may have. A leaden seed refers to a negative comment that someone makes, and that undermines our belief in ourselves, reflecting their judgment that we cannot do something, yet while we believe ourselves that we can.

- Environments that nurture golden seeds are those where children are individualised (rather than stereotyped); where they are given their own voice (rather than having their view of the world defined by adults); and where they are enabled to hold a growth mindset, believing that they can develop themselves and their abilities through effort and hard work (rather than holding a fixed mindset, whereby they believe that what they have is what they have got).

- Enabling children to realise their strengths also requires us, as adults, to allow them room to experiment and to make mistakes. This involves giving children as many and as varied opportunities and experiences as we are able, such that they are able to forge their own understanding of themselves and their strengths and abilities through the crucible of their own experience.

- Parents, teachers and significant others in children's lives have important roles as "climate engineers" that set the tone for the way things are. As such, adults need to be mindful of their responsibility for this role, and to role model what it is that they would like to see in their children: children learn most from copying those around them.

Areas for Reflection and Action

- Can you identify the golden seeds in your own life? What were they? Where were they from? Who gave them to you? Can you trace the impact that they have had on you over the years? Does the person know the positive impact that their comments had?

- Think about the golden seeds that you have given to others. What can you do to give more golden seeds? What can you do to improve the positive impact of the messages that you give?

- How effective are you at creating an optimal environment for your children to realise their strengths? This requires individualising children, allowing them their voice, and helping them to hold a growth mindset, while also allowing them to experiment and explore, and role modelling the behaviour that we would like to see in them. Is there anything that gets in the way of you doing these? If so, what can you do about it?

EIGHT

Making our Greatest Contributions

"…everyone can give something. And there's so much to be done, down the street and around the world. It's never too late or too early to start."

Bill Clinton,
Giving: How Each of Us Can Change the World

WE ALL HAVE strengths, and throughout this book, we have started to look at the ways in which we can realise them – in both of two senses. First, we focused on realising strengths in terms of being aware of what strengths are – which we did by understanding where strengths come from (in Chapter 2), understanding how to use strengths most appropriately and effectively while overcoming our negativity bias (in Chapter 3), and how we can identify our strengths, and those of others, through strengthspotting (in Chapter 4). Second, we explored how to realise strengths in terms of making them real and manifest, both in ourselves and others – developing and building them in ourselves (in Chapter 5), harnessing them at work (in Chapter 6) and growing strengths in children (in Chapter 7). We have seen how strengths are a natural and important part of who we are as individuals and human beings, and we have seen how using our strengths enables us to be happier, more fulfilled, and more effective at work. In essence, through realising our strengths we are able to become ourselves, only better – the best that we are capable of becoming.

Our strengths are our greatest source of power. But with that great power comes great responsibility – a great responsibility that we might consider as *the three pillars of responsibility of the strengths approach*. First, we have *a personal responsibility to use and develop our own strengths*, to be the authors of our own lives, to become the best that we are capable of becoming. Second, we have *a collective responsibility to create the conditions that enable the strengths of others*, to allow them to achieve what they are capable of achieving and, in turn, make their own contributions. Third, we have *a social responsibility to harness strengths for the benefit of wider society*, to build networks and institutions that make the world a better place. Through each of these three pillars, we have the ultimate responsibility for the legacy that we leave the generations who follow us – to make a lasting positive contribution to the world of which we are but a transient part.

Personal responsibility is not a sexy topic – and yet it forms the bedrock of many of the freedoms that are enjoyed in democratic societies. Viktor Frankl recognised this delicate balance between liberty and responsibility when he wrote: "I recommend that the Statue of Liberty on the East Coast be supplemented by a Statue of Responsibility on the West Coast." In testament to the recovery of responsibility in the Western world, this Statue of Responsibility, showing two interlocking hands that represent our interdependency and hence the responsibility we share for one another, has now been commissioned.

As we acknowledge these responsibilities, we are invited, collectively, to create a new set of public goods. And yet, public goods are faced with a unique problem: because everybody benefits from them, no single person wants to pay for them – for example, none of us typically pays directly for the use of a streetlamp or a particular footpath, but we all benefit from having them. Historically, governments have gotten round this problem through taxation and redistribution, which means that as tax-paying citizens we all contribute collectively through our local or national taxes. But even so, nobody likes paying taxes – and if we could legitimately avoid it, the probability is that we would.

Working from our strengths, however, to create these public goods, is a novel proposition that turns these traditional assumptions on their head. When using strengths, people contribute because they have the intrinsic motivation to do so and because they want to – not because they are forced to or feel compelled to do so. In this way, we can start to recast the ways in which we can make our greatest contributions to the public good as being opportunities for us to use our strengths, thereby creating an individual-social double-win that parallels the employee-organisation double-win that we talked about for organisations in Chapter 6. To explore this further, we need to consider, in turn, each of the three pillars of responsibility of the strengths approach – as illustrated in Figure 8.1.

The First Pillar: A Personal Responsibility to Use and Develop Our Strengths

We are faced with many choices throughout life, but perhaps the most fundamental is what we choose to do with the strengths and talents with which we have been endowed. It does not matter what we believe about where those strengths have come from – whether they are

God-given gifts, evolved adaptations, or the result of some random scattering of abilities. Whatever we believe, we are faced with the choice of what we do with them. Do we do nothing, or not enough, and allow them to wither, neglected and irrelevant? Or do we seek to develop and harness them, to build a better life for ourselves and others, to become what we are capable of becoming? Throughout human history and prehistory, mankind has advanced because people made this positive choice, because they opted to develop, to grow, to expand, to build on what they had – in short, to realise their possibilities. But we need not do so: we can choose to ignore them, to be a free-rider, to let others pick up the slack. If we choose this path, however, we are likely foregoing our greatest opportunity for happiness and fulfilment – and as Aristotle decreed, our happiness and fulfilment is the *summum bonum*, or highest good, the only thing that we pursue for its own ends.

An insightful way to approach this question is to take each answer to its most extreme conclusion. For example, what would happen if *nobody* sought to develop their possibilities, build on their strengths, and grow to become who they were capable of becoming? Human life would be stagnant; human development would end. In contrast, what would happen if *everybody* sought to develop their possibilities, build on their strengths, and grow to become who they were capable of becoming? Human life would be a glorious miasma of engagement, fulfilment and growth; human development would be exponential. Recognising this, it is clear that one course leads in a positive, growthful direction, the other leads in a negative path toward decline and decay. As such, we may legitimately argue that each of us has *a personal responsibility to use and develop our strengths,* the first pillar of responsibility in the strengths approach. When we do so, we benefit as individuals, as well as benefiting our wider community and society as a whole.

Another way of viewing this responsibility is through the lens of our evolution, as we discussed in Chapter 2. Strengths originally evolved in us as ways of dealing with problems of survival and reproduction in our environment. Through the actualising tendency, our basic motivational force in the direction of our growth, development, and fulfilment, we were equipped with a psychological compass that guides us in the directions that are right for us. As we have seen, using our strengths is at the heart of those right directions, with people who are using their strengths more showing significantly higher levels of authenticity, engagement, happiness, and fulfilment. Further, people using their strengths more deliver better performance. Using our strengths more effectively delivers better performance in everything that we do – as Charles Handy described it in *The New Alchemists*, a study of people who had created great things from nothing, including Tim Waterstone, who started the Waterstones book chain, and Michael Young, the founder of the Open University: *"All the alchemists played to their strengths. That was one secret of their success."* To be as successful as we can be in our own lives, we should be playing to our strengths wherever we can do so – and where we can't, we should be doing what we can to transform the disabling circumstances into enabling ones.

For these reasons, using our strengths is one of our primary responsibilities to ourselves. When we do so, we are making use of the capabilities with which we have been endowed, we are following the directions that are right for us, we are delivering our best performances, and we are on the way to realising our potentials and possibilities, and becoming all that we are capable of becoming – for many, the goal of a good life and a life well-lived. Using strengths is a responsibility, but a responsibility with a difference. Because using our strengths serves both the individual good, as well as the public good, we achieve another powerful double-win, thereby overcoming one of the key chal-

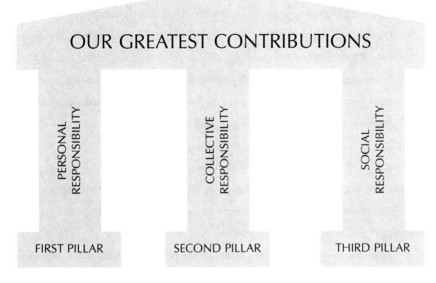

Figure 8.1 The Three Pillars of Responsibility of the Strengths Approach

lenges faced by the provision of public goods - the fact that because everybody benefits, nobody wants to pay. Where strengths are concerned, the investment comes from the individual, who derives their own core intrinsic motivation and value from using strengths, with the wider benefits for the public good being a welcome addition. Using strengths is not only a rewarding personal activity, but also a valuable collective one.

The Second Pillar: A Collective Responsibility to Create the Conditions that Enable the Strengths of Others

As Karen Horney described in relation to our intrinsic growth tendency, when we have found our own opportunities for self-expression and self-realisation, we then want to enable others to do the same:

"...we become free to grow ourselves, we also free ourselves to love and to feel concern for other people. We will then want to give them the opportunity for unhampered growth when they are young, and to help them in whatever way possible to find and realize themselves when they are blocked in their development. At any rate, whether for ourselves or for others, the ideal is the liberation and cultivation of the forces which lead to self-realization."

Applied to strengths development, the corollary is a straightforward one: when we have been able to develop our own strengths and use them more effectively in the service of our goals and aspirations, we will want to do the same for others.

This forms the second pillar of responsibility in the strengths approach: *each of us has a collective responsibility to create the conditions that enable the strengths of others.* When we are using and developing our own strengths, as well as creating the conditions to enable others to do the same, we are taking significant strides both toward realising strengths in ourselves and others – by definition – but also to realising more of the potential and possibility that otherwise lies dormant within the human population. As Muhammad Yunus describes it: *"Unless we create an environment that enables us to discover the limits of our potential, we will never know what we have inside of us."* The action of creating this enabling environment provides a collective impetus that helps propel us toward a better world for everyone.

For example, when I founded CAPP, we selected HOPEHIV (**www.hopehiv.org**) to be our charity partners. Why? The opening quote on their website said it all: "There are 13 million children orphaned by AIDS in Africa. Some see them as Africa's greatest problem. We see them as Africa's greatest hope." Focusing on the solution, rather than the problem, as well as focusing on prevention and building capability, rather than only on treatment, and tackling, rather than ignoring, the causal roots of the problem, are central tenets of the strengths approach.

HOPEHIV is doing both of these, in a way that both tackles the problem and builds solutions for the future. By working with children orphaned by AIDS to provide for their basic needs, to teach them life skills, and to develop their talents and capabilities, HOPEHIV is providing them with the tools to create a better future – both for themselves and others – and the hope that they can do so. Further, they are building a culture of enablement where children who have been given hope then work to empower and enable others, thus perpetuating a cycle of hope and aspiration, rather than one of hopelessness and despair. As James O'Toole describes this concept in relation to giving:

> *"The first order for philanthropists is to understand that the purpose of their actions is to create the conditions under which others can realize their own potential...Hence, the question a philanthropist must ask is the same one a virtuous politician or business leader must ask: 'What can I do to provide conditions in which others can pursue happiness?'"*

HOPEHIV, in developing the strengths of children orphaned by AIDS, and then in turn enabling these children to enable others, are practising this second responsibility of the strengths approach. Consider, for example, the story of Mbali. For ten years she survived as a street girl in South Africa, joining gangs where robbery, violence and sexual abuse were rife, and deadening the pain through sniffing glue. Now, through the efforts of O'Saviour, herself a former street girl, Mbali has joined the Umthombo Street Children team in Durban, South Africa, and spends her time helping other girls to avoid the start to life that she had. HOPEHIV's model of working is predicated fundamentally on enabling people who in turn enable others. While this example is specific to HOPEHIV and their particular context, it illustrates the essential point: the greatest difference we can make is through enabling others to help themselves and, in their turn, subsequently to enable others themselves. Enabling the enablers is key to sustainable social change such as HOPEHIV is working to achieve in Africa, and it is also central to the effective application of the strengths approach.

No doubt you will also be able to think of many examples of your own where this has happened – and will be able to relate to the power and importance of the ripple effect that we create by enabling others who are then able, in their own turn, to enable others themselves. Whether it is as parents seeing our children grow to support and nurture others in turn, as managers seeing promising employees become great managers themselves, as teachers seeing our pupils develop into worthwhile contributors to society, or as community leaders seeing our efforts blossom into better societies for those who are part of them – whatever the context, the subtle power of the ripple effect of good works is at the heart of the second pillar of responsibility in the strengths approach, while also speaking to its wider impact.

The Third Pillar: A Social Responsibility to Harness Strengths for the Benefit of Wider Society

The ripples we create can go far beyond our own immediate sphere – thereby forming the third pillar of responsibility in the strengths approach: *our social responsibility to harness strengths for the benefit of wider society*. Muhammad Yunus had no idea that he was taking the first steps to found a multibillion-dollar bank when he lent a total of less than $27 to 42 people in Jobra, Bangladesh in 1976. To date, Grameen Bank has lent $6.55 billion, and has over 7 million customers, transforming their lives – and not through big money loans, but through micro-credit – loans often of just a few dollars at a time to some of the world's poorest people. Yunus' efforts in micro-credit are indeed an example of doing the smallest thing to make the biggest difference, as thousands of the Grameen Bank success stories will testify. And he did it through enabling others to use their strengths in ways that enabled them to build their own pathways out of poverty and so to transform their lives and the lives of those around them. As ever, enabling the enablers is key to sustainable social change.

For many of us, our sphere of influence will not extend to have anything like the reach of that of Muhammad Yunus. And yet we would be making a grave error, and selling ourselves far short, if we underestimated our potential to have an impact on the world – for good or ill. As Yunus himself writes in relation to the potential effect of the ripples that each of us creates:

> "Each person has tremendous potential. She or he alone can influence the lives of others within the communities, nations, within and beyond her or his own time."

As we discovered in Chapter 7, planting golden seeds in children is an act that has positive repercussions throughout their lives, and which they then, in turn, pass on to others. And those others pass on to others, and they on to others, and those on to others, and others... The ripple spreads, the impact grows, the initiator is usually forgotten – if indeed they were ever known beyond the first ripple of impact that they sent out. But their input, irrespective of domain, time and space, continues to be felt, as Figure 8.2 shows.

Recognising this, we should all acknowledge and take ownership of the fact that we have a contribution to make, and that this contribution can be made best through us deploying our strengths optimally for positive social ends. In the grand scheme of the world, our contribution may be small, it may be great, but it is, above all, our contribution, what we have been able, and enabled to give. This contribution from harnessing and deploying our strengths to greatest effect is the paramount reason for our existence – by doing so, we are developing ourselves, contributing to our societies, and helping to build a better world – a pathway of human evolution that can be traced from our prehistoric origins and aspirations, through our tendency to self-realisation and fulfilment, to our enablement of a more humane world going into the future. Such is the developmental growth path of human civilisation, as it has been for all time. Realising our strengths, enabling strengths in others, and harnessing our strengths for a better world are all reflections of our individual contributions to this path.

When we understand that we all have something to give, we are better enabled to ask ourselves where our greatest contributions might lay. As Bill Clinton implores in *Giving*:

> *"I wrote this book to encourage you to give whatever you can, because everyone can give something."*

Whether we give money, time, ideas, or connections, whatever our gift, if we are contributing through our strengths, then we are making our greatest contributions. Two fine examples abound from two of the richest people on our planet – not *because* they are the richest people on our planet, but because of *how* they have used the strengths that enabled their riches to make, truly, their greatest contributions.

Having made billions of dollars through his business success with Microsoft, Bill Gates has now turned his attention to philanthropic success:

> *"Guided by the belief that every life has equal value, the Bill & Melinda Gates Foundation works to reduce inequities and improve lives around the world."*

The way in which they do so speaks clearly to the idea of the smallest thing that can be done to make the biggest difference, since the focus of the Gates Foundation is on the "problems that cause great harm and get too little attention." Echoing the third pillar of responsibility of the strengths approach, Bill and Melinda Gates explained their reasons for philanthropy thus:

> "We also believe that from those to whom much is given, much is expected. We benefited from great schools, great health care, and a vibrant economic system. That is why we feel a tremendous responsibility to give back to society."

The Bill Gates story also provides another instructive example, from another billionaire. Warren Buffett is, like Bill Gates, one of the richest men in the world – this time having made his billions through stock market investments. And when he turned to major philanthropy, rather than setting out to do it himself, he made the remarkable decision to do it through others, donating $37bn to the Gates Foundation – and explained it in this way, a powerful example of the principle of *kratisto* (to the strongest) in practice:

> "What can be more logical, in whatever you want done, than finding someone better equipped than you are to do it? Who wouldn't select Tiger Woods to take his place in a high-stakes golf game? That's how I feel about this decision about my money."

Buffett's actions are an exceptional example of recognising one's best contribution (in his case, investments) and applying it to the area of greatest need (in his case, giving the money to the Gates Foundation, because it was best placed to achieve what he wanted to achieve). Of course, few if any of us will ever be in a position to take action on the scale that Bill and Melinda Gates and Warren Buffett have done, but the

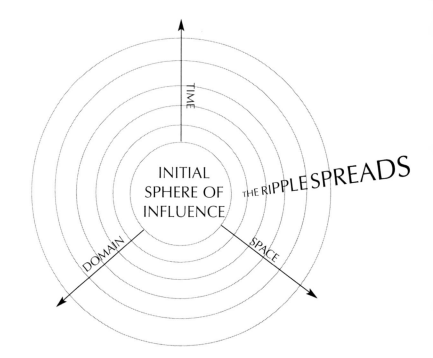

Figure 8.2 The Ripple Effect

principles of their actions remain true, and are equally applicable to us, as we strive to make our greatest contributions – whatever they may be. Remember – through realising our strengths, every one of us has something to contribute.

While we have focused here on Warren Buffett and Bill and Melinda Gates in relation to charity, they did not make their reputations as philanthropists. Instead, they did what they did best – in Buffett's case, stock market investments, and in Bill Gates' case, computer software. Our focus need not be philanthropic for us to make our greatest contributions, but to be effective, it has to be the right thing, for the right reasons, in the right way and at the right time – again, the golden mean. When we do so, we are fulfilling the third pillar of responsibility of the strengths approach: *our social responsibility to harness strengths for the benefit of wider society.*

The World Needs All of Us – And All of Our Strengths

Forces such as the Internet, globalisation, cheap international travel, and ready communications have transformed the world in which we live. From being a dislocated scattering of communities, we talk now of a 'global village.' But just as this global village brings with it opportunities unrivalled in the history of civilisation, so it also brings with it the challenges and threats that reflect the inequalities that exist – and of which we are now only too acutely aware.

Four unprecedented trends represent this cataclysmic shift, none of them reversible – like the proverbial genie, they have been let out of the bottle: (1) the global movement of financial capital, with monetary instruments transferring across markets and time zones instantaneously; (2) the international dispersion of tens of millions of people, whether through travel, migration, or forced immigration; (3) the instant transfer and global accessibility of information on a scale never seen before or even envisaged – through the Internet; and (4) the osmosis of popular culture, such as food, fashion, music, and films across borders, in a way never before witnessed, and yet which we now recognise as the hallmark of globalisation – the fact that we can buy a Big Mac as easily in New Delhi as we can in New York. With globalisation comes global consciousness – an awareness of how others live, what they do, and most impactful of all, the material possessions and opportunities for growth that they have relative to us.

If we do not harness this realisation of global consciousness to reawaken our appreciation of our shared humanity, our collective community, our integral joinedness, then we run the risk of walking blindly into a world that is divided into two halves – with unforgiving and unforgivable consequences – a threat acknowledged only too clearly by Paul Collier in *The Bottom Billion*:

> *"You are a citizen, and citizenship carries responsibilities. In the 1930s the world sleepwalked into the avoidable catastrophe of World War II because electorates in the United States and Europe were too lazy to think beyond the populist recipes of isolationism and pacifism. These mistakes led to the slaughter of their children. It is the responsibility of all citizens to prevent us from sleepwalking into another avoidable catastrophe that our children would have to face."*

The catastrophe to which Collier refers is the unconscionable gulf between the developed and developing worlds.

Yet, there is hope. Overcoming compassion fatigue, and celebrating our common humanity, is made much easier when we pay attention to what it is that unites us, rather than focusing on what divides us. Recognising the strengths of each and every person, wherever they are in the world, and whatever their life circumstances, provides us with a common thread running through our shared humanity. This provides a powerful way of recognising what connects us rather than what separates us - and in a way that levels the playing field more effectively than almost any other.

Every single person in the world has strengths – irrespective of race, colour, creed, religion, belief, sexual orientation or (dis)ability: the people of the world are united by the strengths that they share. Whether slum dwellers in Calcutta, the Maasai in Kenya, the Inughuit in Greenland, the Amish in Pennsylvania, Pacific Islanders parenting children with disabilities, juvenile offenders in Kansas, or the well-educated middle classes in Britain – amongst more than fifty other nations – strengths are universally recognised and valued. Universally recognised and valued – but not universally celebrated or harnessed to best effect, even though the evidence is clear that using our strengths enables both our best performances and our greatest fulfilments. This lack of celebration and effective harnessing of strengths needs to change.

Change needs only a small group of people with the commitment and energy to make the difference. And then others listen. In the UK at least, it may be that they are listening already. David Cameron's Conservative Party has developed a clear social responsibility agenda (with parallels to the three pillars of responsibility of the strengths approach discussed here), while for the Labour Party, "strength" has become a core signature theme of the recently installed British Prime Minister, Gordon Brown. *"Strength to change Britain"* was emblazoned across the pedestal at the Labour Party Annual Conference in September 2007. And in his 354-word speech upon entering 10 Downing Street, the Prime Minister's official residence, Brown dedicated 53 words – 15% - to messages that were fundamentally about the strengths approach:

> *"If we can fulfil the potential and realise the talents of all our people, then I am absolutely sure that Britain can be the great global success story of this century,"*

together with:

> *"I am convinced that there is no weakness in Britain today that cannot be overcome by the strength of the British people."*

We can go further – it is my view that if we are able to harness the strengths of the people of the world, there is not a life circumstance, social problem or economic disadvantage that cannot be overcome:

harnessing strengths effectively provides opportunities for everyone, and it is one of the greatest enablers that we can give.

To be serious about change, we need to be serious about what we measure. As the old adage warns: *"Measure what matters, or what we measure becomes what matters."* If we get the measurement wrong, then our focus ends up being on the wrong thing – and this is especially so when what is important is more difficult to measure than what isn't – so often, we will take the easy option and justify it as being 'pragmatic.' But pragmatism is no substitute for doing the right thing, and as advocates of the strengths approach, we should be adding our voice to the clamour for new governmental measures – but measures of input as well as output. We should be measuring strengths use as well as economic performance, and measuring strengths deployment in tandem with measures of gross national happiness or general well-being. In our post-industrial society, it is time for us to move beyond just industrial age measures of economic capital and output, and to incorporate measures of psychological capital and well-being that are more fitting and appropriate for our new information age, where people, rather than industries, have to be the priority.

Of course, it could be argued that the data are not there yet to warrant this wholesale national assessment of strengths use. To this, there are two responses. First, that often the scientific evidence follows the evidence of experience in many walks of life – psychology most especially included. Second, more can – and should – be done to build this evidence base, and to answer the question as to whether using strengths is – as myself and my colleagues purport – the smallest thing we can do to make the biggest difference. Ongoing longitudinal surveys, such as the UK Household Longitudinal Study in the United Kingdom, the General Social Survey in the United States, or the European Social Survey across 30 European nations, all provide ample, credible and appropriate opportunities to begin to introduce a strengths focus into socially significant questions across national and international boundaries. And the introduction of this strengths focus need not – and should not - mark a wholesale departure from the areas of traditional focus. It could begin, quite simply, with a single question that is tracked over time and linked to other variable of interest as social functioning, physical health, well-being and mortality. This question could be:

> *How much of your time do you spend doing the things that you do best and that you love to do?*

As we found in Chapter 6, a number of major international organisations, operating across geographical and political boundaries, are introducing the strengths approach to their ways of working. With a commercial imperative, they have the incentive to do so. National governments, with their social and political imperatives, could (and should) begin to explore what doing the same could mean for them. Creating the conditions for people to flourish is, quite simply, a vote winner. Creating the conditions that enable the realisation of strengths should be a central tenet of that activity.

As we broaden our minds to consider some of these horizons, intriguing questions present themselves – questions with answers even more intriguing in their possibilities and potential for individual, social and economic transformation. These questions include:

- How would a family function when it was working together and developing its young members on the basis of their strengths?
- What would a neighbourhood, community, or even society look like that was explicitly focused on realising the strengths of its constituents?

- Where can we find schools that have as their explicit aims the realisation of their children's strengths, and the transformation of their potential into performance and contribution?
- Why would an organisation not seek to organise itself in a way that created the working conditions that enabled its members to deliver their best performances through maximising their strengths?
- How would politicians operate, and what would they seek to achieve, if they were selected according to their strengths of social contribution?

As we noted above, these questions are, of course, much easier to ask than they are to answer. But, as Robert Sternberg so insightfully described, the hardest part is most often deciding on the right question to ask in the first place. It is my hope and aspiration that in providing this input, and posing these questions, I have enabled and inspired you to think about how, where, when and why you can make your greatest contributions.

Some people believe – and I am one of them – that if we are able to harness the collective knowledge, experience, expertise and strengths of the world's population, then we will be able to solve the world's problems. The challenge, of course, is in how we go about doing so. It may be a small step, but seeing strengths as a common thread running throughout humanity can be one way of starting to harness this collective potential. It is this that inspired us, in our own small way, to start The Strengths Project.

The Strengths Project – What We Are Doing About It

We cannot stand idly by. I could not stand idly by. When I was an academic, reading – and contributing to – the research corpus of the new field of positive psychology, I was consistently and increasingly struck by how relevant this field was to our everyday lives. I was struck by how much difference this research could make. And I was struck how by writing for other academics, filling tomes that would block up dusty old library shelves, we were missing the opportunity to contribute where it really mattered – and where it was really needed. Academics talk a lot about getting their findings into practice, but in reality, the structural barriers to them doing so are high – they are rewarded and performance managed according to how well they serve the needs of other academics (through high-ranking research journal publications) far, far more than they are for the difference that they have made in the world. Faced with my own choice, I jumped into the world of practice and application – the world where I, and many, many others, are striving to make a difference. This jump began with CAPP, the Centre for Applied Positive Psychology (see **www.cappeu.org**), and the publisher of this book through the CAPP Press. CAPP is a social business, with the mission of *Strengthening the World*. Having read this far in the book, you will know why. The Strengths Project is the next stage in our journey to do just this.

The mission of The Strengths Project is to help underprivileged individuals and groups identify, develop, and use strengths to enhance their quality of life and improve their life circumstances. Our focus through this work is on exploring the strengths of people who otherwise lack opportunities and demonstrating how, despite the barriers they face to their material security and comfort, they still have great personal and social strengths on which they can capitalise. Equally importantly, our focus is on using these stories of strengths in underprivileged settings to overcome compassion fatigue and promote a greater connection and understanding between the people of the developed and developing world.

It was for this reason that in February 2008, Robert Biswas-Diener, Reena Govindji, and myself visited Kolkata (Calcutta) and spent time working with slum dwellers there. You can read more about our trip, our objectives, and the outcomes that we have achieved so far, at **www.thestrengthsproject.org** It is through recognising, appreciating and celebrating each other's strengths as common threads of our shared humanity, and working to create the conditions that will enable and realise those strengths, that we serve our overall mission of *Strengthening the World*.

Strengthening the World works at two levels and has two aims. First, it is about identifying, harnessing and enhancing strengths in everyone in the world. Second, it is about building connection and community through recognition of our commonality, and celebrating each other's successes and strengths across our differing social, cultural and environmental circumstances. In practice, these two aims are achieved simultaneously through the same actions and interactions. Identifying, harnessing and enhancing strengths are largely a function of our dissemination model – of which this book is a significant part. The first stage in the strengths approach is about raising the awareness, but more than just that, generating the interest to create the appetite for exploration and application. When people understand the significance and impact of working from their strengths – and I have seen this thousands of times – the shift can be huge. Once the realisation is there, it cannot be reversed and change has begun. The task facing us is colossal, but every day we take steps forward and help the strengths movement to advance. Strengthening the World? Well, stretch goals can achieve remarkable results.

And to begin…

Strengthening the world begins with each and every one of us as individuals. It begins through the decisions we take each day about how we are going to deploy our abilities, lead our lives, and contribute to those around us and who will follow us in future generations. We all have the potential to send our ripple out into the world, a ripple that can impact far beyond what we might ever have imagined. Every single one of us has the ability to make a contribution. Every single one of us carries the responsibility to do so. As we have discovered through this book, our potential and possibility is nowhere more potent, nowhere more powerful, than when it is drawing from the deepest sources of our being, from who we really are and from how we can best contribute. Every time, this comes through realising strengths in ourselves and others. Thank you.

Key Points

- The first pillar of responsibility of the strengths approach is a personal responsibility to use and develop our strengths. When we do so, we are making most effective use of the capabilities with which we have been endowed, and achieving not only a rewarding personal activity, but also a valuable collective one.

- The second pillar of responsibility of the strengths approach is that each of us has a collective responsibility to create the conditions that enable the strengths of others. As we create the conditions that enable others to realise their strengths, we create a powerful ripple effect, with an impact that lasts far beyond us in both time and space.

- The third pillar of responsibility of the strengths approach is our social responsibility to harness strengths for the benefit of wider society. We all have something to give, and our greatest contributions will come through us harnessing our greatest strengths for positive social change.

- Every person in the world has strengths. Recognising this, wherever people are in the world and whatever their life circumstances, provides us with a common thread running through our shared humanity. The strengths approach enables us to pay attention to what connects us rather than to what separates us, in a way that levels the playing field of comparison more effectively than almost any other approach.

- CAPP's mission of Strengthening the World works on two levels and has two aims. First, it is about identifying, harnessing and enhancing strengths in everyone in the world. Second, it is about building connection and community through recognition of our commonality, and celebrating each other's successes and strengths across our differing social, cultural and environmental circumstances. The Strengths Project was established to help underprivileged individuals and groups identify, develop, and use strengths to enhance their quality of life and improve their life circumstances. It is central to our mission of Strengthening the World.

Areas for Reflection and Action

- To what extent are you already practising the three pillars of responsibility of the strengths approach? What can you do to increase your execution of these responsibilities? How will you do it? And when?

- When you envision a different future for your own sphere of influence, created through the strengths approach, what does it look like? How would it be better? What problems might it solve? What opportunities does it present? What can you do to make this happen?

- How can you make your greatest contribution? When you look at the times where you have been able to do this before, what was it that made it possible? How can you create those enabling conditions again? *Carpe diem* – the world needs all of us – and all of our strengths.

NINE

The Smallest Thing to Make the Biggest Difference

What is the smallest thing that you could do to make the biggest difference?

Share your thoughts with us, and join us in *Strengthening the World* at **www.thestrengthsproject.org**

NOTES

Chapter 1: Average isn't Good Enough

1   "Good is the enemy of great." Collins, J. (2001). *Good to great: Why some companies make the leap – and others don't.* London: Random House. (p. 1).

1   "almost everyone rates themselves as being above average" See: Alicke, M. D., & Govorun, O. (2005). The better-than-average effect. In M. D. Alicke, D. A. Dunning, & J. I. Krueger (Eds.), *The self in social judgment* (pp. 85-106). New York: Psychology Press.

3   "strain every nerve to live in accordance with the best thing in us." Aristotle (1998). *The Nicomachean ethics.* [Trans. D. Ross.] Oxford: Oxford University Press. (p. 265)

3   "...this article proposes to examine what can and may be done to assure better utilization of human talents at the management level..." Haldane, B. (1947). A pattern for executive placement. *Harvard Business Review, 25* (4a), 652-663. (p. 652).

3   "The unique purpose of organization is to make strength productive..." Drucker, P. F. (1967). *The effective executive.* London: Heinemann. (p. 60).

4   "Ronna Chamberlain and Charles Rapp developed the strengths model of case management" See Saleebey, D. (in press). Strengths perspective (social welfare). In S. J. Lopez (Ed.), *The encyclopedia of positive psychology.* Oxford: Blackwell.

4   *The Strengths Perspective in Social Work Practice* Saleebey, D. (Ed.). (2005). *The strengths perspective in social work practice* (4th ed.). Boston, MA: Allyn & Bacon.

4   "if you were a juvenile offender in Riley County, Kansas, after December 1999" Kurtz, D., & Linnemann, T. (2006). Improving probation through client strengths: Evaluating strength based treatments for at risk youth. *Western Criminology Review, 7,* 9-19.

4   "the popular bestseller from Marcus Buckingham and Donald Clifton – *Now, Discover Your Strengths* " Buckingham, M., & Clifton, D. O. (2001).

Now, discover your strengths: How to develop your talents and those of the people you manage. New York: Simon & Schuster.

6   "on August 21, 1999, gave his Presidential Address to the Annual Convention of the APA in Boston, Massachusetts" Seligman, M. E. P. (1999). The president's address. *American Psychologist, 54,* 559-562.

7   "The field of positive psychology at the subjective level is about ... to also building positive qualities" Seligman, M. E. P., & Csikszentmihalyi, M. (2000). Positive psychology: An introduction. *American Psychologist, 55,* 5-14. (p. 5). 8 "Within less than a decade following its inception, positive psychology has attracted many millions of dollars in research funding..." See Linley, P. A., Joseph, S., Harrington, S., & Wood, A. M. (2006). Positive psychology: Past, present and (possible) future. *Journal of Positive Psychology, 1,* 3-16.

9   "when researchers asked a representative sample of 1,000 people in the UK to say what their strengths were..." Hill, J. (2001, March.). *How well do we know our own strengths?* Paper presented to the SMG Section of the British Psychological Society Centenary Conference, Glasgow, Scotland.

12   "In a study conducted with my colleague Reena Govindji..." Govindji, R., & Linley, P. A. (2007). Strengths use, self-concordance and well- being: Implications for strengths coaching and coaching psychologists. *International Coaching Psychology Review, 2* (2), 143-153.

16   "Concepts carry consequences – classifying things one way rather than another has important implications for the way we behave toward such things." Reznek, L. (1987). *The nature of disease.* London: Routledge & Kegan Paul. (p. 1).

Chapter 2: Back to the Beginnings

24   "Without the biologically predisposed mechanisms...." Dahlsgaard, K., Peterson, C., & Seligman, M. E. P. (2005). Shared virtue: The convergence of valued human strengths across culture and history. *Review of General Psychology, 9,* 203-213. (p. 212).

25   "According to Jerome Barkow, editor of *The Adapted Mind: Evolutionary Psychology and the Generation of Culture*" Barkow, J. H. (1992). Beneath new culture is old psychology: Gossip and social stratification. In J. H. Barkow, L. Cosmides, & J. Tooby (Eds.), *The adapted mind: Evolutionary psychology and the generation of culture.* New York: Oxford University Press.

32   "Christopher Peterson and Martin Seligman developed a classification of "character strengths"" Peterson, C., & Seligman, M. E. P. (2004). *Character strengths and virtues: A handbook and classification.* New York: Oxford University Press.

32   "they compared the rankings of strengths that were endorsed by 117, 676 participants..." Park, N., Peterson, C., & Seligman, M. E. P. (2006). Character strengths in fifty-four nations and the fifty U.S. states. *Journal of Positive Psychology, 1,* 118- 129. 34 "the South Pacific blue moon butterfly produced only male offspring..." The blue moon butterfly, *Hypolimnas*

bolina. See Charlat, S., Hornett, E. A., Fullard, J. H., Davies, N., Roderick, G. K., Wedell, N., & Hurst, G. D. D. (2007, 13 July). Extraordinary flux in sex ratio. *Science, 317* (5835), 214.

34   "In December 2001, a hammerhead shark at the Henry Doorly Zoo in Omaha, Nebraska..." The hammerhead shark, *Sphyrna tiburo*. See Chapman, D. D., Shivji, M. S., Louis, E., Sommer, J., Fletcher, H., & Prodohl, P. A. (2007). Virgin birth in a hammerhead shark. *Biology Letters, 3*, 425-427. Also see: No sex please, we're female sharks. Science Daily, May 23, 2007. Retrieved from **http://www.sciencedaily.com/releases/2007/05/070523072254.htm**

34   "And over several decades, Iain Douglas-Hamilton has demonstrated that the tusk sizes of African elephants are decreasing..." Gray, R. (2008, January 20). Why elephants are not so long in the tusk. *The Sunday Telegraph*, News, p. 9.

35   "I've had to question the overall assumption that human evolution pretty much stopped by the time of the agricultural revolution..." Pinker, S. (2008). Second thoughts on life, the universe and everything by world's best brains. The Guardian, January 1, 2008. Retrieved from **www.guardian.co.uk/science/2008/jan/01/sciencenews.evolution**

40   "...What happens if we ask people to list the characteristic of human nature?..." Mandler, G. (1997). *Human nature explored*. New York: Oxford University Press. (pp. 4-5).

41   "It is only after some probing that the positive side of human nature emerges in everyday discourse..." Mandler, G. (1997). *Human nature explored*. New York: Oxford University Press. (p. 5).

42   "strain every nerve to live in accordance with the best thing in us." Aristotle (1998). *The Nicomachean ethics*. [Trans. D. Ross.] Oxford: Oxford University Press. (p. 265).

42   "...we become free to grow ourselves...." Horney, K. (1951). *Neurosis and human growth: The struggle toward self- realization*. London: Routledge & Kegan Paul. (pp. 15-16).

44   "higher levels of authenticity were associated with higher levels of self-esteem and lower levels of anxiety" Sheldon, K. M., Ryan, R. M., Rawsthorne, L. J., & Ilardi, B. (1997). Trait self and true self: Cross-role variation in the big-five personality traits and its relations with psychological authenticity and subjective well-being. *Journal of Personality and Social Psychology, 73*, 1380-1393.

44   "In our own work, we have shown that authenticity is associated with higher levels of happiness..." Wood, A. M., Linley, P. A., Maltby, J., Baliousis, M. & Joseph, S. (in press). The authentic personality: A theoretical and empirical conceptualization, and the development of the Authenticity Scale. *Journal of Counseling Psychology*.

44   "we have demonstrated how using your strengths more is associated with higher levels of authenticity..." Govindji, R., & Linley, P. A. (2007). Strengths use, self-concordance and well- being: Implications for strengths coaching and coaching psychologists. *International Coaching Psychology Review, 2* (2), 143-153.

45   "In one study by Ken Sheldon and Andrew Elliot..." Sheldon, K. M., & Elliot, A. J. (1999). Goal striving, need satisfaction, and longitudinal well-being: The self-concordance model. *Journal of Personality and Social Psychology, 76*, 482-497.

45   "In a second series of studies, Ken Sheldon and his colleagues showed that people who were more successful at attaining their goals..." Sheldon, K. M., & Houser-Marko, L. (2001). Self-concordance, goal attainment, and the pursuit of happiness: Can there be an upward spiral? *Journal of Personality and Social Psychology, 80*, 152-165.

46   "When I was an academic at the University of Leicester, I conducted some research in which I was interested in the question of whether people were more likely to attain their goals..." Linley, P. A. (2003). Unpublished data set – VIA strengths and goals. University of Leicester, UK.

Chapter 3: Our Negativity Bias and the Golden Mean

50   "...Moral virtue is a mean...it is a mean between two vices..." Aristotle (1998). *The nicomachean ethics*. [Trans. D. Ross]. Oxford: Oxford University Press. (p. 45).

51   "In fact, even when researchers have tried to find instances of where, all other things being equal, good may be stronger than bad, they have failed." Baumeister, R. F., Bratslavsky, E., Finkenauer, C., & Vohs, K. D. (2001). Bad is stronger than good. *Review of General Psychology, 5*, 323-370.

52   "Paul Rozin and Edward Royzman identify five other reasons for the negativity bias that seems inherent to all of us..." Rozin, P., & Royzman, E. B. (2001). Negativity bias, negativity dominance, and contagion. *Personality and Social Psychology Review, 5*, 296-320.

54   "...as Roy Baumeister and his colleagues argue, that "bad is stronger than good,"" Baumeister, R. F., Bratslavsky, E., Finkenauer, C., & Vohs, K. D. (2001). Bad is stronger than good. *Review of General Psychology, 5*, 323-370.

56   "Barbara Fredrickson and Marcial Losada examined the extent of positive emotions experienced by people..." Fredrickson, B. L., & Losada, M. F. (2005). Positive affect and the complex dynamics of human flourishing. *American Psychologist, 60*, 678-686.

56   "...marriage researcher John Gottman found that long-lasting, happy and successful marriages reported positive to negative emotion ratios of 5:1 or more..." Gottman, J. (1994). *What predicts divorce? The relationship between marital processes and marital outcomes*. Hillsdale, NJ: Erlbaum.

56   "As my research with Reena Govindji has shown..." Govindji, R., & Linley, P. A. (2007). Strengths use, self-concordance and well- being: Implications for strengths coaching and coaching psychologists. *International Coaching Psychology Review, 2* (2), 143-153.

68   "Many of the strengths that lead high-potential managers to early promotions become weaknesses..." Lombardo, M. M., & Eichinger, R. W. (1989). *Preventing derailment: What to do before it's too late*. Greensboro, NC: Center for Creative Leadership. (p. 1).

68   "Regardless of the particular combination, many future leaders have big strengths and corollary big weaknesses..." Lombardo, M. M., & Eichinger, R. W. (1989). *Preventing derailment: What to do before it's too late.* Greensboro, NC: Center for Creative Leadership. (p. 34).

69   "...our flashbulb memories for these events..." Brown, R., & Kulik, J. (1982). Flashbulb memories. In U. Neisser (Ed.), Memory observed (pp. 344-345). San Francisco, CA: Freeman.

69   "For example, research with 19,187 employees by the Corporate Leadership Council (CLC) showed that..." Corporate Leadership Council (2002). *Performance management survey.* Washington, DC: Author.

70   "the opportunity to use one's strengths at work every day is a core predictor of engagement and performance..." Harter, J. K., Schmidt, F. L., & Hayes, T. L. (2002). Business-unit-level relationship between employee satisfaction, employee engagement, and business outcomes: A meta-analysis. *Journal of Applied Psychology, 87,* 268-279.

Chapter 4: Strengthspotting

72   "Each of us has much more hidden inside us than we have had a chance to explore." Yunus, M. (1999). *Banker to the poor: The story of Grameen Bank.* London: Aurum Press. (p. xvii).

72   "studies to date have shown that only around one-third of people have any meaningful understanding of what their strengths are..." Hill, J. (2001, March.). *How well do we know our own strengths?* Paper presented to the SMG Section of the British Psychological Society Centenary Conference, Glasgow, Scotland.

79   "the same emotional mood that in turn influences productivity and team performance, as studies are beginning to show..." Losada, M., & Heaphy, E. (2004). The role of positivity and connectivity in the performance of business teams: A nonlinear dynamics model. *American Behavioral Scientist, 47* (6), 740-765.

80   "I developed an exercise where I asked someone first to spend about five minutes talking about a weakness..." The findings from these exercises were first reported in Linley, P. A. (2006). *Listening and observing for strengths.* CAPP Pathfinder Paper #2. Coventry, UK: Centre for Applied Positive Psychology.

92   "Even though only around one third of people can meaningfully identify their strengths when asked..." Hill, J. (2001, March.). *How well do we know our own strengths?* Paper presented to the SMG Section of the British Psychological Society Centenary Conference, Glasgow, Scotland.

95   "was known as a leading innovator in career development..." See Duttro, K. (Ed.). (2003). Special issue: The influence of Bernard Haldane. *Career Planning and Adult Development Journal, 19* (3), 1-128. Also see Knowdell, R. (n. d.). The contribution of Bernard Haldane to the career development profession. CareerTrainer. Retrieved from: **http://www.careertrainer.com/ Request.jsp?lView=ViewArticle&Article=OID%3 A113785**

95   "One of the reasons for this neglect and waste of manpower..." Haldane, B. (1947). A pattern for executive placement. *Harvard Business Review, 25* (4a), 652-663. (p. 652).

96   "Mike Pegg and the Strengths Way" See Pegg, M. (2007). *The strengths way: The art of building on strengths.* Cirencester, England: Management Books 2000. See also Pegg, M., & Moore, S. (2005). *Strengths coaching in 90 minutes.* Cirencester, England: Management Books 2000.

96   "Marcus Buckingham and the SIGNs of a Strength" Buckingham, M. (2007). *Go put your strengths to work: Six powerful steps to achieve outstanding performance.* New York: Free Press.

101   "Not only have we delivered substantial organisational benefits, including enhanced retention and improved performance, to clients like Norwich Union..." See the Norwich Union case study on this work: Stefanyszyn, K. (2007, November). Norwich Union changes focus from competencies to strengths. *Strategic HR Review, 7,* 10-11.

105   "the psychological ingredients – processes or mechanisms – that define the virtues. Said another way, they are distinguishable routes to displaying one or another of the virtues." Peterson, C., & Seligman, M. E. P. (2004). *Character strengths and virtues: A handbook and classification.* New York: Oxford University Press. (p. 13).

106   "the UK data for the VIA-IS has been reported by myself and my colleagues..." Linley, P. A., Maltby, J., Wood, A. M., Harrington, S., Peterson, C., Park, N., & Seligman, M. E. P. (2007). Character strengths in the United Kingdom: The VIA Inventory of Strengths. *Personality and Individual Differences, 43,* 341-351.

Chapter 5: Be Yourself – Better

112   "Everything that every individual has ever done..." Tooby, J., & Cosmides, L. (1992). The psychological foundations of culture. In J. H. Barkow, L. Cosmides, & J. Tooby (Eds.), *The adapted mind: Evolutionary psychology and the generation of culture* (pp. 19-136). New York: Oxford University Press. (p. 40).

119   "Even as a young child, I loved putting words on paper..." Gardner, H. (2006). *Five minds for the future.* Boston, MA: Harvard Business School Press. (p. 5).

121   "Cohn discovered that when we compare ourselves with people..." Cohn, M. A. (2004). Rescuing our heroes: Positive perspectives on upward comparisons in relationships, education and work. In P. A. Linley & S. Joseph (Eds.), *Positive psychology in practice* (pp. 218-237). Hoboken, NJ: Wiley.

124   Dweck distinguishes between having a fixed mindset and having a growth mindset Dweck, C. S. (2006). *Mindset: The new psychology of success.* New York: Random House.

124   "Dweck re-tells the story of Christopher Reeve..." Dweck, C. S. (2006). *Mindset: The new psychology of success.* New York: Random House. (p. 22).

125   "It's interesting that those with the growth mindset seem to have that talent." Dweck, C. S. (2006). *Mindset: The new psychology of success*. New York: Random House. (p. 11).

127   "...strength productive...cannot, of course, overcome the weaknesses withwhich each of us is abundantly endowed. But it can make them irrelevant." Drucker, P. F. (1967). *The effective executive*. London: Heinemann. (p. 60).

128   "Recognising and dealing with one's weaknesses is increasingly being identified is a key part of what it takes to be an authentic leader..." Goffee, R., & Jones, G. (2006). *Why should anyone be led by you? What it takes to be an authentic leader*. Boston, MA: Harvard Business School Press.

135   "Research by Chris Peterson and his colleagues, examining the strengths profiles of people across different occupations..." Peterson, C., Stephens, J. P., Park, N., Lee, F., & Seligman, M. E. P. (in press). Strengths of character and work. In P. A. Linley, S. Harrington, & N. J. Page (Eds.), *Oxford handbook of positive psychology and work*. New York: Oxford University Press.

136   "Herminia Ibarra's research on career changes demonstrates the point..." Ibarra, H. (2003). *Working identity: Unconventional strategies for reinventing your career*. Boston, MA: Harvard Business School Press.

137   "we are happier, more fulfilled, more confident, more capable, and more likely to achieve what is most important to us in life..." Govindji, R., & Linley, P. A. (2007). Strengths use, self-concordance and well- being: Implications for strengths coaching and coaching psychologists. *International Coaching Psychology Review, 2* (2), 143-153. Sheldon, K. M., & Elliot, A. J. (1999). Goal striving, need satisfaction, and longitudinal well-being: The self-concordance model. *Journal of Personality and Social Psychology, 76*, 482-497.

140   "something that Mark Muraven and Roy Baumeister looked at specifically in relation to self-control" Muraven, M., & Baumeister, R. F. (2000). Self-regulation and depletion of limited resources: Does self-control resemble a muscle? *Psychological Bulletin, 126*, 247-259.

141   "The Power of Full Engagement"Loehr, J., & Schwartz, T. (2003). *The power of full engagement: Managing energy, not time, is the key to high performance and personal renewal*. New York: Free Press.

141   "Any activity that is enjoyable, fulfilling and affirming serves as a source of emotional renewal and recovery." Loehr, J., & Schwartz, T. (2003). *The power of full engagement: Managing energy, not time, is the key to high performance and personal renewal*. New York: Free Press.

142   "The Seven Habits of Highly Effective People" Covey, S. R. (1999). *The seven habits of highly effective people*. New York: Simon & Schuster.

143   "and as a result, reported increased happiness and lower depression that was sustained over time." Seligman, M. E. P., Steen, T. A., Park, N., & Peterson, C. (2005). Positive psychology progress: Empirical validation of interventions. *American Psychologist, 60*, 410-421.

143   "This is one of a variety of initiatives recommended for the increase of

happiness..." Lyubomirsky, S. (2008). *The how of happiness: A scientific approach to getting the life you want.* New York: The Penguin Press. Sheldon, K. M., & Lyubomirsky, S. (2004). Achieving sustainable new happiness: Prospects, practices, and prescriptions. In P. A. Linley & S. Joseph (Eds.), *Positive psychology in practice* (pp. 127-145). Hoboken, NJ: Wiley.

143   "famously even in the case of people who have won the lottery, or who have been seriously disabled in accidents..." Brickman, P., Coates, D., & Janoff-Bulman, R. (1978). Lottery winners and accident victims: Is happiness relative? *Journal of Personality and Social Psychology, 36*, 917-927. See also Diener, E., Lucas, R. E., & Napa Scollon, C. (2006). Beyond the hedonic treadmill: Revising the adaptation theory of well-being. *American Psychologist, 61*, 305-314.

144   "Builders achieve enduring success when they pour themselves into constructive habits – limiting their 'addictions' to the passions that serve them." Porras, J., Emery, S., & Thompson, M. (2007). *Success built to last: Creating a life that matters.* Harlow, England: Pearson Education. (p. 132).

144   "Our deepest fear is not that we are inadequate..." Williamson, M. (1996). *A return to love: Reflections on the principles of a course in miracles.* London: Thorsons. (pp. 190-191).

146   "Everything that every individual has ever done..." Tooby, J., & Cosmides, L. (1992). The psychological foundations of culture. In J. H. Barkow, L. Cosmides, & J. Tooby (Eds.), *The adapted mind: Evolutionary psychology and the generation of culture* (pp. 19-136). New York: Oxford University Press. (p. 40).

Chapter 6: Harnessing Strengths at Work

149   "...one cannot build on weakness..." Drucker, P. F.(1967). *The effective executive.* London: Heinemann. (p. 60).

149   "type 'work' into an online thesaurus and see some of the synonyms that come up" Source: **http://thesaurus.reference.com/browse/work** I conducted my own search, but borrowed the idea and findings from my colleague Martin Galpin of Work Positive, **www.work-positive.com**, who is focused on redefining these negatives to make people's primary experiences of work much more positive ones.

150   "This book, being about work..." Terkel, S. (1974). *Working: People talk about what they do all day and how they feel about what they do.* New York: The New Press. (p. xi).

151   "in a study of 19,187 employees, drawn from 34 organisations across seven industries and 29 countries, the Corporate Leadership Council (CLC)" Corporate Leadership Council (2002). *Performance management survey.* Washington, DC: Author.

152   "Jim Harter, Frank Schmidt, and Barry Hayes, writing in the *Journal of Applied Psychology*" Harter, J. K., Schmidt, F. L., & Hayes, T. L. (2002). Business-unit-level relationship between employee satisfaction,

employee engagement, and business outcomes: A meta-analysis. *Journal of Applied Psychology, 87,* 268-279.

153   "As one unsuccessful candidate described their recruitment experience..." Stefanyszyn, K. (2007, November / December). Norwich Union changes focus from competencies to strengths. *Strategic HR Review, 7* (1), 10-11. (p. 11).

153   "as reported by Tim Smedley in a *People Management* feature article" Smedley, T. (2007, 1 November). The powers that BAE. *People Management,* 40-42.

153   "the Centre for Applied Positive Psychology (CAPP) developed a 10-point business case for strengths-based organisation" *The Business Case for Strengths-based Organisation.* Downloaded from: **www.cappeu.org/admin/uploadDocuments/strengths_business_case.pdf**

154   "And as our research has shown, using strengths more is associated with significantly higher levels of happiness, well-being and fulfilment" Govindji, R., & Linley, P. A. (2007). Strengths use, self-concordance and well-being: Implications for strengths coaching and coaching psychologists. *International Coaching Psychology Review, 2* (2), 143-153.

154   "research has consistently shown that happier, more fulfilled employees are more productive and perform better across a range of organisational metrics" See Judge, T. A., Thoreson, C. J., Bono, J. E., & Patton, G. K. (2001). The job satisfaction – job performance relationship: A qualitative and quantitative review. *Psychological Bulletin, 127,* 376-407. See also: Wright, T. (in press). More than meets the eye: The role of employee well-being in organizational research. In P. A. Linley, S. Harrington, & N. Page (Eds.), *Oxford handbook of positive psychology and work.* New York: Oxford University Press.

155   "Strengths-based organization is a term used to describe..." Page, N., & Carter, D. (in press). Strengths-based organization. In S. J. Lopez (Ed.), *The encyclopedia of positive psychology.* Oxford: Blackwell.

157   "David McClelland's original approach and rationale for developing competencies..." McLelland, D. (1973). Testing for competence rather than for "intelligence." *American Psychologist, 28,* 1-14.

158   "A team is a small number of people with complementary skills..." Katzenbach, J. R., & Smith, D. K. (2003). *The wisdom of teams: Creating the high performance organization.* New York: HarperBusiness.

158   "To make strength productive is the unique purpose of organization..." Drucker, P. F. (1967). *The effective executive.* London: Heinemann. (p. 60).

159   "Bringing together two or more people with complementary strengths..." Miles, S. A., & Watkins, M. D. (2007, April). The leadership team: Complementary strengths or conflicting agendas? *Harvard Business Review,* 90- 98. (p. 92).

161   "Throughout my life, I've always needed somebody as a counterbalance..." Branson, R. (2005). *Losing my virginity: The autobiography* (updated ed.). London: Virgin Books. (p. 56).

162   "Cheryl is one of my best assets...She's not the person who sorts out my diary; she's very much part of the business." Leighton, A. (2007). *On lead-*

ership: Practical wisdom from the people who know. London: Random House. (p. 117).

162 "social loafing – the idea that people ride on the back of other people's efforts without doing anything themselves" North, A. C., Linley, P. A., & Hargreaves, D. J. (2000). Social loafing in a co- operative classroom task. *Educational Psychology, 20*, 389-392.

164 "Entrepreneurs who want to build businesses of substance and size need to understand what they are good at…" Leighton, A. (2007). *On leadership: Practical wisdom from the people who know*. London: Random House. (p. 23).

165 "in a consulting assignment with the board of the Air Support business unit of BAE Systems" Smedley, T. (2007, 1 November). The powers that BAE. *People Management*, 40-42.

167 "It is only by combining the strengths of everyone in the organization…" Tichy, M. (2005). *The leadership engine: How winning companies build leaders at every level*. New York: Collins Business Essentials. (p. 245).

172 "…should have the intellectual capacity to make sense of unfathomably complex issues…" Ancona, D., Malone, T. W., Orlikowski, W. J., & Senge, P. M. (2007, February). In praise of the incomplete leader. *Harvard Business Review*, 92-100. (p. 92).

172 "Only when leaders come to see themselves as incomplete…" Ancona, D., Malone, T. W., Orlikowski, W. J., & Senge, P. M. (2007, February). In praise of the incomplete leader. *Harvard Business Review*, 92-100. (p. 94).

173 "described by Stefanie Naumann and Nathan Bennett as "climate engineers" " Naumann, S. E., & Bennett, N. (2000). A case for procedural justice climate: Development and test of a multilevel model. *Academy of Management Journal, 43*, 881-889.

174 "As research by Marcial Losada and Emily Heaphy shows" Losada, M., & Heaphy, E. (2004). The role of positivity and connectivity in the performance of business teams: A nonlinear dynamics model. *American Behavioral Scientist, 47* (6), 740-765.

175 "as Barbara Fredrickson and Marcial Losada subsequently demonstrated" Fredrickson, B. L., & Losada, M. F. (2005). Positive affect and the complex dynamics of human flourishing. *American Psychologist, 60*, 678-686.

179 "Builders harvest failure…Sure, they focus most of their energy on passions and strengths, but they don't waste their mistakes by dismissing them." Porras, J., Emery, S., & Thompson, M. (2007). *Success built to last: Creating a life that matters*. Harlow, England: Pearson Education. (p. 128).

180 "With the growing challenges of globalisation…a new Generation Y of workforce entrants…" Cascio, W. F. (in press). The changing world of work. In P. A. Linley, S. Harrington, & N. Page (Eds.), *Oxford handbook of positive psychology*. New York: Oxford University Press. Twenge, J., & Campbell, S. M. (in press). Generation Me and the changing world of work. In P. A. Linley, S. Harrington, & N. Page (Eds.), *Oxford handbook of positive psychology*. New York: Oxford University Press.

Chapter 7: Golden Seeds and Flourishing Children

189   "As Handy describes it, a "golden seed...refers to..." Handy, C. (2001, December 20). *Education for a new world: The third Geoffrey Hubbard memorial lecture.* Retrieved from: **http://www.nec.ac.uk/info/news- item? news_item_id=100437**

190   "Everything that every individual has ever done...". Tooby, J., & Cosmides, L. (1992). The psychological foundations of culture. In J. H. Barkow, L. Cosmides, & J. Tooby (Eds.), *The adapted mind: Evolutionary psychology and the generation of culture* (pp. 19-136). New York: Oxford University Press. (p. 40).

192   "You can read more about Jenny's work in her excellent book: *Celebrating Strengths: Building Strengths-based Schools.*" Fox Eades, J. M. (2007). *Celebrating strengths: Building strengths-based schools.* Coventry, UK: CAPP Press.

199   "My colleagues and I have found strong evidence that people who are more in touch with their true selves..." Govindji, R., & Linley, P. A. (2007). Strengths use, self-concordance and well- being: Implications for strengths coaching and coaching psychologists. *International Coaching Psychology Review, 2* (2), 143-153. Wood, A. M., Linley, P. A., Maltby, J., Baliousis, M. & Joseph, S. (in press). The authentic personality: A theoretical and empirical conceptualization, and the development of the Authenticity Scale. *Journal of Counseling Psychology.*

200   "...children and adolescents need to be actively validated for who they are as a person; they need to be told that they are valued for their personal strengths." Harter, S. (2002). Authenticity. In C. R. Snyder & S. J. Lopez (Eds.), *Handbook of positive psychology.* New York: Oxford University Press. (p. 391).

202   "in one of her studies, Dweck told children who were studying maths about great mathematicians" Dweck, C. S. (2006). *Mindset: The new psychology of success.* New York: Random House. (p. 173).

204   "according to Dweck, the thread that unifies all great parents, teachers and coaches is that they believe in people's ability to grow and develop" Dweck, C. S. (2006). *Mindset: The new psychology of success.* New York: Random House. (pp. 187-190).

208   "the fact that Conn and Hal Iggulden's *The Dangerous Book for Boys* was a runaway bestseller" Iggulden, C., & Iggulden, H. (2006). *The dangerous book for boys.* London: HarperCollins.

212   "Do you quit a lot? Do you think for a minute and then stop?..." Dweck, C. S. (2006). Mindset: The new psychology of success. New York: Random House. (p. 180).

214   "especially when we remember that we need at least three positive interactions" Losada, M., & Heaphy, E. (2004). The role of positivity and connectivity in the performance of business teams: A nonlinear dynamics model. *American Behavioral Scientist, 47* (6), 740-765. Fredrickson, B. L., & Losada, M. F. (2005). Positive affect and the complex dynamics of human

flourishing. *American Psychologist, 60,* 678-686.

215   "I look over at Holly and Sam and realise that I don't want to plan their lives for them. I just want them to be happy." Branson, R. (2005). *Losing my virginity: The autobiography* (updated ed.). London: Virgin Books. (p. 571).

215   *The Samurai in the Teashop* Gawler-Wright, P. (2000). *The Samurai in the teashop; Story sequence one.* London: BeeLeaf Publishing. I heard this story beautifully told on a CD narrated by Dermot Fitzpatrick: *Reflections on Life 1,* TimeOUT Retreats, **www.timeoutretreats.co.uk** My thanks to Pamela Gawler-Wright for her kind permission to reproduce it here.

Chapter 8: Making Our Greatest Contributions

222   "everyone can give something..." Clinton, B. (2007). *Giving: How each of us can change the world.* New York: Knopf. (p. xii).

223   "Personal responsibility is not a sexy topic" See Linley, P. A., & Maltby, J. (in press). Personal responsibility. In S. J. Lopez (Ed.), *The encyclopedia of positive psychology.* London: Blackwell.

223   "I recommend that the Statue of Liberty on the East Coast be supplemented by a Statue of Responsibility on the West Coast." Frankl, V. (1984). *Man's search for meaning: An introduction to logotherapy* (3rd ed.). New York: Touchstone Books. (p. 134).

223   "this Statue of Responsibility, showing two interlocking hands..." Visit the Statue of Responsibility Foundation at **www.sorfoundation.org** if you want to find out more.

226   "All the alchemists played to their strengths..." Handy, C., & Handy, E. (2004). *The new alchemists.* London: Hutchinson. (p. 236).

228   "...we become free to grow ourselves..." Horney, K. (1951). *Neurosis and human growth: The struggle toward self-realization.* London: Routledge & Kegan Paul Ltd. (pp. 15-16).

228   "*Unless we create an environment that....*" Yunus, M. (1999). *Banker to the poor: The story of Grameen Bank.* London: Aurum Press. (p. xvii).

229   "The first order for philanthropists..." O'Toole, J. (2005). *Creating the good life: How to apply the wisdom of Aristotle to the pursuit of happiness in midlife and beyond.* London: Rodale. (p. 290).

229   "Consider, for example, the story of Mbali." HOPEHIV (2007). *HOPEHIV annual review 2007: A generation of hope.* London: HOPEHIV. (p. 12).

230   "To date, Grameen Bank has lent $6.55 billion, and has over 7 million customers" See **http://www.grameen-info.org/bank/GBGlance.htm** at October 2007

231   "Each person has tremendous potential." Yunus, M. (1999). *Banker to the poor: The story of Grameen Bank.* London: Aurum Press. (p. xvii).

232   "I wrote this book to encourage you to give whatever you can." Clinton, B. (2007). *Giving: How each of us can change the world.* New York: Knopf. (p. xii).

232   "Guided by the belief that every life has equal value..." See

http://www.gatesfoundation.org/default.htm

233   "problems that cause great harm and get too little attention."
http://www.gatesfoundation.org/AboutUs/OurWork/OurApproach/def
ault.htm

233   "We also believe that from those to whom much is given, much is
expected."   See
http://www.gatesfoundation.org/AboutUs/OurValues/GatesLetter/

233   "What can be more logical, in whatever you want done..." Loomis, C.
(2006). A conversation with Warren Buffett. *Fortune Magazine*, June 25,
2006, retrieved from: **http://money.cnn.com/2006/06/25/magazines/
fortune/charity2.fortune/index.htm**

235   "Four unprecedented trends represent this cataclysmic shift..." These
trends are adapted from Gardner, H. (2006). *Five minds for the future*.
Boston, MA: Harvard Business School Press. (p. 16).

236   "You are a citizen, and citizenship carries responsibilities...." Collier, P.
(2007). *The bottom billion: Why the poorest countries are failing and what can
be done about it*. Oxford: Oxford University Press. (p. 176).

236   "Whether slum dwellers in Calcutta..." Biswas-Diener, R. (2006). From
the equator to the North Pole: A study of character strengths. *Journal of
Happiness Studies, 7*, 293-310.

236   "Pacific islanders parenting children with disabilities" Haley, J., &
Harrigan, R. C. (2004). Voicing the strengths of Pacific Island parent care-
givers of children who are medically fragile. *Journal of Transcultural
Nursing, 15*, 184-194.

236   "juvenile offenders in Kansas" Kurtz, D., & Linnemann, T. (2006).
Improving probation through client strengths: Evaluating strength based
treatments for at risk youth. *Western Criminology Review, 7*, 9-19.

236   "the well-educated middle classes in Britain" Linley, P. A., Maltby, J.,
Wood, A. M., Harrington, S., Peterson, C., Park, N., & Seligman, M. E. P.
(2007). Character strengths in the United Kingdom: The VIA Inventory of
Strengths. *Personality and Individual Differences, 43*, 341-351.

236   "amongst more than fifty other nations" Park, N., Peterson, C., &
Seligman, M. E. P. (2006). Character strengths in fifty-four nations and the
fifty U.S. states. *Journal of Positive Psychology, 1*, 118- 129.

237   "David Cameron's Conservative Party has developed a clear social
responsibility agenda" Cameron, D. (2007). *Social responsibility: The big
idea for Britain's future*. London: The Conservative Party.

237   "And in his 354-word speech upon entering 10 Downing Street" Brown,
G. (2007, June 27). [Brown's speech] Retrieved June 27, 2007, from:
http://news.bbc.co.uk/1/hi/uk_politics/6246114.stm

238   "UK Household Longitudinal Study in the United Kingdom" See
http://www.iser.essex.ac.uk/ukhls/

238   "the General Social Survey in the United States" See **http://gss.norc.org/**

238   "the European Social Survey across 30 European nations" See
http://www.europeansocialsurvey.org/

240   "as Robert Sternberg so insightfully described" See Robert Sternberg in

Morgeson, F., Seligman, M., Sternberg, R., Taylor, S., & Manning, C. (1999). Lessons learned from a life in psychological science. *American Psychologist, 54,* 106-116.

241 "The mission of The Strengths Project is to help underprivileged individuals and groups…" The Strengths Project grew out of The Other Half Project, a nonprofit organization founded in the United States by Robert Biswas-Diener. See **www.thestrengthsproject.org** for the history and evolution of The Strengths Project so far.

Chapter 9: The Smallest Thing to Make the Biggest Difference

246 Grace Fan, an outstanding executive coach based in the UK but originally from China, is the source of the question "What is the smallest thing that you could do to make the biggest difference?" It is quite simply the most impactful question I have ever heard. Grace works both independently and as part of the CAPP Strengths Coaching Cadre. You can contact her at **gracefan@madasafish.com**

246 The style of this chapter (short *in extremis* and with an invitation to participate) was inspired by the closing chapter of *Wikinomics: How Mass Collaboration Changes Everything,* by Don Tapscott and Anthony D. Williams (Atlantic Books, 2006). The central thesis of *Wikinomics* is about how mass collaboration is changing the world, with open source technology and open source ideas being particular examples. As a result, ideas are flowing between people and being adopted, built on and developed like never before. My use of their idea for a closing chapter is yet another example of this!

INDEX

habits 142–4
habituation 143–4
haiku (Japanese poetry) 216
Haldane, Bernard 3, 95
Ham, Alastair
  on authenticity 43
  and golden mean 66
  and occupational niches 134,
    135, 160–1
  on respect 173
Handbook of Positive Psychology
  (Harter) 199–200
Handy, Charles 189, 193, 226
Hanson, Lord James 162
happiness, increasing 143, 154
Harter, Jim 152
Harter, Susan 198, 199–200
Hayes, Barry 152
headline news 69
Heaphy, Emily 174–5
Hedges, Bill 189, 193, 195, 196
heuristics 197
Hill, Jonathan 73
HOPEHIV 228–9, 230
Horney, Karen 42, 227
human body 52
human nature
  conflict theory 41–2
  constructive or destructive,
    alleged 41, 42
  and strengths 39–43
Human Nature Explored (Mandler)
    40–1
humanistic psychologists 42
Hunter, Sir Tom 164
Hutchinson, Clive 145

Ibarra, Herminia 136
identification of strengths *see*
  strengthspotting
Iggulden, Conn and Hal 208
ILT (Inspirational Leadership Tool)
    106–7
inauthenticity 43, 199
Incisive (strength) 17
Individual Strengths Assessment
  (ISA) 74, 86–95
    see also strengthspotting
  as conversation 87–8, 91–2
  experiences 92

as open-ended approach 97
  sample questions 89–90, 90–1
  value of 94
inescapable weaknesses 169–70,
    182
Inspirational Leadership Tool (ILT)
    106–7
interactions, positive 174–5
internalised messages 201–4
interviewing, strengths-based
    97–103
  competency-based interviews
    98
  consistency across responses
    100
  experiences 101
  questions 99–100
  warm up 98
ISA (Individual Strengths
  Assessment) *see* Individual
  Strengths Assessment
  (ISA)

job shaping 135
John Lewis Partnership 154
Joseph, Stephen 146
Juvenile Intake and Assessment
  Case Management
  (correctional program) 4

Kaiser, Rob 64, 120
Kaplan, Bob 64, 67
Katzenbach, Jon 158
Kauffman, Carol 117
kratisto (ancient Greek principle)
    164, 166, 233

labels and labelling 2, 3, 16
Labour Party (UK) 237
language, effect of 15–18
Lay, Kenneth 69
leaden seeds 190, 191, 212
leadership roles 103, 172–3
  attributes of leadership 106–7
The Leadership Engine (Tichy) 167
Leeson, Nick 69
Leighton, Allan 158, 162
liberty, and responsibility 223
life skills 125
Lift (strength) 17, 79, 120

STRENGTHS GLOSSARY

THIS STRENGTHS GLOSSARY provides brief descriptions of the strengths that have been introduced in the book, which are in turn a small subset of our overall strengths database. To use our comprehensive online strengths identification and development tool, Realise2, please visit www.realise2.org

Alignment	working out how to get things done by bringing together the ideas, people, passions and resources to make it happen
Balance	seeing both sides of any argument and being able to plot a wise middle course as a result
Bounceback	using negative experiences as a springboard that inspires future achievement and success
Bravery	standing up to challenge, threat, or pain; standing up for your beliefs in the face of challenge or controversy
Connector	joining people with people, or people with ideas, or ideas with ideas, always making connections and seeing what comes of those connections
Contact	thriving on the initial contact with a new person; loves meeting new people
Counterpoint	looking at things in different ways to provide alternative perspectives; playing the role of 'devil's advocate' constructively
Creativity	coming up with novel ways of doing things and solving problems

Curiosity	interested in finding out more about things and wanting to learn more, whatever those things may be
Emotional intelligence	recognising and understanding one's own emotions as well as the emotions of other people
Empathy	sensing what other people are feeling and seeing things fromtheir perspective
Enabler	focusing on helping other people to do things for themselves
Esteem Builder	seeing what people do well and helping them to realise it themselves, enhancing their self-esteem and confidence as a result
Explainer	explaining complex issues to people in a simple way so that they understand
Incisive	seeing to the heart of the issue with a penetrating clarity of insight
Lift	having a positive emotional mood that lifts the mood of others around you
Planful	Focusing on what needs to be done and by when, establishing priorities and schedules to ensure that deadlines are met
Rapport	Making a connection with people quickly and easily, and using that connection to build rapport
Relationship	building deep, enduring relationships that last over time
Relationship Investor	a combination of the ability to get to know people while also building and maintaining deep relationships with them over time
Rightfinder	seeing the good in people and finding the best in what they have to offer
Spotlight	being the centre of attention and revelling in being the focus of other people
Time optimizer	making the most of every minute of every hour of every day, exceptionally efficient use of time
Unconditionality	accepting and valuing people for who they are, without attaching any conditions to that valuing

Acknowledgements

THANK YOU to my colleagues at CAPP who gave input to so many drafts and provided so many different ideas throughout the writing process: Tony Andrews, Robert Biswas-Diener, Jenny Fox Eades, Reena Govindji, Nicky Page, Janet Willars, and Linda Woolston. Particular thanks are due to Dominic Carter for consistently playing his *Counterpoint* strength, and serving as my copy editor for the volume.

Thanks are due also to the many people who gave their time to be interviewed as part of my research for this book: Alex Bailey, Parminder Basran, Vernon Bryce, Adam Eaton, Arvinder Dhesi, Jill Garrett, Ginger Gregory, Alastair Ham, Bill Hedges, Jonathan Hill, Rob Kaiser, Bob Kaplan, Richard Lancaster, Karen Stefanyszyn, Kerry Thorley, Mike Westcott, Roy White, Tracy Wood.

And to all those in organisations and in schools who have taken the strengths approach into practice with us, thank you. Your stories are here, and more will certainly follow.

Martin Mullin was integral to the formative stages of the CAPP Press, and also to the shape this book finally took. Thank you, Martin. Patrick Armstrong was always on hand to deal with typesetting, and Avril Ehrlich undertook the indexing. Thank you both.

Over many years, and in many different life circumstances, I have been inspired by golden seeds from many important people in my life. For your belief in me, thank you all: Nigel Aspland, David Davies, Graham Davies, Michael Humphrey, Stephen Joseph, Martin Seligman, Lorraine Sheridan, and, of course, from the beginning, my mother and father.

And finally, as any author will know, it is often those closest to you who bear the greatest burden during the creative process. That is true in my case, and I am especially grateful to my wife, Jenny, and children, Jack, Lucy, Sophie, and Ben, for their support and forbearance while I was writing this book. I hope the times away and the often distracted air of my existence will be worth the sacrifice you all made. Thank you.

ABOUT THE AUTHOR

A LEX LINLEY is a psychologist and social entrepreneur. After time spent working first in business and then in academia, in 2005 Alex founded the Centre for Applied Positive Psychology (www.cappeu.org), where he is now Director. CAPP is a social business, registered as a not-for-profit company limited by guarantee, and is focused on the applications of strengths in organisations and schools. CAPP's profits are reinvested in its mission of *Strengthening the World*.

Alex holds the position of Visiting Professor in Psychology at the University of Leicester, and is an international speaker on strengths and positive psychology, having delivered keynote presentations throughout Europe and in the Caribbean, the United States, and India. He has written, co-written, or edited more than 80 research papers and book chapters, and four books, including *Positive Psychology in Practice* (Wiley, 2004) and *Positive Therapy: A Meta-theory of Positive Psychological Practice* (Taylor & Francis, 2006).

He is an Associate *Editor of the Encyclopaedia of Positive Psychology and the Journal of Positive Psychology*, as well as Co-Editor of the *International Coaching Psychology Review*, and a regular reviewer for a number of journals, publishers, and grant awarding bodies.

Alex's first degree in psychology was from the University of Leicester, UK, where he graduated with first class honours and the Sluckin Prize, before reading for his PhD in Psychology at the University of Warwick, UK. In the early days of positive psychology, Alex was a Founding Committee Member of the European Network for Positive Psychology, and later served as its Chair. He is now a Founding Trustee of The Strengths Project, and a Parent Governor of Templars Primary School. His time outside work is spent with his wife and four children.

Lightning Source UK Ltd.
Milton Keynes UK
11 March 2010